INSIDERS' GUIDE® SERIES

INSIDERS' GUIDE® TO
PALM SPRINGS

CAROLYN PATTEN

D1288021

INSIDERS' GUIDE®

GUILFORD, CONNECTICUT
AN IMPRINT OF THE GLOBE PEQUOT PRESS

The prices and rates in this guidebook were confirmed at press time. We recommend, however, that you call establishments before traveling to obtain current information.

INSIDERS' GUIDE®

Text design by LeAnna Weller Smith
Maps created by XNR Productions, Inc. © Morris Book Publishing, LLC

ISSN: 1933-2637
ISBN-13: 978-0-7627-3904-2
ISBN-10: 0-7627-3904-5

Manufactured in the United States of America
First Edition/First Printing

CONTENTS

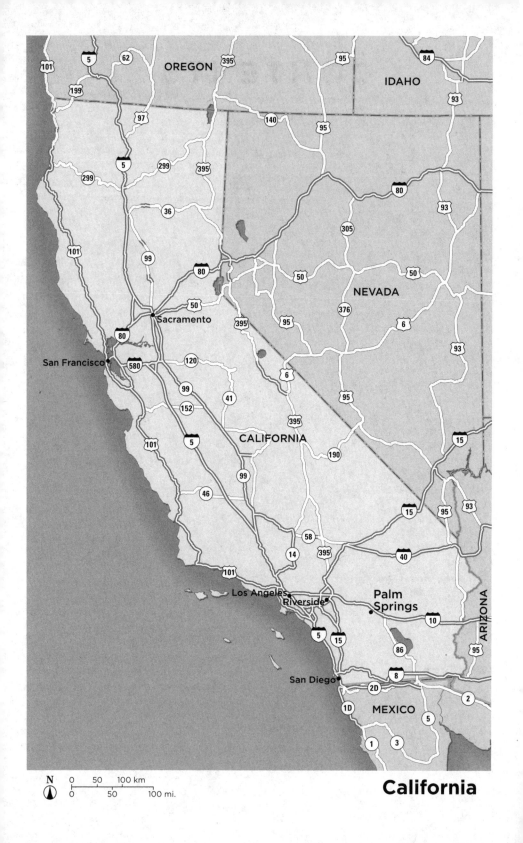

California

Palm Springs Area

Joshua Tree National Park

Little San Bernardino Mountains

Indio Hills

Desert Hot Springs

Dillon Rd.

62

Dillon Rd.

Indian Canyon Dr.

Palm Dr.

Palm Canyon Dr.

10

111

Palm Springs Aerial Tramway

Mt. San Jacinto State Park and Wilderness

Palm Springs

Desert Regional Medical Center

Indian Canyons

San Jacinto Mountains

Cathedral City

Rancho Mirage

Ramon Rd.

Children's Discovery Museum

The River

Eisenhower Medical Center

College of the Desert

Coachella Valley Preserve

California State Univ, San Bernardino, Palm Desert Campus

Washington St.

Dillon Rd.

Indian Wells

Palm Desert
The Gardens on El Paseo

Living Desert Zoo & Gardens

Indian Wells Tennis Garden

74

La Quinta

Santa Rosa and San Jacinto Mountains National Recreation Area

Jefferson St.

Ave. 52

Indio

10

John F. Kennedy Memorial Hospital

Empire and El Dorado Polo Clubs

86

111

111

195

111

Palms to Pines Hwy.

74

371

243

San Bernardino National Forest

N

0   5   10 km
0   5   10 mi.

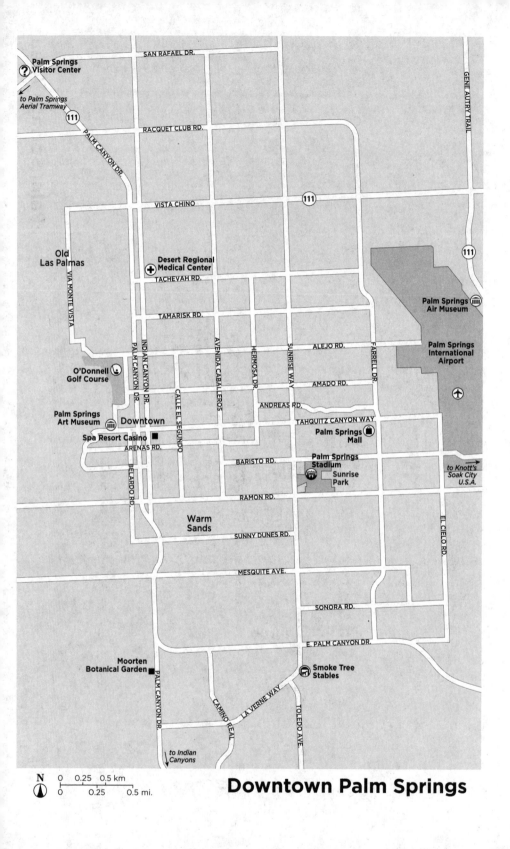

Downtown Palm Springs

ACKNOWLEDGMENTS

When I worked promoting Palm Springs to visitors all over the world, I was often struck by the absence of a good guidebook to the desert. Sure, there were lots of books about Southern California, but they relegated Palm Springs to a chapter or two, covering the usual bits about weather and golf. The desert is so much more than that. It is an incredibly complex and interesting spot, with its own quirks, foibles, and delights. I hope this book will encourage newcomers, frequent visitors, and even longtime residents to do a bit more exploring.

It was a pleasure and an honor to work on this book, and I have many people to thank. First of all, Mark Graves at the Palm Springs Desert Resorts Convention & Visitors Bureau is an inexhaustible source of news and encouragement, and a pleasure to work with. *Gracias, amigo!*

Donna Curran, editor of the *Desert Guide* and a longtime desert insider, has been happy to share her vast knowledge and resources with me, as well as her friendship. Donna is a true desert treasure.

My dear friend Bruce Poynter was the individual who introduced me to the desert more than 20 years ago. His enthusiasm and love of the area inspired me in many, many ways and continue to do so today. Another dear friend, Linda Vivian, has been my last-minute hero in tying up loose ends and sharing her own insider tips.

Milt Jones, publisher of *Palm Springs Life Magazine,* and Sally McManus at the Palm Springs Historical Society are the ultimate Palm Springs insiders, and I thank them for their clear-eyed view over the years.

Greg Purdy of the Fabulous Palm Springs Follies, JP Allen at the Palm Springs International Film Festival, and public relations pro Anne North were all especially gracious in providing news, photos, and more.

Any errors or omissions are strictly my doing, and not that of these excellent individuals.

Finally, I must thank my wonderful daughter, Jasmine. She was the reason I came to Palm Springs, she cheered me on over the course of writing this book, and she remains my favorite person on earth.

PREFACE

Welcome to Palm Springs! I must have said those words hundreds of times in the past 18 years, welcoming visitors from all over the world to one of the world's most beautiful vacation spots.

When I moved here to take a job with a small publishing company, I had only the vaguest notion of what I would find. In my mind, Palm Springs was a glamorous, terribly romantic spot full of movie stars and palm trees, endless sun and sand. The years haven't changed that impression so much as added to it. It has been my good fortune to work with some of the people who made the desert what it is today, from Palm Springs' "Cowboy Mayor" Frank Bogert to its "Movie Star Mayor" Sonny Bono. Milt Jones, the publisher of *Palm Springs Life Magazine* and the acknowledged behind-the-scenes power broker of a multitude of deals and public policies, was one of my first employers and the one who let me catch a glimpse of the desert's complex and fascinating character.

Murrell Foster, a man who started the city of Palm Springs' first agency aimed at attracting individual leisure travelers, had a lot to do with my love of the desert, since he gave me the amazing job of telling the desert's story to travelers from all over the world. It was my job to lure travel writers to the city, enchant them with its beauty and personality, and help them get the facts and experiences that would lead to press coverage later on.

This was truly an absorbing and exciting job, and it kept me on the run, always looking for new angles on the age-old story of sun and sand. I traveled all over the valley and took every tour, from riding horses in the Indian Canyons to bouncing across the San Andreas Fault in an open-top jeep. I learned how to spot the plants that are native to the desert, found out when the rare wildflower blooms were likely to happen, and lived through the days of out-of-control spring break weeks.

My guide to the wonders of the hills and deserts around the developed areas was Bruce Poynter. The writers fell in love with this adorable man's ready wit and encyclopedic knowledge of history, geography, Native American lore, plants, and animals. Bruce starred in many a travel documentary and feature story and inspired many visitors to the desert to venture out beyond the country clubs.

Of course, one of the questions I heard over and over again was, "Where do the movie stars hang out?" It's true that famous people of every profession hang out in the desert, but today's stars are much more cautious and wary than the ones who made the place famous 70 years ago. I learned that stars come to Palm Springs to relax, not to pose for photos and promote their newest projects. They check in to hotels under assumed names, keep a low profile, and go into relaxation mode. And, for the most part, the locals respect that. I remember often seeing Bob Hope and Kirk Douglas downtown, having lunch or running the occasional errand. Sure, they got some looks, but the looks were discreet and respectful. When Liberace died at his home and the national press set up camp in a parking lot across the street, the desert was scandalized. This was a man who opened his home each year for trick-or-treaters. He deserved to be treated as a beloved resident, with dignity and affection.

One of the wonderful parts of living in Palm Springs today is the fact that the city and the desert are so young. Many of the original "pioneer children" are still here, and they have marvelous stories to tell. Clark Moorten is one of those pioneer kids who has seen the desert's population double repeatedly and can tell you the pivotal moments in that growth.

For all its surface sophistication, the Palm Springs area still has a good bit of the small-town flavor at its heart. If you take your time to search out the natural beauty beyond the swimming pools and golf courses and to listen to the stories of the old-timers, you just may begin to see the attraction that has kept them here all their lives. And you'll be hooked. Welcome to Palm Springs!

HOW TO USE THIS BOOK ?

For such a young city, Palm Springs has grown up pretty fast. In little more than a hundred years, the little dirt-street village has bloomed into a world-class resort and tourist destination, attracting more than two million visitors each year. And even though there are now several cities flourishing next to the original, the entire desert area of the Coachella Valley is fondly referred to as Palm Springs. Major streets are named for movie stars and presidents, development is creeping ever farther out into the desert, and the resort is becoming more and more attractive as a year-round home. The economy, once entirely dependent on tourism and agriculture, is changing slowly as Southern California's burgeoning population looks for affordable housing and a relaxed lifestyle without big-city traffic, crime, and stress. Cal State University is offering four-year degrees. Indian casinos that rival those in Las Vegas are luring even more visitors. Change is in the air.

But for all this, Palm Springs and its neighbors still have the quirky small-town charms that originally attracted actors and actresses looking for a place to let down their hair and let down their guard. Part of it, of course, is the incredible weather—less than 6 inches of rain every year and more than 350 days of sunshine. Part of it is the abundance of natural wilderness that surrounds the desert and offers respite from any demand of civilization. Palm Springs is an easy place to visit and an easy place to put down roots.

The *Insiders' Guide to Palm Springs* is designed to be your companion in enjoying this unique desert treasure, whether you are here for a few days or a few years. This is a book to take with you—keep it in the car, stuff it in your backpack, mark it

up, and use it to show you the many faces of Palm Springs. The chapters are organized thematically, covering everything from hotels and restaurants to relocation and retirement. Each chapter varies a bit in its structure, depending on the content. For example, the Annual Festivals and Events chapter has sections on film festivals, golf resorts, ongoing events, and annual events by month. The Accommodations chapter lists hotels alphabetically within the categories of resorts, hotels and motels, RV parks, and vacation rentals.

Although the Palm Springs area has seven separate cities laid out from west to east—Palm Springs, Cathedral City, Rancho Mirage, Palm Desert, Indian Wells, La Quinta, and Indio—the book treats the area as a whole. You won't even notice when you move from one city to the next, but you will need to know which city you're talking about when you are interested in real estate, schools, and government. When it's important to know, we will always point out these distinctions.

The first few chapters will get you oriented to the area by providing information about history and transportation and giving you a geographic and political overview, plus some insight into local quirks and "Palm Springs–ese."

If you are a visitor, this book will be your resource for locating the places where the stars hang out, the best hiking and horseback riding trails, the most entertaining family outings, and the best bargains for each season of the year. The next few chapters will help you choose among hundreds of excellent hotels, from budget to luxury, and will give you some of the area's best choices for dining out, from moderate family cafes to once-in-a-visit elegant restaurants.

The number and variety of golf courses, naturalist tours, cultural and recreational attractions, casinos, spas, nightlife options, and special events can be bewildering; but this Insiders' Guide will help you plan a memorable visit at any time of year. Several chapters are devoted to exploring and detailing every possible activity at all times of the year. And we haven't forgotten shopping, with information on everything from designer outlet stores to farmers' markets.

If you're considering making your home in the Palm Springs area, this book will give you a good overview of the basics—education, medical and health care resources, real estate, parks and recreation, and retirement. For quick reference, information on local governments, safety, media, and local laws and regulations is easy to locate and understand.

Within the chapters, you'll find lots of cross-referencing and even some cross-listings, just to make your search for information easier. One of this book's outstanding features is its many Insider tips—tips that even some locals don't know about—aimed at giving you a comfortable feeling right away; just look for the ■. We've also included a number of Close-ups that look at some of the people, places, and events that give Palm Springs its own distinctive personality.

Some basic maps are provided to help you with orientation, but you will probably want to purchase some additional maps to help you navigate neighborhoods and make sure you find that special restaurant in time for your 7:00 P.M. reservation.

AREA CODES AND LONG-DISTANCE CHARGES

The entire valley has one area code—760—but you may still be charged a toll for calls made within the 760 coverage area, generally if you are calling a number that's 15 miles or more away. You don't need to dial either "1" or "760" anywhere in the valley, but we have included the area code with all phone numbers, just to make it easier when you're using the book outside the desert.

LOOKING AHEAD

Don't just take our word for it. Use this guide to help you explore for yourself the charms of Palm Springs. This beautiful area is always changing, adding new attractions and businesses, closing down others, and expanding existing ones. You may discover some of these changes in your own travels, and we hope you'll let us know those that ought to be reported in future editions. If, in your journey to becoming an Insider, you find you have something to tell us, please write to us in care of the Insiders' Guides, P.O. Box 480, Guilford, Connecticut 06437-0480, or visit us online at www.insiders.com.

AREA OVERVIEW

One of the many quirks about the Palm Springs area is the variety of ways people describe the collection of cities, and what that can tell you about the person doing the describing. Locals will generally say either "the desert" or "the valley." Those using the "valley" designation are usually year-round residents. People who call the entire area "Palm Springs" are almost always vacationers—if you live here, you quickly learn the political distinctions among cities and the jealous regard each has for its own particular name. To a local, Palm Springs always means the city, not the area. When you hear people saying "The Springs," you can bet that they're from the Los Angeles area and attached to the movie industry in some way, if only in their imaginations.

People who say "Coachella Valley" fall into two groups. Those who pronounce it correctly (co-chell-a) know their way around the area and may be involved in government or politics, where this term is more common. Those who mispronounce it (co-a-chell-a) have done enough reading to be aware of the proper geographic designation but are certainly not residents or even frequent visitors. One particular term, "down-valley," is used almost exclusively by Palm Springs residents and dates from the days when there wasn't much of anything to the east of that city.

This sense of place is what defines the politics, culture, and social climate of the valley and each of its cities. When California passed the infamous Proposition 13 more than 20 years ago, property taxes were frozen on each piece of private property until that property was sold, thus choking a huge revenue stream down to a trickle. All manner of public projects and services, from roads and schools to prisons and health care, took a big hit. Cities that had counted on a healthy share of the property tax revenue found themselves in the red. The sales tax kept them going for a while, but the deficit kept building and the state began taking a larger percent of that revenue to meet its obligations. Several cities have actually declared bankruptcy, and many have stood on that cliff for years.

In the valley, each city gets a share of the sales tax generated within its own boundaries, although that amount varies widely from year to year. The one tax that stays within each city and is never shared with the state is the Transient Occupancy Tax (TOT), or hotel tax. Because the valley is primarily a tourist destination, the cities with the most visitors are able not only to stay out of the red but also to flourish. If a city has both a good visitor base and a strong retail trade, the present and the future are rosy indeed. Palm Desert is the perfect example of this. With the valley's huge concentration of retail business and a number of strong convention hotels, the city consistently runs a budget surplus and can provide the parks, recreation, and infrastructure upkeep that make the quality of life there perhaps the best in the valley for all ages.

Palm Springs and Indio, the valley's two oldest cities, struggle daily with budget problems and financial near-disasters. Palm Springs has a large inventory of hotels.

Looking for information on starting a business in California? Want to find out the average price for an apartment rental in Riverside? Need information on state parks and campgrounds? Go to www.ca .gov/state/portal/myca_homepage.jsp. This is the official Web site for the state, and it has an exhaustive store of information about virtually everything you could possibly want to know about California.

Because most are older and smaller than the megaresorts down-valley, they tend to have a lower room rate and lower occupancy overall, so increasing the TOT is a struggle. With most of its available land already built out, Palm Springs doesn't offer good prospects for new hotel development. For retailers, the city's location at the western edge of the valley makes it less attractive than Rancho Mirage or Palm Desert, which sit dead center and are easy to reach from all the other cities.

Indio, which began life as a bustling agricultural city, has also languished because of its remote location, on the far eastern end of the valley. The city never developed a strong visitor or retail base. Although it is working mightily to increase awareness and traffic with a steady stream of well-attended events, Indio remains a blue-collar town with financial challenges.

Located in between Palm Springs and Rancho Mirage, Cathedral City is the valley's "working-class town," with challenges similar to those in Indio—practically no tourism and a light retail base—though it has scored in recent years by luring major auto dealers into town. A strong redevelopment effort is making strides in creating an actual downtown out of a previously rundown area, and the city is becoming known for its livable family neighborhoods.

Rancho Mirage—with its high concentration of country clubs, the Eisenhower Medical Center campus, a couple of very upscale hotels, and the new River shopping/entertainment complex—is set financially and has the potential to become a leading voice in valley politics. Indian Wells, between Palm Desert and Indio, is the valley's fastest-growing city. It has virtually exploded with new housing developments, country clubs, golf courses, restaurants, and shopping options in the past few years. Time will tell if the city's relatively young government is up to the task of creating a master plan to shepherd this growth in the most profitable direction.

In the area of master planning, Palm Desert can give the entire valley a good example and lesson on how it's done right.

The city recently revamped its general plan, a document that guides overall development for the next few decades. A key part of that plan is the construction of the first University of California campus in the valley. With a four-year university in the works, most community leaders say that the valley is in for big changes. They envision moving from an economy that relies solely on tourism and agriculture to a broader base of year-round businesses and light industry.

Each of these cities has its own government, mayor, council members, and personality, making the valley a much more diverse and complex area than it appears to the casual visitor. Over the years, many efforts to consolidate governments have died on the planning table, killed by the more affluent cities that don't see the advantage in sharing their riches with the others. This has led to a real problem in one particular area. Highway 111 runs right through the middle of every desert city. It and I-10, well to the north of the city centers, are the only straight paths from west to east. Slice it how you will, it takes from 45 minutes to an hour to drive from Palm Springs to Indian Wells. Only in recent times has the Coachella Valley Association of Governments pulled together to try to improve traffic flow from one end of the valley to the other. Its partial solution, the Mid-Valley Parkway, is an attempt to add another main artery, but it runs through residential and business areas, with numerous stoplights and frequent delays.

Problems aside, the constant competition among the cities may make the entire valley a better place to live, and it certainly provides a lot of choice in lifestyle.

Palm Springs has always been the hot Hollywood hangout, even when it lost some of its luster in the 1970s and 1980s. Now the hipsters are back, buying up homes, pouring money into new restaurants and boutiques, and bringing a sharp air of vitality to the town.

Cathedral City has finally focused its priorities and is working hard to provide the type of town that will attract and keep young families. Rancho Mirage is hitting a new stride with The River and trendy new restaurants attracting locals and visitors alike. Palm Desert's upward path seems unstoppable, with the new university, retail that grows stronger each year, and a commitment to quality-of-life services for its residents.

Indian Wells and Indio are the new hot places to buy a home, and the once-empty desert land is fast filling up with year-round residents who want a suburban lifestyle. The entire valley is benefiting from an overheated housing market in Southern California, attracting homebuyers who will trade a long commute for an affordable place to live in a beautiful spot.

Lots of locals and newcomers lament the changes in the once-sleepy summer resort, arguing that nothing good can come of this explosive growth. Of course, the cities will grow and evolve, but owing to some truly visionary old-timers, the breathtaking combination of pristine desert and mountains around the valley will be preserved for many decades to come.

Back in 1970, several prominent citizens anticipating urban development and wanting to protect the natural desert convinced the Palm Springs Art Museum to establish an interpretive trail and preserve on 360 acres in Palm Desert. That area became today's 1,200-acre Living Desert Wildlife and Botanical Park, the number one open space recreation attraction in the Coachella Valley. The Living Desert was the inspiration for a wide-ranging open-space plan that regulates development from the San Jacinto Mountains in the west to the Coachella Valley Preserve in the east, extending north to encompass Joshua Tree National Park and south to the Imperial Valley.

Setting up these wilderness areas has been a complicated project and a stellar example of how several different organizations can create great things together. The Coachella Valley Mountains Conservancy, Friends of the Desert Mountains, Center for Natural Lands Management, the Nature Conservancy, the Wildlands Conservancy, and the Living Desert have worked to purchase and save as wilderness areas several hundred thousand acres of unspoiled desert and mountain land. This land is off-limits to development, ensuring that the valley cities will remain surrounded with natural vistas free of homes, hotels, and businesses.

Vital Statistics

Population: The Coachella Valley includes nine incorporated cities: Palm Springs, Palm Desert, Rancho Mirage, Desert Hot Springs, Indian Wells, Cathedral City, Coachella, La Quinta, and Indio. Unincorporated areas and towns in the valley include Bermuda Dunes and Thousand Palms in the west end of the valley, with Indio Hills, Sky Valley, North Palm Springs, and Garnet along the northern rim, and Thermal, Valerie Jean, Vista Santa Rosa, Oasis, and Mecca to the southeast. The Cabazon Band of Mission Indians, Twentynine Palms Band of Mission Indians, Agua Caliente Band of Cahuilla Indians, and the Torres-Martinez tribe each have reservations in the area.

According to the most recent census, there were 111,700 people living in the east valley as of the end of 2003. The population is projected to reach 197,000 by 2020.

Economy: Tourism is the main industry in the valley, bringing millions of visitors and hundreds of millions of dollars into the local economy each year. Agriculture is a close second. The valley is the primary date-growing region in the United States, responsible for more than 90 percent of the nation's crop. Table grapes, peppers, avocados, artichokes, corn, citrus fruits, grain, and cotton are also big products here.

When to go: November and early December are delightful in the desert—the annual lawn and golf course reseeding is all done, the weather is reliably warm and clear, and the tourist season rush has not begun. From mid-January through early April, the population of the valley doubles as people flock in to enjoy sunny days by the pool and crisp evenings filled with stars. This is the most expensive and crowded time to visit. The "season" begins tapering off in April, and by Memorial Day it's relatively quiet in the desert cities. Take your pick: lots of action, crowds, and high rollers in the winter; sleepy nights and casual days in the summer; or a near-perfect mix of both in the late fall.

Weather: Daytime temperatures begin topping 100 on a regular basis in June and may stay in the triple digits all the way through October.

The Coachella Valley is the beneficiary of the "rain shadow" effect, with the San Jacinto and San Bernardino Mountains acting as shields that block both pollution and rainfall moving inland from the coast. The Palm Springs area is a true desert—less than 6 inches of annual rainfall, most of it in December, January, and February.

According to the Palm Springs Convention & Visitors Authority, these are the average daily minimum and maximum temperatures:

Average Daily Minimum/Maximum Temperature

	Fahrenheit	Celsius
January	43/70	6/21
February	45/72	7/22
March	53/80	11/26
April	67/87	19/31
May	64/93	17/33
June	70/102	21/39
July	76/108	24/42
August	79/109	26/42
September	73/101	23/38
October	62/90	16/32
November	52/76	11/24
December	43/70	6/21

A common myth about the desert is the assertion that the humidity is increasing because of the many golf courses and the watering needed to keep them green. Annual rainfall determines the actual humidity, and that has been stable for many, many years.

Geography: The desert sits at sea level, sloping slightly below sea level far to the east around the Salton Sea, and is surrounded by mountain ranges on all sides. To the east of Indio and the Salton Sea, the infamous San Andreas Fault has created a fascinating jumble of shapes and colors around the area called Painted Canyon. The entire desert area was once under the sea. In fact, that oceanic history is the source of the valley's name—Coachella. Thousands of tiny seashells are visible throughout the desert, particularly in sandy washes. When the original maps of the area were drawn up, local lore has it that the mapmakers misspelled the valley's name, which was "conchilla," or "little shell."

The Indian Canyons just south of Palm Springs are North America's largest natural palm oases, and home to the only palm trees that are native to this continent, the *Washingtonia filifera*. The groves of date palms here were originally imported from the Middle

East and are now grown from parent plants in nurseries located in the eastern valley's agricultural zone.

Foreign currency exchange: In Palm Springs, Anderson Travel Agency exchanges British, Canadian, and Swiss currencies and the euro and also provides foreign-currency traveler's checks.
Anderson Travel Agency
700 East Tahquitz Canyon Way
(760) 325-2001

Liquor laws: Alcohol is sold throughout California in bars, restaurants, grocery stores, and liquor stores. The legal drinking age is 21.

Smoking: You must be 18 to buy any tobacco products. California law prohibits smoking in all public buildings, restaurants, and bars and on public transportation.

Sales taxes: California state sales tax is 7.75 percent on all sales transactions. Some municipalities impose an additional percentage, so tax rates may vary throughout the state.

Time zone: California observes daylight saving time and is in the Pacific time zone.

Palm Springs is such a diverse area when it comes to politics, lifestyles, and cultures that it's defied the efforts of generations to describe it succinctly. To the casual visitor, "Palm Springs" may be simply the desert, but to those who live here it's a rich mixture of immigrant farm workers, retirees, artists, presidents, and movie stars. The Palm Springs lifestyle can be lived out on a horse farm in Indio, a retro-style condo in Palm Springs itself, a lavish country club home in Bermuda Dunes, or a family neighborhood in Cathedral City. We hope this book will inspire you to explore the many sides of this fascinating land.

GETTING HERE, GETTING AROUND

The city of Palm Springs is located 110 miles southeast of Los Angeles and 140 miles northeast of San Diego in the Coachella Valley. The cities of the valley are laid out in a string along the foothills of the San Jacinto and Santa Rosa Mountains. Moving east from Palm Springs, Highway 111 runs right through the middle of the cities of Cathedral City, Rancho Mirage, Palm Desert, Indian Wells, La Quinta, and Indio. The small communities of Thermal and Mecca are situated south of Indio, and the city of Desert Hot Springs is a few miles to the north of Palm Springs.

Historically separate, each city early on developed its own government and created its own road system without input or overall planning from the other cities. The result is that there are only two major arteries moving cars from the west end of the valley to the east—I-10 and Highway 111. And because Highway 111 is really the main street in each of these cities, it comes complete with traffic signals and speed limits that work to slow traffic dramatically. I-10 sits relatively far to the north of each city center, so, even though you can drive faster on the interstate than on Highway 111, you won't be saving much overall travel time.

Locals have developed their own shortcuts from place to place, but I've found that most of these will shave off only a couple of minutes on a valley-wide drive. In recent years the Coachella Valley Association of Governments has been working to find remedies to the traffic problem. So far, it hasn't happened. The local bus company, Sun Bus, is heavily subsidized but still can offer only rudimentary service. Like the rest of Southern California, the Palm Springs area is woefully lacking in modern public transportation. If you're going to be here for any length of time, rent a car and be prepared to take around 45 minutes to drive from Palm Springs to Indian Wells—more if a major event is taking place that will spill extra cars onto the streets.

Using taxis to get around just isn't practical. They're both expensive and hard to find. The only place where you can actually hail a taxi is at the airport. Otherwise, you must call one of the companies and request one.

Some other quirks: Highway 111 running through Palm Springs is named Palm Canyon Drive on street signs and maps. Some Cathedral City businesses use the Palm Canyon Drive name and others choose to use Highway 111. It's all the same street.

Unless you're really on the lookout, you won't be able to tell when one city ends and the other begins. Speed limits can vary a bit from spot to spot, so keep an eye on those signs. If you're driving slowly and trying to find a street address, stay to the far right and pay attention to your signaling skills. Rush hours in the morning and evening can be particularly busy as local residents try to get to work, so be considerate (and safe!) and let these speeders pass you.

Bike lanes are becoming more common as the various cities work on alternative transportation modes. Bike lanes are always on the far right of the regular lanes. Stay out of these unless you are about to turn right. Never use them for passing or slowing down and always keep your eyes open for bike riders, who may be hard to spot in congested areas. In Palm Desert, golf carts are legally allowed on city streets, but only on very limited parts of Highway 111. In residential areas where golf cart crossings are marked, the carts have the right of way.

AIR TRANSPORTATION

Palm Springs International Airport is located just a few minutes from downtown Palm Springs and is a $35–45 cab ride from the other valley cities. Major airlines that consistently fly into Palm Springs include American, America West, Alaska, Continental, Delta, Northwest, and United. Service may be provided on smaller planes by American Eagle, Delta Connection, and United Express. Other smaller U.S. airlines flying into Palm Springs include Horizon Air and Sun Country. Harmony Airways has service to Vancouver, British Columbia, and WestJet flys to Calgary, Alberta.

Summer service is less frequent, and some airlines may stop flying to Palm Springs in the summer months. Major hubs serviced from Palm Springs include Atlanta, Chicago, Dallas/Fort Worth, Houston, Las Vegas, Los Angeles, Portland, Salt Lake City, San Francisco, and Seattle.

A good alternate airport is Ontario International Airport, 70 miles west off I-10. Ontario is a major airport with consistent service year-round, so it's easier to find inexpensive restricted tickets if you're willing to fly in here. Southwest Airlines also services Ontario and offers good prices from its hub cities in the Midwest and Southwest. Shuttle service from

The Web site for the Palm Springs International Airport has a section of tips on getting the best airfares into the valley. Visit www.palmspringsairport.com. The airport's public information and marketing office does a lot of research on the ever-changing airfares for the different airlines, and they continually update the site with the latest changes.

Ontario to Palm Springs is available on a prearranged basis and usually costs around $100 per person for a one-way trip.

Palm Springs International

Palm Springs International Airport (PSP)
3400 East Tahquitz Canyon Way
at El Cielo
(760) 318–3800
www.palmspringsairport.com
The airport is a beautifully decorated facility with an excellent restaurant/lounge, gift shops and art galleries, comfortable waiting areas, and a compact baggage claim area adjacent to the rental car concessions. It even has a free, mini-putting green to pass the time while you're waiting to board. The parking lot has undergone extensive security upgrades and changes since 9/11, but it's still extremely close and convenient. Parking is $1.00 for each 20 minutes, with a daily maximum of $8.00.

Customs service is available 24 hours a day with a four-hour notice to clear international general aviation flights. The service is provided on a user-fee basis and is very popular with chartered corporate and privately owned aircraft. Call (760) 778–8455 for general inquiries Monday through Friday 8:00 A.M. to 5:00 P.M.

Private Plane Facilities and Services

Atlantic Aviation
145 South Gene Autry Trail
(760) 320-7704
Unicom: 122.95
Atlantic Aviation, on the east side of Palm Springs International Airport, offers fuel, supplies, towing, maintenance services, and aircraft storage. Other features include a conference room with wireless Internet access, lounges, a pilots' lounge, flight planning room, game room, pool and spa, cafe, and concierge service. The facility is being expanded to offer 16 individual hangars for turbo props and midsize jets. It is open from 6:00 A.M. to 10:00 P.M.

Million Air La Quinta
56-850 Higgins Drive, Thermal
(760) 399-1855, (800) 235-9876
Unicom: 122.95
www.millionair.com
A full-service fixed-base operator with hangars, jet and avgas fuel, and other aviation services, this facility features a four-acre ramp and 8,500-foot runway. This airport services corporate and private aircraft only.

Signature Flight Support
210 North El Cielo Road
(760) 327-1201
Unicom: 122.95
www.signatureflight.com
Signature is located next to the commercial airline terminal at Palm Springs International Airport and offers fueling, ground handling, passenger services, maintenance, repairs, towing, storage, aircraft sales, and charters. Other services include in-flight catering, business meeting facilities, limousine and car rentals, and a concierge. Signature is open from 6:00 A.M. to 10:00 P.M., with call-out after 10:00 P.M.

GROUND TRANSPORTATION
Rental Car Companies

Alamo
530 Vella Road
(760) 778-6271, (800) 327-9633
Airport pickup and drop-off at no charge.

Avis
(760) 778-6300, (800) 331-1212
Located at the airport.

Aztec Rent-A-Car
477 South Palm Canyon Drive, #4
(760) 325-2294

74-527 Highway 111, Palm Desert
(760) 341-1995
www.aztecrentacar.apg.com

Budget Rent A Car
(760) 778-1956, (800) 842-5628
www.budget.com
Located at the airport.

Dollar Rent A Car
(866) 434-2226
www.dollar.com
Located at the airport.

Enterprise Rent-A-Car
4041 Airport Center Drive
(800) 736-8222
www.enterprise.com
Airport pickup and drop-off at no charge.

Foxy Wheels Car Rental
440 El Cielo, #16
(760) 321-1234
Call for airport pickup and drop-off.

This is one of few areas in the country where you can rent a convertible from the national car rental agencies. And if you want to really break out of the normal car rental routine, some companies rent classic cars, luxury cars such as Jaguars and Rolls-Royces, and even Hummers on occasion.

Hertz
(760) 778-5100, (800) 654-3131
Located at the airport.

National
(760) 327-1438, (800) 227-7368
Located at the airport.

Trains and Buses

TRAINS
Amtrak
(800) 872-7245
www.amtrak.com
Train service into the valley has never been good, even back in the days when Indio had a regular depot. After much cajoling from the cities, Amtrak built a lone platform at North Palm Canyon Drive just south of I-10. Service is spotty, and there are no facilities other than a public phone. The area is isolated and trains may stop here in the middle of the night, so it is absolutely necessary to call for a schedule and reservations and to make pickup arrangements.

Amtrak also provides daily bus service to and from the Bakersfield station with stops in Indio at Jackson Street and the Southern Pacific tracks, in Palm Desert at Westfield Shoppingtown, and in Palm Springs at Palm Springs International Airport.

BUSES
Greyhound Bus Lines
311 North Indian Canyon Drive
(760) 325-2053

45-524 Oasis, Indio
(760) 347-5888

LOCAL BUSES
SunBus
(760) 343-3451, (800) 347-8628
(866) 311-7433 for mobility-impaired service
www.sunbus.org
SunBus has daily, regularly scheduled routes throughout the valley. Wheelchair

If you're parking your car outside during daylight hours in the summer, do what the locals do and bring along gloves, a towel, or even oven mitts to handle the super-hot steering wheel until the air conditioning cools it off.

lifts and bike racks are available. Fares are $1.00, plus 25 cents for transfers. Exact fare is required. Schedules are available from bus operators, hotels, restaurants, and other tourist information centers.

Limousines, Shuttle Services, and Taxis

Limousines and shuttle services always require advance reservations. Rates run around $100 per hour for limos and $100-plus per person for shuttle service to Ontario International Airport. Limousines can be reserved for any time, but the shuttle services usually run on preset schedules.

Unless you are getting a taxi at the airport, plan on calling ahead for one. Despite the number of taxi companies listed here, you will have a very hard time just hailing a taxi anywhere in the valley. Also keep in mind that many of the taxi companies shut down during the summer months—June through mid-September—and thus the wait time for a cab ride might be as long as 45 minutes, depending on where you are and where the taxi is. All taxis that take passengers to and from the airport are licensed by Sunline Transit Agency and required to have standard insurance and pass annual inspections for safety. Some of the larger hotels offer airport pickup service, which

The Palm Desert Shopper Hopper is a great way to get to all of that city's shopping areas. Just park near one of their stops and jump on—this open-sided, trolley-like bus runs all day.

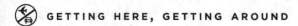

can be a bargain, considering that you'll pay upwards of $35 for most down-valley destinations. The airport drop fee is $3.75, and standard per-mile rates are $2.32.

LIMOUSINES

American Limousine
(760) 340-1051

A Votre Service
(760) 408-0208
www.jeancharles88.com

Cardiff Limousine and Transportation
75-255 Sheryl Avenue, Palm Desert
(760) 568-1403, (800) 669-0355
www.cardifflimo.com

Classic Transportation
(760) 322-3111

First Class Limousine
(760) 343-4910

Good Life Transportation
(760) 343-2221

Heyden Limousine
(760) 327-5466

Kenny J. Limousine
(760) 770-0790

Limo 4 U
(760) 322-1881
www.limo.com

Lion Transportation
(760) 771-0201

Luxury Limo
42-335 Washington Street, Suite 323
Palm Desert
(760) 345-6556, (800) 546-6555
www.luxurylimoservice.com

Palm Springs Resort Transportation
(760) 578-8060

Personalized Transportation
(760) 346-9344
Presidential Limousine
(760) 320-7707

Red Carpet Limousine
(760) 325-4116

Royal Limousine
(760) 346-7333

Sahara Limousine
(760) 251-7904

West Coast Transportation
41-951 Corporate Way, Palm Desert
(760) 862-1220, (888) 862-1218
www.westcoasttrans.com

SHUTTLE SERVICES
At Your Service
(760) 343-0666, (888) 700-7888

Desert Valley Shuttle
(760) 251-4020, (800) 413-3999
www.palmspringsshuttle.com

TAXIS
A few taxi companies do not accept credit cards. We have not listed them here.

AAA Limousine
(760) 322-4454

Ace Taxi
(760) 321-6008

American Cab
(760) 775-1477

A Valley
(760) 340-5845

Bighorn Taxi
(760) 321-4599

California Cab
(760) 578-3076

City Cab
(760) 321-4470

ClassicCab
100 South Sunrise Way, Suite 500
(760) 322-1111, (888) 644-8294

Executive Taxi
145 South Gene Autry Trail, Suite 8
(760) 864-1500

La Quinta Taxi
(760) 564-7575

Mirage Taxi
(760) 322-2008

R&C Express Cab
(760) 567-2780

Sun Taxi
(760) 567-5460

USA Taxi
(760) 416-1200

VIP Express Taxi
(760) 322-2264

Yellow Cab
(760) 345-8398

Services for the Mobility-Impaired or Seniors

Disabled Transportation Services
(760) 360-2068

SunDial
(760) 341-6999
SunDial is a daily, curb-to-curb service operated by SunBus for the mobility-impaired. ADA certification is required. The cost is $1.50 within your city and $2.00 outside your city.

Valley Care Transport
(909) 658-7611

There isn't a single parking meter in the Palm Springs desert area, but keep your eye out for time-limited parking zones in downtown Palm Springs parking lots.

IMPORTANT PHONE NUMBERS
Emergency Assistance

Emergency police, fire, or medical assistance Dial 911, free from any telephone

Fire and medical aid for all cities in the Coachella Valley (800) 472-5697

POLICE
Bermuda Dunes, Indian Wells, North Palm Springs, Rancho Mirage, and Thousand Palms (800) 950-2444

Cathedral City (760) 770-0300

Desert Hot Springs (760) 329-2904

Indio (760) 347-8522

La Quinta (760) 836-3215

Palm Desert (760) 836-1600

Palm Springs (760) 323-8116

EMERGENCY ROADSIDE ASSISTANCE
AAA Automobile Club of Southern California
(800) 400-4222

Hospitals and Care Centers

Desert Regional Medical Center Emergency Room
1150 North Indian Canyon Drive
(760) 323-6511

Eisenhower Medical Center
Emergency Room
39000 Bob Hope Drive, Rancho Mirage
(760) 340-3911

EMC Immediate Care Centers
78-822 Highway 111, La Quinta
(760) 564-7000

67-780 East Palm Canyon Drive
Cathedral City
(760) 328-1000
The centers are open from 8:00 A.M. to
8:00 P.M. Monday through Friday and from
8:00 A.M. to 4:00 P.M. Saturday and Sunday.

John F. Kennedy Memorial Hospital
Emergency Room
47-111 Monroe, Indio
(760) 347-6191

General Information

Phone directory assistance 411
Road conditions (800) 427-7623
Weather (760) 345-3711

VISITOR CENTERS AND VISITOR INFORMATION:

City of Palm Springs Official Visitors
Information and Reservation Center
2901 North Palm Canyon Drive, at the
intersection of Highway 111 and
Tramway Road
(760) 778-8418, (800) 347-7746
www.palm-springs.org

---

*If you're visiting Palm Springs from out-
side the country, change your foreign
currency before you arrive, preferably at
the airport where you clear customs.
The desert has limited currency
exchange facilities, mostly for euros,
pounds, and Canadian dollars.*

City of Palm Springs Uptown
Visitors Center
777 North Palm Canyon Drive, Suite 101
(760) 327-2828
Both of these centers are operated by the
City of Palm Springs and serve all the
hotels, restaurants, and other businesses
in the city, plus all valley attractions. The
visitor center at Highway 111 and Tramway
Road is located in the historic "Frey gas
station," one of architect Albert Frey's
gems and one of the most significant
examples of midcentury architecture in
the desert.

Both facilities offer hotel information
and reservations, brochures on visitor
attractions and activities, Internet, e-mail,
restrooms, ATMs, maps, gifts, and refreshments. There is bus and RV parking at the
2901 North Palm Canyon location. Each
staff member is an expert on the valley,
and you can depend on the information
you pick up here.

The Official Visitors Center is open
Sunday through Thursday from 9:00 A.M.
to 5:00 P.M. and Friday and Saturday from
9:00 A.M. to 5:30 P.M. The Uptown Visitors
Center is open daily from 10:00 A.M. to
4:00 P.M. September through May, and Friday and Saturday from 10:00 A.M. to 4:00
P.M. June through August.

Joshua Tree National Park
Visitors Center
74485 National Park Drive
Twentynine Palms
(760) 367-5522
Located at the north entrance to the
national park, this visitor center is also a
great little gift shop, featuring art from
locals, photography of the park, books,
pamphlets, and very-specific-to-the-
desert souvenirs, as well as good maps
and postcards.

Palm Desert Visitors Information Center
72567 Highway 111, Palm Desert
(800) 873-2428
www.palm-desert.org
This conveniently located center—right on
Highway 111 as you drive into Palm

Desert—stocks brochures and pamphlets on Palm Desert hotels, restaurants, and businesses, as well as for attractions and events throughout the valley. There is a nice selection of Palm Desert logo merchandise, such as hats and polo shirts. The visitor center is open from 9:00 A.M. to 5:00 P.M. Monday through Friday and from 9:00 A.M. to 4:00 P.M. Saturday and Sunday. It is closed on major holidays.

Palm Springs Desert Resorts Convention and Visitors Authority 70-100 Highway 111, Rancho Mirage (760) 770-9000, (800) 967-3767 www.palmspringsusa.com
This visitor center is a bit hard to find and not really geared up to handle large numbers of tourists, although it does offer brochures and information about its members. You will probably get better assistance from either their Web site or printed visitor guide. Pick up the guide at the CVA office or request that it be mailed to you before your visit.

Santa Rosa and San Jacinto Mountains National Monument Visitor Center 51-500 Highway 74, Palm Desert (760) 862-9984
The Santa Rosa Mountains Scenic Area forms Palm Desert's southern boundary. The visitor center, located on Highway 74 at the north base of the Santa Rosa Mountains, provides information on the nature, culture, and history of the area. It also serves as a gateway to myriad hiking, biking, and horseback riding trails. In addition, the center is home to a Cahuilla garden of plants used by Native Americans. This is a good spot to pick up maps that concentrate on the area's natural features and to talk with the staff about the most scenic spots to photograph on the way up Highway 74 to Idyllwild. The center is open daily from 9:00 A.M. to 4:00 P.M.

HISTORY 🏛️

It took Palm Springs little more than a hundred years to grow from a dusty dirt-street town of cowboys, pioneers, and Native Americans to a world-famous resort that attracts more than two million visitors a year. The stories of how those cowboys, pioneers, and Native Americans built their dreams out of sand and palm trees are in turn flamboyant, mundane, courageous, cowardly, inspiring, and dispiriting. It's a fascinating tale that explains a lot about the character of the Palm Springs area today.

INDIAN HERITAGE

When Spanish army captain Juan Bautista de Anza passed by the Indian Canyons in Palm Springs on his way to the Los Angeles Basin in 1774, the ancestors of the present-day Cahuilla people had been living there for perhaps 2,000 years. At the time, they were divided into around a dozen clans, each of which owned large areas of land—mountain areas where they summered and desert areas for the winters. A peaceful and complex society, the Cahuilla lived by hunting and gathering and had strong ties with other tribal groups as far away as the California coast and into Arizona.

ℹ️ *Street names in Palm Springs tend to honor influential members of the Agua Caliente Band of Cahuilla Indians as well as early pioneers: Andreas, Arenas, Amado, Belardo, Lugo, Patencio, Saturnino, and Chino are all Cahuilla surnames; Murray and McCallum were early pioneers. Farrell Drive is named for actor and Racquet Club founder Charlie Farrell.*

The Agua Caliente Band of Cahuilla Indians spent much of the summer in the cool oases of the Indian Canyons, just a few minutes from downtown Palm Springs. In the winter, social and religious life centered around the Agua Caliente hot springs, site of today's Spa Resort Casino downtown. At the eastern end of the Coachella Valley, other Cahuilla villages flourished in the palm oases along the San Andreas Fault near present-day Indio.

As the Spanish began setting up missions, the Cahuilla strengthened their political control by confederating clans, and, as late as 1860, the Cahuilla outnumbered Europeans in the desert. But in 1862 a smallpox epidemic swept the desert, a wave of settlers from the East Coast began arriving, and the Cahuilla found themselves at the beginning of a 100-year struggle to regain control of their land.

In 1864 Congress gave huge areas of the desert to the Central Pacific and Union Pacific railroads as incentives to complete the lines to the coast. The presence of an Indian labor force was considered another plus for construction, and in 1872 Indio was selected as the division point for the new Southern Pacific Railroad.

In Palm Springs the railroads got a checkerboard—10 alternating mile-square sections on each side of the right of way. In 1876 the first trains from Los Angeles pulled into Indio, and a year later the final link in the southern transcontinental route was completed to Yuma, Arizona. That same year the government set up almost a dozen reservations on the land not owned by the railroads—almost half of Palm Springs, a third of Cathedral City, and smaller areas in the eastern part of the valley. Although the Indians now owned 48 sections of land throughout the valley, the government held every square inch of it "in trust," making it impossible for the tribes to sell or set up long-term leases to earn money from their holdings.

With land as their only asset, the Agua Calientes in Palm Springs fought to have their 32,000 tribal acres divided among individual members. The Mission Indian Relief Act of 1891 gave the Secretary of the Interior authority to do just that, but he refused.

In the early part of the last century, when heat and sun were thought to be cures for tuberculosis, Palm Springs began attracting notice as a spot for health seekers. Many a pioneer family came for a visit with ailing children and then put down roots as the little community grew.

All this time, the Cahuilla stayed focused on their land. Finally, after tribal leader Lee Arenas took the battle all the way to the Supreme Court in 1944, most members were allotted 47 acres each. In Palm Springs the tribe retained ownership of the Indian Canyons and most of Section 14, which encompassed the hot springs, the tribal cemetery, and most of present-day downtown. That same year, the city bought the landing strip area from the tribe. It is now the site of Palm Springs International Airport.

Even after the allotments, the land division was unequal, with some individuals owning parcels on mountain land that held virtually no development potential and others owning the land under such revenue producers as the Canyon Country Club and major downtown hotels. At last, in 1959, President Eisenhower signed an equalization bill that gave each tribal member an allotment worth no less than $335,000.

By this time many of the Cahuilla's rituals and sacred songs had been lost, discarded by generations trying to rise out of enforced poverty and adapt to a different culture. But as the tribal members who were small children in the 1960s grew up, they began to look for ways to preserve the language and traditions for their own children. Using the income from admission fees and film location permits for the Indian Canyons, they slowly put aside money for a cultural center and museum.

The tall palm with fanlike fronds that trail shining "threads" in the breeze— Washingtonia filifera—*is the only palm native to North America and grows abundantly in the natural palm oases of the desert. For the Cahuilla Indians, it provided food, shelter, fuel, and material for beautiful baskets.*

Tahquitz Canyon, a beautiful wild area butting up to the western edge of Palm Springs just 2 blocks from downtown, had been scarred by graffiti and littered with trash for years, but the tribe lacked the funds to patrol and clean the area. Planning carefully, the tribe first fenced off the area and then enlisted the help of local volunteers to clean it and keep transients away.

In 1987 the legal system that had kept the Cahuilla in second-class status for so long suddenly opened the door to enormous riches. The U.S. Supreme Court ruled that California could not bar gambling on Indian land. Despite intense lobbying from Nevada gaming interests, the state eventually legalized Indian gaming, and in 1995 the Agua Caliente Cahuilla brought slot machines into the Spa Hotel in the very heart of downtown Palm Springs. Built on Section 14 land that was virtually worthless just 60 years before, it is the only Indian casino in the middle of a city. Following the lead of the Agua Calientes, the Morongo, Augustine, Cabazon, and Twenty-Nine Palms bands all have desert casinos that generate wealth and stability for their members.

The Agua Calientes now own and operate the $90 million Spa Resort Casino in downtown Palm Springs and the elaborate Agua Caliente Casino just off I-10 in Rancho Mirage. They have set up scholarships and provided full health coverage for members, invested wisely, and created their own bank. As a sovereign nation, they hold absolute authority over zoning and building on tribal land, making their decisions of prime importance to the City of Palm Springs.

Today Tahquitz Canyon is home to a beautiful interpretive center where rangers lead hikes to the impressive waterfalls and give visitors an appreciation of the Cahuilla heritage. The tribe is one of the valley's most generous and consistent benefactors, donating hundreds of thousands of dollars to local charities each year. The Cahuilla language is being taught in special classes, and oral histories are being recorded.

The Agua Caliente Tribe of Cahuilla Indians is widely regarded as being the country's wealthiest tribe, per capita, of Native Americans.

AGUA CALIENTE BECOMES PALM SPRINGS

In 1884 this little oasis and stage stop was still known as Agua Caliente. That year John Guthrie McCallum became the first non-Indian to settle here permanently. A San Francisco lawyer looking for a warm, dry climate to help his son's tuberculosis, McCallum had big dreams for the desert. He bought more than 6,000 acres, set up the township that today makes up downtown Palm Springs, and founded the Palm Valley Land and Water Company, building ditches to bring water into the new Palm City.

Land sales boomed, and Dr. Welwood Murray moved in from Banning to build the Palm Springs Hotel across from the McCallum house, which now sits on the Village Green downtown and is headquarters for the Palm Springs Historical Society.

In 1893 a record 21-day downpour

washed out crops and irrigation ditches, only to be followed by an 11-year drought. Murray and his family were among the handful of residents to stay on, running the hotel until his death in 1914. By that time another generation of pioneers had sunk roots, building hotels and attracting writers and artists who first came for their health and later returned for the beauty and small-town camaraderie.

In 1901 *The Riverside Press* newspaper reported that amusements included "tennis, croquet, baseball, mountain climbing, and tramps along desert." A warm, dry climate was prescribed by physicians for those with respiratory diseases, and Nelson's Health Camp, near the Southern Pacific railroad depot in Indio, was one facility that provided a place for invalids to recuperate.

HOLLYWOOD COMES TO THE DESERT

By 1925 more than 35,000 tourists were visiting each winter. And Hollywood discovered the desert. Former Palm Springs mayor Frank Bogert, who came to Palm Springs as an 18-year-old horse wrangler and soon became the city's most famous and successful public relations spokesperson, was on the spot to chronicle the stars at play through the 1950s. "In the early days," he writes, "Hollywood studios were used only for close-up scenes; Palm Springs served as a location site for Arabia, North Africa, Mexico, and other global areas. As many as ten movies were made each season and both guests and townsfolk turned out to watch the proceedings."

With its close proximity to Hollywood, the city became the favored playground for stars who wanted to escape the prying eyes of the press and let down their hair. El Mirador Hotel, now the site of Desert Regional Medical Center, was at the center of the action, and Bogert was their star, not only snapping photos of celebrities but also starring in a few of those photos himself with siren Clara Bow and other lovelies.

i

Horseback riding and hiking were the original entertainments in the desert, decades before the first golf course was built. For trail maps and regulations, contact the Santa Rosa Mountains Visitor Center (760-862-9984) or the City of Rancho Mirage (760-324-4511).

Hollywood's Love Affair with the Desert

Some of the films and television programs shot in the Palm Springs area:

The Hoax (2006)
Bone Dry (2005)
Mission: Impossible III (2005)
Alpha Dogs (2004)
Phat Girls (2004)
Alias (2003)
Curb Your Enthusiasm (HBO, 2003)
Santa Trap (2002)
Ocean's Eleven (2001)
The Opposite of Sex (2001)
The Princess and the Marine (2001)
Fugitive Nights (1997)

Beverly Hills 90210 (1994)
P.S. I Love You (1990)
After Dark, My Sweet (1990)
Funny About Love (1990)
General Hospital (1985)
Dressed to Kill (1979)
6 Million Dollar Man (1977)
Columbo (1972)
Kotch (1971)
Mission Impossible (1969)
Hanging by a Thread (1964)
Lost Horizon (1937)
Lone Star Rush (1915)

Before long, film stars Charlie Farrell and Ralph Bellamy built the Racquet Club on the north end of town, and it soon became a hot rival for El Mirador's famous guests. The Racquet Club's tennis, cocktails, and glamorous parties attracted some of Hollywood's most popular stars, as well as scores of hopeful would-be starlets. Legend has it that Marilyn Monroe was discovered by the Racquet Club pool. Rudolph Valentino, Shirley Temple, Theda Bara, and what seemed like the entire cast of every movie shown in town were familiar faces on the streets.

In the late 1930s and early '40s, bigtime stars started investing in second homes in the desert. Cary Grant, Bob Hope, Frank Sinatra, Wiliam Powell, Daryl Zanuck, and dozens of others made the Las Palmas neighborhood their winter home.

In 1930 Indio incorporated, becoming a city at the beginning of the Depression era's largest construction project. With Indio as their distribution base, mining crews built 92 miles of tunnel through the eastern mountains for the Metropolitan Aqueduct to carry water from the Colorado River into the Los Angeles Basin.

The aqueduct transformed Los Angeles into a major city but had little impact on the sleepy desert, which remained a charming winter playground for Hollywood stars and those in their orbit.

In 1938 Palm Springs became a city, and the tourists just kept coming. With nine stables, the O'Donnell Golf Course, and several tennis courts, the city boasted that it had more swimming pools than any other place in the country. Neighboring Cathedral City was a mecca of nightclubs and gambling.

Hollywood had adopted Palm Springs as its permanent playground, and not even World War II could dim the desert's glamorous aura. El Mirador Hotel was commandeered to become a hospital, and the soldiers and their visiting families turned the village into a year-round resort. When the war ended, the tourists were back with a vengeance, and the real land boom was on.

Frank Bogert was a partner in the desert's first golf course country club, Thunderbird Ranch, in Rancho Mirage. Jacqueline Cochran Odlum built the second golf course in the Coachella Valley in

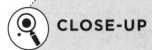

Midcentury Architecture

Endless sunshine and clean, uncluttered vistas were a natural backdrop for post-war modern architecture, with its stripped-down lines and generous use of natural materials. In fact, what has come to be called "the modern idiom" was being practiced in Palm Springs well before the 1940s.

Rudolph M. Schindler, one of Frank Lloyd Wright's disciples, built the first truly modern house here in 1922, using concrete, wood, and canvas in an echo of the house he built for himself in Los Angeles the same year. In 1937 Richard J. Neutra built his first residential commission in the desert, the Miller House. It was considered his best small house of the 1930s and was included in the 1938 Museum of Modern Art traveling exhibition.

Other significant homes of the 1930s included the 1933 home designed by

The former Tramway Gas Station, designed by famed architect Albert Frey and now the home of the city's visitor information center, is an important part of Palm Springs' architectural history. PHOTOGRAPH PROVIDED BY THE PALM SPRINGS BUREAU OF TOURISM

William Gray Purcell (a disciple of Louis Sullivan) and Evera Van Bailey; the grand 1936 Davidson House designed by Los Angeles architects Eric Webster and Adrian Wilson; and the 1934 Kocher-Sampson Building. The Kocher-Sampson Building was a collaboration between A. Lawrence Kocher, then managing editor of *Architectural Record,* and Albert Frey, the first of Le Corbusier's disciples to build in America. It was featured in the Museum of Modern Art's 1935 exhibition, "Modern Architecture in California."

A native of Switzerland, Frey moved to Palm Springs from New York to supervise the Kocher-Sampson construction. He stayed on, starting a partnership with architect John Porter Clark that lasted almost 20 years.

E. Stewart Williams and William E. Cody arrived in 1946 and 1945, respectively. With Frey and Clark, they created a substantial body of work, and much of their midcentury modern architecture remains today. Along with Neutra, John Lautner, William Burgess, A. Quincy Jones, Frederick E. Emmons, Craig Ellwood, Donald Wexler, and Ric Harrison, they were responsible for such elegant public buildings as Palm Springs High School, the Palm Springs Art Museum, and the downtown Bank of America and Washington Mutual Bank buildings, all superb examples of modernist architecture.

Albert Frey's legacy is especially important in Palm Springs. His Frey House 2 is now owned by the Palm Springs Art Museum and has been restored to its original simplicity and purity, wrapped around a mountain overlooking the city below. His designs for the Palm Springs City Hall, the Palm Springs Aerial Tramway Lower Station, and the Tramway Gas Station (now the Palm Springs Visitor Center) are just three of the most visible and public of his works. The Gas Station has become a recognizable emblem of the city, with its sweeping parabolic roofline and almost cartoonlike simplicity.

Adele Cygelman, writing in her book *Palm Springs Modern,* says, "The impact that these architects and homeowners had on the desert oasis between the 1940s and the 1960s is immeasurable. The town's current revival as a 'hot' hot spot and the worldwide acclaim being accorded its architecture [are] gratifying to those who thought their work had gone undiscovered or, worse, ignored. Now it has come full circle, for some in their own lifetime."

SUGGESTED READING

Ainsworth, Katherine. *The McCallum Saga: The Story of the Founding of Palm Springs.* Palm Springs: Palm Springs Public Library, 1996.

Bean, Lowell John, with Sylvia Brakke Vane and Jackson Young. *The Cahuilla Landscape.* Menlo Park, Calif.: Ballena Press, 1991.

Bogert, Mayor Frank M. *Palm Springs First Hundred Years: A Pictorial History.* Palm Springs: Palm Springs Associates Heritage Printers, 1987.

Cygelman, Adele. *Palm Springs Modern.* New York: Rizzoli International Publications, 1999.

Hubbard, Doni. *Favorite Trails of Desert Riders.* Redwood City, Calif.: Hoofprints, 1991.

Rosa, Joseph. *Albert Frey, Architect.* New York: Rizzoli International Publications, 1990.

The General George S. Patton Memorial Museum on the summit of Chiriaco Hill on I-10 east of Indio is a treasure house of World War II memorabilia. It sits on the site where Patton's troops trained for the North African campaign. Outside, you can still see tracks left by the tanks. Call (760) 227-3483 for more information.

1947 on her ranch just south of Indio. Not far off, a group of investors bought 1,600 acres for a hotel, country club, homes, and offices. Thirty years later this became the city of Palm Desert.

Desi Arnaz helped build the first resort hotel in Indian Wells—close to the site of the present-day Miramonte Resort on Highway 111. After his first visit to the desert in 1954, President Dwight D. Eisenhower returned to Washington to sign the Equalization Bill that finalized the Agua Calientes' land allotments. He made Indian Wells his winter residence and contributed his name and considerable fund-raising clout to the Eisenhower Medical Center in Rancho Mirage.

Since President Eisenhower's visits, each sitting U.S. president has spent time here in the winter, many staying over New Year's at Walter Annenberg's sprawling walled estate in Rancho Mirage. But the terrorist attacks of September 11, 2001, coupled with Walter Annenberg's death the next year, ended that tradition, perhaps for good.

BEYOND THE "VILLAGE" OF PALM SPRINGS

As the 1960s began, the valley's growth slowly shifted away from the City of Palm Springs and moved east, where vast stretches of vacant land and less restrictive development regulations held the promise of lucrative investment.

Cathedral City, which had long sought to become a part of Palm Springs, was a solid middle-class city of its own now. Indio was still the desert's largest city, and the communities in between—Rancho Mirage, Palm Desert, Indian Wells, and La Quinta—were on the way to becoming world-class cities with huge residential areas, exclusive country clubs, and, most importantly, prime retail areas. Desert Hot Springs, a little community in between the "high" and "low" desert areas, was being discovered as a place with abundant natural hot springs, sweeping views, and great land values.

The city government in Palm Springs, responding to the wishes of its residents, was extraordinarily strict in its building standards, banning neon, high-rises, and drive-through restaurants and regulating paint colors and virtually every aspect of a building's appearance. The so-called "cabaret" ordinances kept live music off the streets and dining off the sidewalks until the City Council approved the Thursday night VillageFest in 1991.

With such tight control, it was no surprise that the desert's first big indoor mall was built in Palm Desert after being rejected by Palm Springs in the early 1980s. The mall would have completely changed the city's downtown. Without it, Palm Springs could no longer compete for the tourist dollar, and many of its high-end boutiques moved east to Palm Desert, relocating in the mall or on that city's burgeoning El Paseo Drive.

Palm Springs opened the now-vacant Desert Fashion Plaza in 1984, but the die had been cast. Following the trend eastward, new megaresorts and golf courses opened in virtually every other desert city in the early 1980s, leaving Palm Springs in the shadow of newer, more glamorous developments. The Bob Hope Chrysler Classic opened in Indian Wells in 1960. Today every major sports tournament in the valley is played outside of Palm Springs.

The desertion of money and fame had some unexpected good news for Palm Springs. Without name recognition of their own, many of the other desert cities relied on the name of Palm Springs in their marketing and promotion, efforts that indirectly paid off for a city strapped for cash.

The tight development and sign ordinances also were responsible for bringing back some of the vanished Hollywood cachet, in the form of Sonny Bono. Bono, who owned a second home in the city, was embarking on a second career as a restaurateur. Stymied in his efforts to build a flamboyant entrance for his new restaurant, he jumped into politics and was elected mayor in 1988.

Over the next four years, Palm Springs and Sonny Bono were constantly in the headlines. Trying to end a boisterous spring break tradition, Bono banned thong bikinis in public. He presided over the creation of VillageFest, which successfully attracted tourists and locals from all over the desert. Under his leadership the city launched its own promotion department, taking the story of the city to the rest of the country and overseas. Most significantly, Bono founded the Palm Springs International Film Festival in 1990. The festival now marks the beginning of "high season" in January and attracts thousands of stars, movie industry decision makers, and film buffs from all over the world.

All through the 1980s, as development fever raged in the east end of the valley, Palm Springs seemed caught in a time warp, desperately trying to re-create a

Frank Bogert, "the cowboy mayor," still rides his horse every day and often leads trail rides in South America. The bronze statue of a rider on a galloping horse in front of Palm Springs City Hall is none other than Frank, modeled from a photo of him taken in the 1930s.

past that had moved on. Then, as the century came to a close, "midcentury" architecture suddenly became hugely popular all over the country. Palm Springs discovered that it was blessed with dozens of extraordinary buildings that had been spared from demolition simply because the developers' attention was elsewhere.

Every major travel magazine and newspaper rediscovered the city as "hip, hot, and happening." Film people and investors from Los Angeles snapped up ranch-style homes that had been empty for years. A new group of hoteliers came to town, restoring old motels and buying homes themselves.

In the last 10 years, Palm Springs has taken on a new life as a charming reminder of a gentler, more carefree past. Hollywood stars and players are once again buying homes in the "village," and another land boom is on.

ACCOMMODATIONS

It's generally accepted wisdom that the population of the desert doubles in high season, with a large part of this seasonal influx accounted for by second homeowners. In the desert cities there are around 15,800 hotel rooms, so even in the most crowded times, you're sure to find a place to lay your head. How much you pay for that place will vary wildly, from rock-bottom rates at small motels in the middle of summer to sky-high prices at megaresorts in February. If you can plan your visit for November, December, April, or May, you'll have a good chance of getting good rates and good weather at the same time. If you don't mind 100-degree-plus days and want the best value, book June through October.

Palm Springs has been a vacation mecca for almost a century. Virtually every national and international hotel company is represented here, from budget places like Super 8 and Howard Johnson's to super-luxurious resorts like The Lodge and the Hyatt Grand Champions. Midsize, mid-priced hotels such as the Embassy Suites, Hilton, and Marriott Courtyard are a good value for business travelers and others seeking a central location and predictable level of quality.

The valley has its share of small inns and boutique hotels, as well as accommodations catering to specific niche markets such as gay men and women and travelers looking for clothing-optional places.

Hotels number in the hundreds in the desert. We have not listed every single one but rather have chosen to highlight those that are outstanding in some way and are consistently recognized as clean, comfortable, and reputable. Instead of listing hotels by city, we are listing them by type of accommodation. Please note that if you are looking for familiar national chains such as Super 8, Motel 6, Howard Johnson's, the Marriott Courtyard, and Embassy Suites, these are well represented in the desert.

Boutique Hotels and Inns include those that are small—always less than 100 rooms—and offer a high level of individuality, personal service, and quality. These are "personality places" with lots of charm, good locations, and often an intriguing bit of history.

As a result of economic forces that first came into play in the 1980s, the overwhelming majority of boutique hotels and inns are in Palm Springs. During the 1980s megaresorts were the trend in hotel construction. A lack of empty land and a restrictive building code kept these huge resorts out of Palm Springs. For years the city was passed over in favor of cities to the east when it came to any new hotel development.

Then, when Palm Springs was "rediscovered" as a hip and charming little village in the 1990s, little mom-and-pop inns found that they were suddenly very attractive, to both visitors and developers. A renewed interest in midcentury architecture and a tourism trend that saw more sophisticated travelers looking for a personal touch all came together to lift the little hotels out of obscurity and into the level of "hot, hot, hot." Today many little places that were first opened in the 1930s, '40s, and '50s have been restored, face-lifted, and groomed to appeal to a new generation of traveler.

The Midsize Hotels category includes hotels that are larger than 100 rooms and offer a level of service and amenities above that which would be found in a basic motel. They have restaurants and room service, and often such extras as concierge service, gift shops, and valet parking.

Resorts are destination spots, places where you could spend your entire vacation without ever stepping outside the property. They have full concierge service, gift shops, restaurants and room service, spas, and fitness centers. They either have full business centers or offer basic business services such as faxing and copying. They also often feature tennis courts and golf courses. The desert resorts are like cruise ships: if you want to take a "shore visit" to see the rest of the area, fine; if you want to leave your car in the parking lot and call the hotel home, you will want for nothing.

Finally, the desert has a good number of accommodations that fall into the Specialty Lodging category. These include hotels that cater specifically to gay men and women, places that are clothing optional, and RV resorts. Condo and home rental companies will offer a variety of long-term (from a week to several months) options, from celebrity homes to simple studios on a golf course.

Because the desert is such a seasonal destination, hotels are highly competitive with rates and packages, and they spend a lot of time checking rate structures and offerings at comparable places. This means that you won't find a great deal of variation in rates if you're comparing hotels of roughly the same size and level of quality. Still, it pays to shop around, particularly at the larger resorts that do a lot of convention business. Cancellations or group confirmation numbers that are smaller than expected will open up space for leisure travelers and give you some bargaining power. You take your chances by waiting until the last minute, and we wouldn't advise doing that in high season, but you may get a great bargain at other times of year.

Another quirk that Palm Springs shares with many resort destinations is the ebb and flow of visitors during the week. Weekends are almost always busy, even in summer, when travelers from Southern California leave the urban areas to spend a few bargain days in the desert. If you're staying just a few days, try to make those days Monday through Thursday—you'll get a better rate. Finally, if you're visiting during high season, you may find that hotels require a minimum stay of two or even three days.

The hotel tax—called the Transient Occupancy Tax (TOT) in California—is not included in the quoted rates when you book a room, so be sure to factor that in. In a local quirk that owes everything to politics and the fact that the TOT is the only California tax that cities can keep to themselves without sharing with the state, the amount you'll be charged on your hotel bill varies from a low of 9 percent for all hotels in Palm Desert to a high of 13.5 percent for convention hotels in Palm Springs. Indian Wells charges 9.25 percent for all hotels. Indio, Desert Hot Springs, and Rancho Mirage charge 10 percent for all hotels. La Quinta charges 10 percent for non-convention hotels and 11 percent for convention hotels. Cathedral City levies 11.5 percent for all hotels, and Palm Springs charges 11.5 percent for non-convention hotels. Confused? Well, sure. Just remember that the tax is there—it won't show up on your quoted rate or in most published rate cards, but you'll definitely see it on your final bill.

The TOT is applied on all vacation rentals of fewer than 29 days. If you're staying in any rental accommodation for more than 29 days, you've just saved yourself a nice piece of money.

Two other charges you should know about are rarely included in the quoted rate. The first is the "resort charge" that some hotels impose to cover such things as parking, the morning paper, a continental breakfast, and so on. The second is a "utility surcharge" that hotels may tack on to compensate for the extremely high cost of electricity in the desert. Both of these charges usually show up only when you're confronted with the final bill, so avoid a surprise and ask about them when you make your reservations.

Accessibility is an issue that able-bodied travelers take for granted. In some hotels, "accessibility" may mean that one or two guest rooms are suitable for individuals in wheelchairs, but the dining room, pool area, and other facilities have too many physical barriers.

Several years ago in Palm Springs, two of that city's tourism "pioneers" took it upon themselves to publish the *Mobility Impaired Traveler's Guide to Palm Springs.* Philip Kaplan, ADA coordinator for the City of Palm Springs, and Murrell Foster, executive director for Palm Springs Tourism, set out with a camera and notebooks, taking almost a year to get the first guide in print. Hotels listed in the guide have participated on a volunteer basis, and there are fewer than 20 in the current printing. The guide includes photos and detailed information on parking, the main entrance, public areas, dining, conference rooms, recreation facilities, guest rooms, bathrooms in wheelchair-accessible units, and provisions for guests with hearing impairments. This is the kind of detail every hotel should have, but few do. For a copy of the guide, call Palm Springs Tourism at (800) 347-7746.

PRICE CODE

The price codes represent rates for two adults for one night in a standard room during high season, which is generally considered to begin in mid-January and end sometime in May. Many hotels will have three published rate structures: one for low season, in the summer; one for "shoulder season," from the fall through early January; and one for the winter months. Hotels in the desert have a history of experimenting with extra amenities, such as allowing pets, but this service is spotty and may be nonexistent in high season. If you are planning to travel with a pet, always double-check the hotel's policy and extra charges, if any. Most hotels offer rooms for smokers. If you are a non-smoker, be sure to specify a nonsmoking room when you make your reservations. Unless otherwise noted, all hotels take major credit cards. All listings are in Palm Springs, unless otherwise noted.

The following symbols indicate the price range for each accommodation listed. Price ranges do not include the Transient Occupancy Tax, resort charge, or utility surcharge. Inquire about these add-ons when you make your reservations.

$	less than $100
$$	$100 to $199
$$$	$200 to $299
$$$$	$300 and up

BOUTIQUE HOTELS AND INNS

Ballantines Hotel $$
1420 North Indian Canyon Drive
(760) 320-1178, (800) 485-2808
www.ballantineshotels.com
One of the first small hotels to get in on the midcentury Modern revival, Ballantines is cool kitsch, with each of its 14 rooms done in a different '60s theme. Create your own fantasy and check into the Pretty in Pink Suite, billed as a place Marilyn Monroe favored for private getaways. It's done completely in pink, with rose-colored melamine dishes and a 1950s radio, decorated with Monroe movie posters, and stocked with a 1,000-piece Marilyn jigsaw puzzle. All the rooms have kitchenettes and minifridges and front the small pool. It's a house-party atmosphere where you're always likely to run into a few Hollywood types and Los Angeles hipsters. Reservations are required.

Caliente Tropics Resort $$$
411 East Palm Canyon Drive
(760) 327-1391, (866) 468-9595
www.calientetropics.com
The Caliente Tropics Resort, a prime, kitschy example of the Polynesian-themed motels from the 1960s, was closed for a number of years. It reopened in 2001 after

a $2 million restoration that added tiki decor and furnishings and revamped the large private pool area. The site attracts tiki fans from all over country, particularly for the annual festivities that usually feature tiki carving, revelry around the pool, and a showing of an appropriate period movie or TV show such as *Hawaii 5-0*. The hotel has 90 rooms, which are quite large and have coffeemakers and minifridges. It's located on East Palm Canyon, a fair drive from downtown but conveniently located near the Sunrise shopping center, with a grocery store, post office, and small shops. Pets are allowed.

Calla Lily Inn $$
350 South Belardo Road
(760) 323-3654, (888) 888-5787
www.callalilypalmsprings.com
A 1950s-era motel converted into a charming tropical-themed inn, Calla Lily has nine oversized rooms around a pool and is surrounded by a wall for privacy. The owners are always on-site and delight in offering the kind of personal service rarely found in any large hotel, including complimentary cordials in the evening. Rooms have coffeemakers and refrigerators. The inn is located in the old Tennis Club area, along with many other small boutique places. Pets are allowed.

Casa Cody $$
175 South Cahuilla Road
(760) 320-9346
www.casacodypalmsprings.com
Built around a collection of 1930s adobe-style bungalows that have been nicely restored with a Santa Fe–style decor, wood-burning fireplaces, and full kitchens, Casa Cody is one of the original Palm Springs hotels. It's just a block or two from downtown and is set against the foothills in the area the locals call the Tennis Club neighborhood. The two pools and private patios make this a comfortable spot to spend more than a few days. The quality of the 23 rooms can vary widely, so it's a good idea to ask for visuals before you book and to check out the

room when you arrive. There is a two-bedroom 1910 adobe available to visitors. A four-bedroom house is still in the making.

The Chase $
200 West Arenas Road
(760) 320-8866, (877) 532-4273
www.chasehotelpalmsprings.com
Located 1 block off Palm Canyon in the heart of downtown, the Chase is another of the many midcentury-style hotels that make this area so unique. It was built in the late 1940s and has the clean, simple lines of that period. All 26 rooms face the saltwater pool and have full kitchens. Relax and play a few games of shuffleboard, then grill some steaks and pour a martini—you've just traveled back to the golden years of the old Palm Springs. Pets are allowed.

Coyote Inn $
234 South Patencio Road
(760) 327-0304, (888) 334-0633
www.coyoteinn.net
A newly renovated, Spanish Mission–style inn, the Coyote is walled and gated for lots of privacy. The seven suites, which face the pool and a beautiful mountain view, all have full kitchens, raised fireplaces, a hardback library, charming iron beds, and slick tile floors. It's another of the many small hotels in the Tennis Club neighborhood.

Del Marcos Hotel $$
225 West Baristo Road
(760) 325-6902, (800) 676-1214
www.delmarcoshotel.com
The Palm Springs Modern Committee gave the Del Marcos its 2005 Design Preservation Award. Designed by famous desert architect William F. Cody, this hip little spot features the classic motel-with-

Every hotel in the desert has at least one pool, and many have two or three. Don't worry—they're all heated in the winter months and ready for a dip.

pool design where rooms surround a courtyard and pool. Its 16 spacious rooms are decorated in clean midcentury style, and the Tennis Club neighborhood is the perfect spot to take a spin on one of the hotel's vintage bikes.

Ingleside Inn $$
200 West Ramon Road
(760) 325-0046, (800) 772-6655
www.inglesideinn.com

Once the home of the heirs to the Pierce-Arrow automobile fortune, the 1925-era Ingleside is a local landmark, a favorite place to have Sunday brunch at Melvyn's restaurant, and a magnet for Hollywood types who want a nostalgic hideaway. It's just off Palm Canyon Drive, a few blocks from the center of town in a quiet location across the road from Tahquitz Canyon. Rooms are all different, furnished with an eclectic mix of 1940s to 1960s antiques and bric-a-brac. The service is wonderful and personal—they will never forget a name here. Melvyn's is the site of an old-time piano bar and hosts a regular Sunday evening jam session that attracts local blues and jazz artists. Suites have private terraces, fireplaces and minifridges stocked with complimentary snacks fruit and cold drinks. The inn has 30 suites and villas, as well as a pool.

Korakia Pensione $$
257 South Patencio Road
(760) 864-6411
www.korakia.com

Owner/architect Doug Smith spent a lot of time operating a restaurant in the Greek islands, where he made a lot of connections with the rich, famous, and very hip, who frequent this Moroccan-style oasis just a few blocks from downtown. The main building was built in the 1920s by Scottish painter Gordon Coutts to remind him of his life in Tangiers. After Coutts died, it languished as an apartment house for many years. Then Doug got his hands on it and proceeded to work magic, cleaning and buffing and adding authentic bits and bobs from Greece and Morocco.

The 20 spacious rooms are a TV-free zone, and the guests often gather in the main courtyard for a freshly cooked, full American breakfast or impromptu cocktail party. Doug has also restored the little adobe-style villa across the street and added guest bungalows to create a uniquely simple and luxurious compound that is consistently full. Rooms have minifridges and coffeemakers, and there are two pools. Deposits are required when you book. There is a two-night minimum on weekends and a strict cancellation policy—give at least two weeks' notice (45 days on holidays) or lose the deposit.

Lake La Quinta Inn $$$
78120 Caleo Bay, La Quinta
(760) 564-7332, (888) 226-4546
www.lakelaquintainn.com

This gorgeous 13-room bed-and-breakfast overlooking the tranquil Lake La Quinta was among the top winners in the 2005 Best of Bed and Breakfast.com Awards. Selected as the Most Romantic, it was touted as a great place for a honeymoon. With its enormous cushy beds, tasteful country-estate decor, a fresh to-order breakfast every day, and private patios that encourage idling and daydreaming, this inn is indeed romantic. It also has a pool. One big potential drawback is the lack of soundproofing, which can make the proximity of eager honeymooners a bit uncomfortable.

La Mancha Private Villas
and Court Club $$$
La Mancha Sur II $$$$
444 North Avenida Caballeros
(760) 320-0398, (800) 593-9321
www.la-mancha.com
www.lamanchavillas.com

Just a block from the Palm Springs Convention Center, this luxury, gated compound has a total of 47 one- and two-bedroom villas, each with its own pool and spa. La Mancha was once Elizabeth Taylor's favorite desert escape, and the privacy is absolute. Most of the staff have been here for years, and their warmth and discretion are legendary. Many villas have outdoor wet bars and come with cabanas to escape the noon sun, a stereo system, DVD and VHS players, and projection TVs. These are fully appointed, homelike villas with a Mediterranean influence in the architecture and decor. La Mancha Sur II offers five super-large, super-deluxe villas. Guests can get room service from the La Mancha Resort Dining Room and take advantage of the nearby putting green, tennis courts, and croquet lawn. Pets are allowed.

L'Horizon $$
1050 East Palm Canyon Drive
(760) 323-1858, (800) 377-7855

One of the most gracious of the old Palm Springs hotels, the 22-room L'Horizon fronts busy East Palm Canyon Drive and looks for all the world like a tiny little inn from the street. Inside, you'll find a two-acre oasis of landscaped lawn and flowers; a low building housing spacious rooms and suites and a separate two-bedroom, two-bath house with a pool; a sunken fire pit; and a martini bar that was a favorite of the Rat Pack years ago. Decor is classic midcentury Modern, with cool white brick walls, plantation shutters, and clean-lined furniture. The staff is exceptionally warm and helpful. The main office/lobby also offers a library, classic table games, and bikes for roaming around town.

Orbit In/Oasis & Hideaway $$
562 West Arenas Road
(760) 323-3585, (877) 996-7248
www.orbitin.com

When the midcentury craze hit Palm Springs, a Portland, Oregon, couple bought two older bungalow motels a few doors apart and created a totally hip, charming little spot with lovely 1950s decor (furnishings by Eames, Noguchi, and Risom), a day spa, saltwater pools, a convivial atmosphere at breakfast and happy hour, and an attitude of laid-back luxury. The inn has 18 rooms. The cruiser bikes are a good excuse to leave your car in the parking lot and explore the town in the open air. It's located in the Tennis Club neighborhood, where most of the cute little inns have popped up in the past 10 years.

Orchid Tree Inn $$
261 South Belardo Road
(760) 325-2791, (800) 733-3435
wwww.orchidtree.com

Located in the Tennis Club area of small historic hotels, the Orchid Tree sprawls over several acres. It has 40 bungalows, suites, studios, and rooms as well as three pools. Its cluster of tile-roofed Spanish bungalows was built in 1934. An authentic and beautiful restoration and expansion entered its final phase in 1999. Once seven separate smaller properties, Orchid Tree is composed of 19 separate buildings representing each decade from the midteens through the late 1950s, including a building designed by noted Swiss modernist architect and Palm Springs resident Albert Frey. The grounds are landscaped with citrus and other trees, flowers, and cacti. Hummingbirds, mockingbirds, roadrunners, and quail take advantage of the many bird feeders, baths, and birdhouses. The bungalows have full kitchens, and everywhere you turn there is an exquisite attention to detail that has taken years to accomplish.

Pepper Tree Inn Palm Springs $$
622 North Palm Canyon Drive
(760) 318-9850, (866) 887-8733
www.peppertreepalmsprings.com

A recent renovation has transformed a drab little motel into a charming Spanish Colonial–style retreat, with 34 guest rooms built around a central pool and surrounded by high walls and gates. The location is in the town's antiques district, with some interesting shops, galleries, and restaurants a stroll away. The pool is filled with saltwater rather than the usual chlorine-saturated wet stuff. Rooms have refrigerators and coffeemakers. Some have fireplaces and Jacuzzis.

Smoke Tree Ranch $$$$
1850 Smoke Tree Lane
(760) 327-9490, (800) 787-3922
www.smoketreeranch.com

Once a private resort where the cottages were all owned individually, Smoke Tree has modernized and opened to the traveling public. It's a western-style property, with spare desert landscaping that's a stark contrast to the overwatered, brilliant green lawns and flower beds of most Palm Springs hotels. All accommodations are in 51 little cottages with refrigerators and basics such as Internet access. Many have fireplaces. In the "Ranch House," meals are served daily, and guests gather to swap tales of a rough day on the golf course. Amenities include use of the adjacent Smoke Tree Stables, a kids' playground, and old-fashioned fun such as croquet, lawn bowling, and horseshoes. The property also has a pool, fitness center, guest laundry, clubhouse, basketball, tennis, and putting green. Smoke Tree is open only from October through April.

The Springs of Palm Springs Hotel
& Spa $$
227 North Indian Canyon Drive
(760) 327-5701
www.thespringsofps.com

Built in 1935 and gorgeously renovated to the Spanish Revival and Craftsman styles of that era, the Springs, like many other motels-turned-inns in the desert, has rooms that face a central courtyard. This courtyard is definitely a cut above the rest, with a shaded lounge area and out-door fireplace. Rooms have graceful iron beds, elegant custom cabinetry and furniture, fireplaces, minifridges, microwaves, and coffeemakers. The Springs has 25 rooms and a pool, small spa and fitness center, and hair salon.

Sundance Villas $$$
303 Cabrillo Road
(760) 325-3888
www.sundancevillas.com

Located in the city's north end, in a quiet residential area, Sundance was originally built as timeshares and private homes. It's a sprawling gated compound of 19 spacious two- and three-bedroom villas with enclosed courtyards, private pools, and such homelike amenities as gas barbecues, two-car garages, washers, and dryers. Sundance also offers tennis and a large community pool. For a family or group of friends who want to stay a while and have all the comforts of home, this is an excellent value. The only drawback is its distance from downtown. A car is a must.

Viceroy Palm Springs $$
415 South Belardo Road
(760) 320-4117, (800) 670-6184
www.viceroypalmsprings.com

Formerly the Spanish Mission–styled Estrella Inn, the 68-room Viceroy is a collection of bungalows, suites, and rooms built around a beautifully landscaped, sprawling property with three courtyards and pools. The bungalows date from the 1930s and have been redone in a glamorous, rather over-the-top "Hollywood Regency" style heavy on mirrors and a color scheme of black, white, and yellow. The small spa and fitness center are sparkling and modern, and the Citron bar/restaurant is a local favorite for evening drinks or desserts. It's located in the Tennis Club area, just a block from downtown.

Villa Royale Inn $$$
1620 Indian Trail
(760) 327-2314, (800) 245-2314
www.villaroyale.com

---

i *Although wireless Internet is gaining popularity in the desert, it's still got some kinks. Some hotels offer it only in the lobby, and some of the providers offer software that works with PCs, but not with Macs. Indeed, some of the hotel Internet connections work only with PCs. If all else fails, visit a local Kinko's, where modern electronics prevail.*

This Mediterranean-style compound once was the estate of a Palm Springs old-timer. Reimagined and rebuilt by a Palm Springs City Council member who had been a Hollywood set designer, it's an unexpected bit of whimsy in the desert. The 30 rooms and suites are each decorated in the style of a different European city or region, and no two have the same theme. Several courtyards, fountains, and garden areas, plus a charming poolside bar and the award-winning Europa Restaurant have made this a favorite for romantic getaways. Rates include full American breakfast.

The Willows $$$$
412 West Tahquitz Canyon Way
(760) 320-0771, (800) 966-9597
www.willowspalmsprings.com
The Willows is the only AAA Four-Diamond property in Palm Springs, and it's a beauty. With just eight rooms, this has got to be the most luxurious and personable small hotel in the entire desert. Gloriously restored from the days when it was a private home hosting such luminaries as Carole Lombard, Clark Gable, Marion Davies, and Albert Einstein, the Mediterranean-style villa has won a pile of awards, including Condé Nast's "Most Outstanding Inn in North America" and USA Today's "Top Ten Romantic Inns." Each room is different and lovingly furnished with antiques, fine linens, fireplaces, hardwood floors, handmade tiles, and luxurious baths, as well as up-to-the-minute electronics. A hillside garden and waterfall, small pool, cozy parlor, and outdoor dining area complete the hideaway. Catered meals from neighboring restaurant Le Vallauris are always available. The hotel is open only to registered guests, so the privacy is complete. It's right next door to the Palm Springs Art Museum, yet nestled up against the foothills away from the bustle of downtown.

MIDSIZE HOTELS

Best Western Las Brisas $
222 South Indian Canyon Drive
(760) 325-4372, (800) 346-5714
www.bestwesterncalifornia.com
On busy Indian Canyon Drive near downtown, this 90-room property is an affordable step above a basic motel. Rooms are sparkling clean and roomy, with light desert colors. Refrigerators and coffeemakers in every room, free American breakfasts, and a well-priced lunch make it a good choice for budget-minded travelers and families who want a little something extra. The Las Brisas also offers a pool, lounge, and restaurant.

Desert Hot Springs Spa Hotel $$
10805 Palm Drive, Desert Hot Springs
(760) 329-6000, (800) 808-7727
www.dhsspa.com
One of the oldest spa hotels in Desert Hot Springs, this one is a favorite for fans of natural hot mineral springs. Everything—including the 50 rooms, lounge/bar, and restaurant—is centered around the pool area. An Olympic-sized main pool and seven smaller soaking pools plus a large Jacuzzi offer a lot of soaking and sunning. The hotel also has a fitness center. Rooms are basic and serviceable, with decor and soft goods that date back several years.

Fantasy Springs Resort Casino $$
84-245 Indio Springs Parkway, Indio
(800) 827-2946
www.fantasyspringsresort.com
The Fantasy Springs Casino has been building and improving from day one, and its newest addition is this 12-story, 250-room hotel aimed at vacationers and business groups. It feels for all the world like Vegas, with the racket of slot machines, multiple restaurants, a golf course, a sparkling pool, and an entertainment center that books many of the same names appearing on the Strip. Rooms have flat-screen TVs, minifridges and coffeemakers, and crisp new furniture and soft goods. The hotel also offers a fitness center and

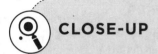

Smoke Tree Ranch

Perhaps the desert's most exclusive and hidden getaways since the 1930s, Smoke Tree Ranch had its beginning in 1887, when a group of land speculators bought hundreds of acres on the north side of Smoke Tree Mountain. Their elaborate plans called for a new city—to be called Palmdale—with parks, homes, a narrow-gauge railroad to connect with the Southern Pacific, and acres of citrus orchards, grapes, and melons. A stone irrigation ditch was built, the narrow-gauge tracks were laid, and the project was set for prosperity when an extended drought set in, turning the growing fields to dust and scattering the dreamers.

Adobe ruins on the Ranch grounds today are all that remain of the spot's early history. Forty years went by before Fred and Maziebelle Markham bought the property and quietly began building a desert legend. A woman who prided herself on being a gracious and welcoming hostess in homes the couple had in Altadena and Balboa Island, Maziebelle thought of the Ranch as another version of a well-run home with extended-stay houseguests. She and her husband created the many cottages as a place where their friends and like-minded acquaintances could count on family-style holidays in exclusive surroundings.

For these highly successful and well-connected businesspeople, the Ranch must have been a bracing change from their lives on the "outside." Ranch life was simple and spare. The roads were dirt, kept in check by a roving sprinkler and scraper team. Barbed wire separated the property from the surrounding desert, and the landscaping was pure nature. The cowboys from Smoke Tree Stables, also owned by the family, led horseback rides and sang songs around the bonfires at night.

In 1945 the Markhams sold the entire property—400 acres—to the Colony, as the steady visitors had named themselves, and new Colonists could come in only with the approval of the entire group. Walt Disney was one of the newcomers. He bought a cottage in 1948 and used it as a place to relax and plan his new Southern California dream park. While he was imagining, he had his designers create six cottages that still exist on the site today. Walt loved this place so much that he snuck a little reminder of the Ranch into Disneyland. The statue of Disney that stands outside Sleeping Beauty's Castle has the brand insignia of Smoke Tree Ranch.

Life at the Colony was a several-months affair for many of the owners, who settled in from October through May. Children spent the mornings at the Ranch's school, whose three buildings and playground stood along the western border, not far from today's gate. Afternoons were free for sports or studies, then an early dinner with the teachers. At 6:30 P.M. on the dot, adults came together for a family-style dinner on the long wooden tables in the Ranch House. Each diner had a special branded clothespin hanging on the dining hall wall to use as a place card, napkin holder, and emblem of prior visits—each visit earned a hash

The little cottages at Smoke Tree Ranch, one of the desert's most exclusive original accommodations, are now open to the public. PHOTO COURTESY OF SMOKE TREE RANCH

mark, and the more marks your pin had, the greater your status.

A rodeo field hosted professional rodeos and gymkhanas, and cowboy crooners were called on to lead songs in the evenings. In many ways it was a make-believe western world, created in the minds of men and women raised with the images of Roy Rogers and Gene Autry, and it was the polar opposite of the Palm Springs lifestyle sought by most other affluent visitors.

Today, though the Ranch is open to the traveling public, more than 300 acres are reserved for the Colony's 85 homes,

many of which are enjoyed by the children and grandchildren of the original Colonists. The Markhams' descendants continue to be involved in the Ranch, which still retains its simple, western dude-ranch aura.

Walt Disney's cottages and 51 other bungalows are available to visitors, who can also opt for a full meal plan or just enjoy the surroundings. Cowboy singers still entertain at night around a bonfire, and the days hold long, lazy hours for swimming, playing tennis, wandering the nature trails, and dreaming the Hollywood western dream.

beach volleyball, and a concierge is ready to help guests. The Avalon Bay boutique in the new shopping concourse is the most recent boutique addition, selling resort-type clothing. A new Starbucks coffee bar has just opened, the better to stay awake to play the odds in the 96,000-square-foot casino.

Hilton Palm Springs Resort $$$
400 East Tahquitz Canyon Way
(760) 320-6868, (800) 522-6900
www.hiltonpalmsprings.com

This mainstay near downtown has just renovated the public space, all the guest rooms, and its main dining room, which is a favorite of locals for a fresh, hearty breakfast. Rooms are oversize and offer all the amenities you'd expect in a midlevel city hotel, such as desks, two-line phones, and coffeemakers. The pool is one of the most convivial in town, with a well-run pool bar and a good central location. The hotel has 266 rooms and 71 suites as well as a concierge, restaurant, lounge, business center, fitness center, massage salon, and gift shop.

Holiday Inn Palm Mountain Resort $
155 South Belardo Road
(760) 325-1301
www.palmmountainresort.com

Definitely one of the most upscale Holiday Inns you'll come across, this one is in the old Tennis Club area of Palm Springs, just a half block from the center of downtown. Rates are affordable, the grounds are gorgeously landscaped and always in bloom, and the rooms are just large enough not to induce claustrophobia. You'll probably be out walking, anyway, as this is very close to all the downtown attractions, restaurants, and bars. The adjacent bar/restaurant is operated separately and has gone through a dizzying number of incarnations, from seafood restaurant to trendy bar to family cafe. The hotel has 122 rooms—each with a microwave, refrigerator, and coffeemaker—and a pool and fitness room.

Hyatt Regency Suites Palm Springs $-$$
285 North Palm Canyon Drive
(760) 322-9000, (800) 554-9288
www.palmsprings.hyatt.com

This place caused quite a commotion when it opened in the early 1980s as a venture of Pierre Cardin. It was the first structure in town that was more than three stories, and it was part and parcel of the Desert Fashion Plaza, an indoor shopping mall that was shuttered in 2001 and has become the city's biggest white elephant. The Hyatt is an all-suite hotel, with 600-plus-square-foot suites opening onto a central atrium lobby/dining room. The dining room and adjacent bar are great places for people-watching, as the hotel is right on Palm Canyon Drive and is a regular stop for locals and celebs looking for a cool drink or a generous happy hour. The pool is a tiny slice of water on the back of the hotel, which commands a spectacular view of the San Jacinto Mountains foothills that tower over the nearby Palm Springs Art Museum and O'Donnell Golf Course. The 194 suites have been recently remodeled, replacing the dated mauves of the original with fresh new desert tones. The hotel offers a business center, concierge, putting green, exercise studio, and day spa.

Indian Wells Resort Hotel $$
76661 Highway 111, Indian Wells
(760) 345-6466, (800) 248-3220
www.indianwellsresort.com

Preferred tee times and privileges at Indian Wells Country Club and the Golf Resort at Indian Wells are the main attractions here. The hotel itself has not been kept up and has gotten a local reputation for spotty service and tired decor. The presidential suite is billed as the largest in the desert, with 4,500 square feet, four bedrooms, five large marble baths, two floors with a private elevator, a full kitchen, a marble bar, a fireplace, and a huge living/dining/entertaining area. The property has 155 guest rooms plus a pool, two golf courses, and three restaurants.

Palm Court Inn $
1983 North Palm Canyon Drive
(760) 416-2333, (800) 667-7918
www.palmcourt-inn.com
A good spot for families and budget travelers, the 107-room Palm Court is a bit far from the center of town, but it offers a wonderful mountain view, good basic rooms, and usually one of the best rates around. Rooms aren't stocked with refrigerators, microwaves, coffeemakers, or hair dryers, but these are usually available for no fee. The hotel has a large pool with a children's wading pool, a coin laundry, and an exercise room, and there's a diner-style restaurant next door.

Ramada Resort & Conference Center $$
1800 East Palm Canyon Drive
(760) 323-1711, (800) 245-6907
www.psramada.com
Primarily a business and convention hotel, the 255-room Ramada is very competitively priced. The lobby has been recently renovated, and 14 suites have been refurbished, but the guest rooms are overdue for deep cleaning and replacement of soft goods. The pool area is enormous. The restaurant and bar have a new Art Deco style and a run-of-the-mill menu that doesn't take advantage of the area's abundant fresh produce and available seafood. This is a good spot for the business traveler who's just passing through and needs a predictable, inexpensive place to stay that's a cut above the chain motels. Rooms have refrigerators and coffeemakers.

Spa Resort Casino $$
100 North Indian Canyon Drive
(888) 999-1995
www.sparesortcasino.com
Originally built in the 1960s as the first development on Indian-owned land, the Spa has undergone a transformation from a basic but boring hotel into a stylish, bustling hub for locals and visitors. Part of the draw is the world-famous Spa, built around the city's original hot mineral springs, and its Well Spirit Fitness Center.

The pool is one of the largest and most social in town, and the neighboring, $95-million casino has added a sharp dose of Vegas-style excitement. More than 900 slots, 30 table games, and a high-limit gaming room, along with six restaurants and lounges, attract hopeful gamblers at all hours and keep a steady buzz going. A $2.3-million renovation of the hotel's 228 guest rooms was completed in 2003, giving the rooms a "California desert" theme, with warm earth tones and touches of dark wood and leather.

Wyndham Palm Springs $$$
888 Tahquitz Canyon Way
(760) 322-6000, (800) 996-3426
www.wyndham.com
Although it's one of the city's largest hotels, with 410 rooms, the Wyndham is also the headquarters hotel for the Palm Springs Convention Center and is geared to conventions and meetings rather than the traveler looking for a luxurious vacation escape. A moderate ($5 million) renovation has just been finished, polishing up the lobby and the lounge area, adding Wi-Fi throughout the hotel, and updating guest rooms. Amenities include a pool with children's area, a restaurant, a lounge, and a business center.

RESORTS

**Desert Springs JW Marriott
Resort & Spa** $$$$
74855 Country Club Drive, Palm Desert
(760) 341-2211, (800) 331-3112
www.desertspringsresort.com
Situated on 450 acres of lavishly landscaped grounds and lagoons, this sprawling oasis-style resort opened with an over-the-top splash in 1987 and is still one of the largest resort and convention complexes (with 884 rooms) in the southwestern United States. From the flock of flamingos feeding in the saltwater streams by the entrance to the massive lobby where guests board little boats to navigate the waterways that lead to restau-

Most of the large resort hotels have multilingual staff and can provide a basic translation service for visitors who are not fluent in English. If you know you or your traveling companions will need this, call ahead to make arrangements.

rants, to the expansive spa and golf course, everything here is big and bold. Several gift shops sell the glittery resort clothes that ladies seem to wear only on vacation. There's a Starbucks in the lobby and a new Sculpture Walk that displays international artwork for sale. The hotel is even on the schedule of the free Palm Desert Shopper Hopper shuttle bus, so you can hop aboard, shop till you drop all over town, and take the bus back in time to get ready for cocktails and an elegant dinner. The rooms are midsize and tastefully if predictably furnished with the familiar "desert" colors of rose and tan. They have minibars but no coffeemakers. The hotel offers three pools, two 18-hole golf courses, an 18-hole putting green, 20 tennis courts (hard, clay, and grass), a spa and fitness center, a hair salon, basketball courts, croquet, biking, a business center, a Kids' Klub for children 4 to 12, 17 shops, and 13 restaurants and lounges. A concierge is available to assist guests.

Doral Desert Princess Resort $$$
67-967 Vista Chino, Cathedral City (760) 322-7000, (888) 386-5672 www.doralpalmsprings.com
The 285-room Doral is located in the middle of Cathedral City on a 27-hole championship golf course and offers both traditional guest rooms and condo rentals at the sister Desert Princess Country Club. This is a good place for the avid golfer who wants a desert vacation with lots of golf and doesn't want to pay the top dollar charged at the better-known resorts. The property is kept up well and has just put a little over $1 million into fluffing up

the public areas and guest rooms. The condos are a good value, especially with the golf. Country Club amenities include a full pro shop, driving range, two putting greens, and a clubhouse with a dining room and lounge. Rooms have coffeemakers and minifridges. The property has a pool, a fitness center, a spa, tennis, hot tubs, volleyball and racquetball courts, and a restaurant.

Hyatt Grand Champions Resort and Spa $$$$
44-600 Indian Wells Lane, Indian Wells (760) 341-1000, (800) 554-9288 www.grandchampions.hyatt.com
With a $65 million renovation completed in 2003, the 479-room Grand Champions remains a strong contender for the title of "best megaresort" in the valley. The once-famous tennis stadium has been replaced with an enormous spa that not only offers the expected skin and body services but also encompasses the Medical and Skin Spa. Here, guests can get a host of noninvasive cosmetic procedures done—Botox, skin peels, laser treatments, and fillers such as Restylane. Golf is provided a short cart's drive from the main hotel at the Golf Resort Indian Wells, with two championship courses designed by Ted Robinson. The Hyatt is also home to the Callaway Golf Performance Center and Pro Shop, a state-of-the-art facility that focuses on a combination of technology and personal instruction to improve your golf game.

The hotel's gift shop sells resort clothing, jewelry, and souvenirs, as well as the usual magazines and sundries. The Hyatt is also on the schedule for Palm Desert's free Shopper Hopper shuttle, which makes the rounds to the city's major shopping areas each day. Rooms are spacious—550 square feet—and furnished in the popular "desert tones" of browns and sunset shades. All have coffeemakers, minifridges, and upscale toiletries. There's also a high-priced, private access floor with more spacious rooms, more luxurious amenities, its own concierge, and complimentary breakfast and evening cocktails/hors d'oeuvres. Amenities at the Hyatt include seven pools and whirlpools, a waterslide, tennis, a fitness center, a business center, Camp Hyatt for children, a concierge, a beauty salon, and five restaurants and lounges.

La Quinta Resort & Club $$$$
49-499 Eisenhower Drive, La Quinta
(760) 564-4111, (800) 598-3829
www.laquintaresort.com

The desert's first resort, La Quinta was built in 1926. At the time, it was a true hideaway—surrounded by miles of empty desert and a very long hike from Palm Springs. Today it's in the heart of fast-growing La Quinta and has itself grown to encompass hundreds of acres and 90 holes of some of the country's best golf, including the famous Stadium Course at PGA West and the picturesque Mountain Course at La Quinta Resort itself. This is a true destination resort—one where you can hand over the car keys at check-in and pick them up days (or weeks) later when you tear yourself away. The spa is a brilliant combination of indoor and outdoor treatment spaces, a huge fitness center, and Yamaguchi Salon, one of the desert's best full-service beauty salons. Also located adjacent to the spa is the Wellmax Center for Preventive Medicine, a facility that features a wide array of tests and medical evaluation procedures, supervised and performed by doctors on staff at local hospitals. This is aimed at those who want to seriously evaluate and adjust their lifestyles and has become increasingly popular with high-stress executives.

Accommodations are in guest rooms, casitas, suites, or villas. The 840 rooms are decorated in Early California style, with rugged wrought-iron and wood furniture and warm earth tones. All rooms have coffeemakers and minifridges; some have fireplaces. The casitas and villas have private patios and a lot of room. Some come with private pools and kitchens, and they've become favorites for writers and business types who need a beautiful secluded spot to work. The five restaurants offer every-

thing from juicy hamburgers to elegantly prepared French cuisine. The central Plaza is a lovely spot landscaped like a Spanish courtyard with flowers, fountains, and handmade tiles. Surrounded by an assortment of shops and the hotel's restaurants, it feels like the center of a small town. Other amenities include tennis, a fitness center, a business center, and a concierge.

Le Parker Meridien Palm Springs $$$$
4200 East Palm Canyon Drive
(760) 770-5000
www.parkermeridien.com

The Parker has had a lot of incarnations over the years. As the Gene Autry, it spent many years as a local landmark, where locals came to have a belt at the bar and admire the Singing Cowboy's silver-trimmed saddle in the lobby. It was later purchased by Givenchy and revamped with a huge rose garden and faux-French decor, but it never caught the imagination and struggled with low vacancy rates. Today's Parker is the result of a $27-million renovation, which was completed in 2004. The rose garden is gone, replaced with a central area that's become a social center, drawing the Hollywood "in" crowd and featuring palenque and croquet, fire pits, oversized outdoor furniture, and paths that wind through the desert-style landscaping and a huge tropical palm garden. The 13-acre, 117-room property is done up in high "Rat Pack" style, with decor and ceramics specially designed by Joseph Adler and a high level of service (including a concierge) where virtually every staff person knows your name within minutes of check-in. The large rooms feature feather beds, sheepskin throw rugs, and photos of such '60s icons as Warren Beatty and Julie Christie. Gene Autry's original residence is now available for rent as well. The Palm Springs Yacht Club spa and fitness center has been recently upgraded and offers a full range of skin and body treatments.

Lovely details like no added charges for parking, free wireless Internet and in-room modem access, and the offer of a complimentary bottle of water as you drive off for the day make this hotel feel much warmer than any of the megaresorts. The Parker attracts a younger, hipper, happier crowd than the megaresorts as well. Children and conventions are welcome, but they are not the main scene, and they don't take over the landscape. The details that are not so lovely include the lack of coffeemakers and informational materials in the rooms. The idea is to have a service staff person at your beck and call, but sometimes a person just wants to have a cup of coffee alone and plan the day without chatting up a stranger. The hotel offers two pools (one saltwater), tennis, two restaurants, a bar, and an 18-hole golf course.

The Lodge at Rancho Mirage $$$$
68-900 Frank Sinatra Drive
Rancho Mirage
(760) 321-8282, (888) 367-7625
www.lodgeatranchomirage.com
The Lodge at Rancho Mirage is currently closed for renovatons and is not scheduled to reopen until December 2007. This resort began life as the Ritz-Carlton, Rancho Mirage, an anomaly in the desert with its marble floors, oriental carpets, and formal 19th-century-Boston decor. It was recently acquired by Rock Resorts out of Vail. This elegant resort is perched on 24 acres in the Santa Rosa Mountains foothills, with a spectacular view overlooking the entire valley floor. There are 240 rooms on three levels. The rooms and suites are oversize, all boasting large patios or balconies. The ultimate luxury, the Club Level, is a concierge floor with a

Families with small children should ask if the hotel is set up for children or if it is more appropriate for adults. Since an "adults-only" policy violates California's strict antidiscrimination laws, this will never be spelled out. Of course, kiddie pools and children's menus signal that a hotel welcomes small ones.

private lounge, personal concierge service, and four complimentary food events each day—as close to a cruise ship as you can get in the desert. If you've just won the lottery, you might want to spend a few nights in the Gerald Ford Suite, soaking in the Jacuzzi, playing a few tunes on the baby grand, and calling for butler service when the mood strikes. Other amenities include tennis, a spa, two restaurants, a pool, a fitness center, a croquet lawn, a gift shop, and a 24-hour business center. Guests have privileges at Mission Hills Country Club, including preferred tee times on the club's golf course.

Miramonte Resort & Spa $$$
45-000 Indian Wells Lane, Indian Wells
(760) 341-2200, (800) 237-2926
www.miramonteresort.com
Miramonte really has created its own category—that of small luxury resort. It has no golf course but has specially trained golf and tennis concierge staff who will make preferred tee-time reservations at many top courses, set up lessons, and arrange pairings and foursomes. Styled after a Tuscan country estate, the hotel has arranged its 222 guest rooms in several villa-style buildings scattered over 11 acres of gardens and citrus groves. Winding paths, fountains, and small courtyards give the property a feeling of quiet and privacy. One of the large pool areas is set up for children and their parents and is situated well away from the adult area, which has private cabanas, just a few steps from the outdoor patio and bar. An extensive renovation in 2005 included the guest rooms and lobby restaurant/bar as well as construction of a new spa, The Well. Miramonte also offers a gift shop and a business center.

Palm Springs Riviera Resort
and Racquet Club $$$
1600 North Indian Canyon Drive
(760) 327-8311
www.psriviera.com
The Palm Springs Riviera Resort and Racquet Club is currently closed for renova-

tons and is not scheduled to reopen until the fall of 2007. A fixture in Palm Springs since the 1960s, the "Riv," as it's known locally, was that era's most famous celebrity hangout and was the site of many scenes in the movie *Palm Springs Weekend*. Those freewheeling days are long gone, and the most frequent guests are now business travelers. This 476-room resort has been one of the host hotels for the annual Easter Bowl Junior Tennis tournaments, as well as the yearly White Party, a gay men's circuit event. It's a good idea to ask about large groups or events booked into the hotel when you call for reservations. An unusual feature here is the hotel's cogeneration plant, which provides electricity year-round. Amenities include tennis, a putting green, a fitness center, basketball and volleyball courts, a restaurant, and poolside dining.

Rancho Las Palmas
Resort and Spa $$$$
41-000 Bob Hope Drive, Rancho Mirage
(760) 568-2727, (800) 458-8786
www.rancholaspalmasresortandspa.com
Often overshadowed by the glitzy resorts at the eastern end of the valley, the 444-room Las Palmas actually has one of the best locations. Almost dead center between Palm Springs and La Quinta, it's right across the street from The River, the huge entertainment/dining complex that packs in the tourists and locals all year. If you're staying here, you can stroll across the street and back, casting a smug glance at the dozens of cars circling the lot looking for prime parking spots. A 27-hole Ted Robinson–designed golf course and large spa/fitness center are the big draws. Rooms are standard Marriott—neither spacious nor cramped and done in tasteful if bland desert colors. Rooms all have coffeemakers and minifridges. The beauty salon has an excellent reputation among the locals for expert haircuts and nail services. The hotel also offers two pools, tennis, a business center, concierge service, and four restaurants/lounges.

Renaissance Esmeralda
Resort and Spa $$$$
44-400 Indian Wells Lane, Indian Wells
(760) 773-4444
www.renaissanceesmeralda.com
Between 2002 and 2003, the Esmeralda put $31 million into renovations and upgrades, including new mattresses, TVs, seating areas, and decor in the guest rooms. The new furnishings have a touch of the desert's popular midcentury Modern style mixed with touches of leather and dark wood to warm it up. Rooms have coffeemakers and minifridges. The spa was added at the same time and has won awards in its size category (14,000 square feet). Indoor and outdoor treatment areas provide serene spaces for a wide menu of massage and skin and body treatments, as well as waxing and nail services. The main pool is stunning, located right off the central lobby area and sited to take advantage of the sun all day. This 560-room hotel is set up to handle a lot of convention and group business but somehow avoids feeling like a "by the number" hotel. It hosts not only the desert's prestigious Town Hall series of lectures, which book world-famous political figures, but also many of the glitziest charity events. Sirocco restaurant received "Best Italian restaurant in the Desert" honors from Zagat in 2005. Amenities include three pools, two golf courses, a clubhouse, tennis, a fitness center, a business center, concierge service, five restaurants/lounges, and children's programs.

The Westin Mission Hills
Resort and Spa $$$$
71333 Dinah Shore Drive, Rancho Mirage
(760) 328-5955, (800) 228-3000
www.westin.com
Situated well away from the town centers, the 512-room Westin sprawls over 360 acres, most of it taken up by two excellent golf courses. The 18-hole Gary Player Course is owned by the hotel and thus always saves its prime tee times for hotel guests. The Westin is primarily a group

and convention business hotel, with a great deal of meeting space and a somewhat cold, impersonal feeling. It is amenity-heavy, though (with three pools, a pro shop, a clubhouse, tennis, three restaurants/lounges, a fitness center, a business center, concierge service, and children's programs), and good for an anonymous escape in luxurious surroundings. Count on driving while you're here, as the valley's action—shopping, movies, theater, exotic dining, and even the relatively nearby Agua Caliente Casino—is well down the road. The rooms are comfortable and tastefully furnished in uniformly unforgettable style—browns and beiges. All have coffeemakers and minifridges. Small dogs are permitted.

SPECIALTY LODGING
Gay Hotels

Palm Springs has been a gay-friendly destination for decades, and you won't find any hotel that discourages gay visitors or treats them with anything but respect and warmth. In addition, more than 35 hotels and inns in Palm Springs and Cathedral City cater specifically to gay and lesbian travelers. These are all small and mostly gay-owned and/or -managed. Most of them are in Palm Springs and are located in three neighborhoods, none of which are more than a mile or so apart.

Warms Sands, just a few blocks east of Palm Canyon Drive, is the most established gay residential neighborhood, with a number of gay men's properties. A few blocks to the south in the Deep Well community and on San Lorenzo Road are several more groups of gay and lesbian hotels. Just north of downtown near the old Movie Colony neighborhood is a third scattering of hotels and spas for the gay traveler.

Many of these small hotels are still finding their particular niches in the gay tourism business—wild and rowdy or quiet and more dignified. On occasion, a previously gay-oriented hotel will change hands

and do an about-face, marketing to the general tourism industry. And, every year, a small inn or two changes its emphasis from general travelers to gay travelers.

The Palm Springs Tourism and the Desert Gay Tourism Guild have worked together for years to promote gay tourism to the valley. They publish an excellent and informative *Gay Tourism Guide* that lists gay-oriented hotels, and they also have up-to-date information on the DGTG Web site, www.dgtg.org. For reservation information on gay hotels, contact the Palm Springs Visitor Information Center at (888) 866–2744 or visit www.palm-springs.org.

Since 1989 the White Party in Palm Springs has been promoted all over the world as the premier event on the gay party circuit. It's the biggest annual tourism-revenue-generating event for the city, stretching over nine days and attracting as many as 25,000 revelers. Festivities are held every Easter Week, with the actual White Party held on Saturday night at the Palm Springs Convention Center.

With so many partygoers in town, several of the city's large hotels have capitalized on the crowd by offering up their entire hotel for the duration, hosting afternoon pool parties that are the daytime highlights of the week. Downtown hotels such as the Hilton, Wyndham, Hyatt, and Spa get in on the action, as does the Riviera at the north end. The White Party is generally confined to downtown Palm Springs, with more mainstream Easter Week vacationers booking into the hotels in other cities. For complete information about each year's White Party, visit promoter Jeffrey Sanker's Web site, www.jeffreysanker.com.

A few of the outstanding gay hotels are listed below.

Casitas Laquita $$
450 East Palm Canyon Drive
(760) 416–9999, (877) 203–3410
www.casitaslaquita.com
This lesbian-friendly inn is a one-acre-plus compound done in Old Mission style, with charming small bungalows built around a

courtyard and pool area. All rooms have full kitchens, and many have large Southwestern-style fireplaces. The hotel is close to downtown and has great mountain views. A pool, barbecue areas, catering, and spa services are available.

Desert Paradise Resort Hotel $$
615 Warm Sands Drive
(760) 320-5650, (800) 342-7635
www.desertparadiseresorthotel.com
The 14 suites are named after famous diva/actresses like Cher, Barbra Streisand, Elizabeth Taylor, and more. Furnishings are simple and clean, and the suites all include wide-screen TVs and full kitchens. All rooms are built around the central area, which contains a pool, fire pit, gazebo, and breakfast patio. Guests can enjoy the Jacuzzi. A complimentary continental breakfast is provided. Clothing is optional.

El Mirasol Villas $$
525 Warm Sands Drive
(760) 327-5913, (800) 327-2985
www.elmirasol.com
One of the desert's most venerable gay hotels, El Mirasol has been around for 25 years and is said to have been built by Howard Hughes in the 1940s. The grounds are walled and gated like all the gay hotels and feature winding paths, lush landscaping around the two pools, and an outdoor steam room/shower. The lanai and fireplace are the central gathering spot for breakfast, lunch, and evening get-togethers. The rooms, located in newly remodeled bungalows, are spare and clean. Wet bars, kitchens, and private patios are available. Complimentary breakfast and lunch are provided, and clothing is optional.

The Hacienda at Warm Sands $$
586 Warm Sands Drive
(760) 327-8111, (800) 359-2007
www.thehacienda.com
Out & About magazine included this on their first list of "Top 10 North American Gay Guesthouses." It's small, like all of the gay hotels, with 10 spacious guest suites

Many larger hotels and a surprising number of small ones are pet-friendly. They have designated rooms set aside for pets and somewhat higher rates to cover the extra work and potential cleaning. If you're traveling with a pet, be sure to check on this and ask about any limitations, such as the size or type of pet allowed.

opening onto two pools and a Jacuzzi. Rooms include full gourmet kitchens, two-man showers, teak and bamboo furniture, and well-chosen antiques. The larger suites have fireplaces. An extensive continental breakfast and full lunch are included in the price. There's a concierge, a large library of movies and books, beautifully kept grounds, and the option of in-room massage by local therapists. The hotel is clothing-optional.

INNdulge Palm Springs $$
601 Grenfall Road
(760) 327-1408, (800) 833-5675
www.inndulge.com
A consistent winner of the *Out & About* Editor's Choice award, INNdulge is party central for many gay visitors to Palm Springs. There are 22 poolside rooms built around the pool and what is billed as a "22-man Jacuzzi." A full gym is open at all hours. A complimentary breakfast is included, and clothing is optional.

Inn Exile $$
545 Warm Sands Drive
(760) 327-5413, (800) 962-0186
www.innexile.com
One of the desert's "party hotel" spots for gay men, this is a two-and-a-half acre walled compound with four pools, two hot tubs, a full gym, a billiard room, an outdoor fireplace, and the "Gang Walk" social room. Rooms are basic, with generic furnishings and decor. Complimentary breakfast and lunch are provided. Clothing is optional.

La Dolce Vita Resort $$
1491 South Soledad
(760) 325-2686
www.ladolcevitaresort.com
The gated and walled inn features 16 rooms that open onto the central pool and three garden area rooms, private cabanas around the grounds, an outdoor gym, and a steam room. Rooms come with refrigerators and microwaves, upscale bath amenities from Aveda, and hardwood floors. Guests enjoy complimentary breakfast and evening cocktail hours. Clothing is optional.

Terrazzo Palm Springs $$
1600 East Palm Canyon Drive
(760) 778-5883, (866) 837-7996
www.terrazzo-ps.com
In the Deepwell area near grocery shopping and restaurants not far from downtown Palm Springs, Terrazzo has gotten several awards from *Out & About* magazine. Its 12 rooms are nicely furnished in bamboo-tropical style, and all face the pool. Most have microwaves and refrigerators. Clothing is optional.

Clothing-Optional Hotels

With more than 360 days of sunshine each year and a dry, warm climate, the desert is the best place in California to run around naked. Even Albert Frey, the famous Swiss-born architect who lived and designed here until his death in his 90s, was a confirmed "naturist."

And it's fitting that one of Frey's designs is now a popular clothing-optional hotel, the Terra Cotta Inn. Located in the quiet north end of town, the Terra Cotta has been the recipient of numerous awards for its service and standards. The desert's other two clothing-optional places, the Desert Shadows and Morningstar, are always booked.

Although many of the gay hotels are also clothing-optional, the atmosphere couldn't be more different. These places are quiet, private, and on the up-and-up, catering primarily to couples.

Desert Shadows Inn $$
1533 Chaparral Road
(760) 325-6410, (800) 292-9298
www.desertshadows.com
This place is the site of the famous "nude bridge" that spans Indian Canyon Drive to connect the hotel's two sites. Building of the bridge caused quite a flap a few years ago, mostly because the city gave it a nice subsidy. Those looky-loos hoping to get a glimpse of bare suntans scampering across the bridge were soon disappointed. The high sides provide complete privacy. This is a modern Southern California–style hideout with lots of fans inside and out and misted pool areas. The 93 spacious rooms have full kitchens, coffeemakers, and microwaves. Other amenities include tennis, a restaurant, and a bar.

Morningside Inn $$
888 North Indian Canyon Avenue
(760) 325-2668, (800) 916-2668
www.morningsideinn.com
With just 10 rooms, the Morningside Inn caters to couples and has a convivial, social atmosphere. The rooms are just a few steps up from a basic motel, with microwaves and VCRs. Some have full kitchens. The inn has a pool. The service is personable and warm, and the location is not too far from the middle of downtown.

Terra Cotta Inn $$
2388 East Racquet Club Road
(760) 322-6059, (800) 786-6938
www.sunnyfun.com
The 17 oversize rooms have sitting areas, minifridges, microwaves, and coffeemakers. Suites offer full kitchens, private patios, sunken tubs, and big-screen TVs. On-site spa services are available in the rooms or in the poolside gazebo and include massage, waxing, facials, and nail services. The central pool is the site of a daily complimentary breakfast. Guests can use the barbecue or call for catered meals.

Vacation Rentals

There are a few excellent companies that specialize in handling rentals for condos and homes throughout the desert. They provide turnkey service and often will be happy to add on such services as stocking the refrigerator, making dinner reservations, and recommending a good local doctor. Options are extremely wide, from simple studios near downtown to lavish homes on golf courses. Daily, weekly, and monthly rates are available, and you can often find good package deals during holiday or slow-season periods. These agencies are a great choice for families and groups who want privacy, security, and home-style amenities and who want someone else to do the footwork.

Some of the larger country clubs in the area also offer rentals throughout the year.

Finally, the desert has a number of timeshare properties that offer rentals to the public. These rentals are handled by the parent timeshare company, so you must contact them directly rather than through a rental agency.

Two rental companies—Desert Condo Rentals and McLean Company Rentals—consistently have the best selection and service.

Desert Condo Rentals, Inc.
4741 East Palm Canyon Drive, Suite D
(760) 320-6007, (800) 248-2529
This is an excellent company with a wide selection of condo rentals throughout the desert, from economical studios to luxury spreads with access to golf courses. The staff is friendly, reliable, and resourceful and will help you make a selection based on your budget, preferred location, and length of stay.

McLean Company Rentals
4777 South Palm Canyon Drive
(760) 322-2500, (800) 777-4606
www.ps4rent.com
Mike McLean, a former football star, brings the same level of intensity to his business as he once did on the field. His company offers a huge variety of condo and private home rentals, all in top shape. If you want to spend the week in the home of a now-deceased and once-famous Hollywood star, this is the place to go. Condos in virtually every country club in the desert are on the rental rolls, and the staff will do everything from stocking the fridge with goodies before you arrive to arranging theater tickets and dinner reservations.

Timeshares

Club Intrawest $$$
1 Willow Ridge, Palm Desert
(760) 674-1200, (877) 258-5852
www.clubintrawestresorts.com
Desert Willow is a stunning architectural combination of Anasazi and Mexican Riviera influences, all cool plaster walls and slick tile floors. Right across the street from the Marriott Desert Springs and situated along the fairways of the Desert Willow Golf Course, this is a refreshing departure from the sometimes overdone Southern California style of many desert resorts. The service is exceptional, and the setting couldn't be better. Extras, besides the expected pool and fitness center, include a mini-basketball court, a private movie theater, children's game rooms, and tennis courts.

Marquis Villas $$$
140 South Calle Encilia
(760) 322-2263, (877) 288-5463
www.marquis-villas.com
Once part of the Marquis Hotel, which is now the Hotel Zozo, the property has 63 extremely spacious (900 square feet) one-bedroom villas just a block from the heart of downtown Palm Springs. Since being acquired by Sunterra Resorts, the rooms and public areas have received a much-needed sprucing up and are both comfortable and elegant, with full kitchens, fireplaces, wet bars, and private balconies. The resort also has a small fitness center and tennis courts.

The hotel reservation service operated by Palm Springs Tourism offers reliable, seven-day-a-week service and the best rates. It's good for last-minute deals and can be a big help when rooms are tight. Unfortunately, it only books Palm Springs hotels, and there are no comparable services for other desert cities. Call Palm Springs Tourism at (800) 347-7746.

Marriott's Shadow Ridge Resort $$$
9003 Shadow Ridge Road, Palm Desert
(760) 674-2600

Marriott's Desert Springs Villas
1091 Pinehurst Lane, Palm Desert
(760) 779-1200
www.vacationclub.com
Guest rooms and one- and two-bedroom condo-type accommodations are available at all of these Marriott timeshares. The newest, Shadow Ridge, is quite a ways from the center of the valley and is in the midst of a major expansion that will bring a total of more than 900 villas, several more pools, and other amenities to the 12-acre property. The property has a Faldo-designed 18-hole championship golf course, along with tennis courts, a fitness center, a minimarket, a casual restaurant, a children's pool and activity center, and two restaurants. The Desert Springs Villas are adjacent to the monster resort, Marriott's Desert Springs, and share its facilities, including a golf course, tennis, a stand-alone spa, gift shops, and multiple restaurants.

Oasis $$
4190 East Palm Canyon Drive
(760) 328-1499, (800) 525-5894
www.sunterra.com
A Sunterra resort, the Oasis is an older property that has been recently upgraded to replace worn furnishings and generally spiff up the exterior. There are several pools, tennis courts, a spa, and a barbecue area. Accommodations all have full kitchens, washer/dryers, and other condo-style amenities. It's a good choice for families wanting a taste of the good life and room to spread out without an outrageous price tag.

Shadow Mountain Resort & Club $$
45750 San Luis Rey, Palm Desert
(760) 346-6123, (800) 472-3713
www.shadow-mountain.com
This older resort is just a few blocks from trendy El Paseo. The rooms and studios have kitchenettes, and the one-, two-, and three-bedroom condos have full kitchens. The resort is showing its age and could use some newer decor, a good painting inside and out, and a bit of fluffing up on the landscape. Still, the location is one of the best for timeshare/condo rentals, and the rates are affordable. A bonus is the 18-court tennis facility and golf nearby at the private Shadow Mountains Golf Club.

RV Resorts

In recent years, the number of RV resorts has dropped dramatically, just as desert real estate has skyrocketed in value. Little mom-and-pop places have all but disappeared, muscled out by the two big resorts. These book up well in advance of the season and cut their services to the bone in the summer months. The few little RV parks are more campground than resort and offer hookups but not much else.

Emerald Desert Golf & RV Resort $
76000 Frank Sinatra Drive, Palm Desert
(760) 345-4770, (800) 426-4678
www.emeralddesert.com
This is very likely the poshest RV resort in Southern California, with pools, a golf course, clubhouses, fitness centers, a pro shop, a minimarket, complete laundry facilities, telephone and Internet access, sparkling bathrooms and showers, fax and copy service, and even indoor, climate-controlled storage for folks who want to

leave their super-luxury RVs on-site all year. Those people who know the RV lifestyle will love this place. There's a full calendar of activities through the week, from bridge and watercolor painting to line dancing, water aerobics, yoga, and golf lessons. Barbecues, horseshoe pits, billiards, bocci ball, and croquet courts are part of the amenity-crammed site. The full amenities are only available October through May, however, and the resort has a strict policy about children under 18. With few exceptions, they are not allowed. Although hotels can't get away with this, the RV courts have found a way around it. This is not a family-oriented place but rather is geared toward older adults. The property has 760 spaces.

Shadow Hills RV Resort $
40655 Jefferson Street, Indio
(760) 360-4040
www.shadowhillsrvresort.com

 Across the street (or freeway) from Sun City and its public golf course, this RV mecca has all the amenities that vacationers in 45-foot RVs have come to expect when they put down roots for the season. There's a huge clubhouse and fitness center, a pool and spa, a full kitchen, bathrooms and showers, and an Internet and small business center. The resort has 100 sites.

RESTAURANTS

There are literally hundreds of places to eat out in the Palm Springs area, from taco shacks to opulently decorated haute cuisine restaurants. Plenty of places are suitable for families, too, with reasonable prices, varied menus, and a welcoming atmosphere.

Because it's impossible to list every restaurant in the desert, we've chosen those that are beloved by locals and popular with visitors because of their food, service, price, atmosphere, or some other outstanding feature.

To help you find your way to a great meal, we've organized the restaurant listings in three main categories: Family Fare, Casual Eats, and Fine Dining. Within each broad category, you're sure to find a good selection of cuisines and styles.

Family Fare includes places that offer low to mid-priced food, a wide range of menu choices, and a relaxed atmosphere. Most of these restaurants offer lunch and dinner, and many also serve breakfast. Reservations are not required and often not taken.

Casual Eats are restaurants that fall in between the Family Fare and Fine Dining categories. They may cater to the sports bar, lounge-dancing, or after-golf crowds and rarely have special children's menus. You will be perfectly comfortable dining here without a suit jacket or cocktail dress,

and these restaurants may be appropriate for families with older children or teenagers.

In Fine Dining you'll find establishments that pride themselves on gourmet food and fine wines as well as a high standard of presentation and decor. The Fine Dining spots do not cater to children, usually require reservations, and have the highest prices.

At most desert restaurants, prices and menu choices vary widely with the seasons, with the summer and early fall offering the best values. With a few exceptions, we do not list dining spots inside casinos or hotels, as these tend to go through frequent changes. We also do not list fast-food places or national chains but instead concentrate on those restaurants that are unique to the desert. Rest assured, you will be able to find all of your favorite fast-food places here, including McDonald's, Pizza Hut, Domino's, El Pollo Loco, Jack in the Box, Wendy's, Taco Bell, Dairy Queen, Arby's, Burger King, and more. The moderately priced chain restaurants, such as Denny's, Ruby's Diner, Tony Roma's, Hamburger Hamlet, IHOP, California Pizza Kitchen, and Marie Callender's, are all represented here and offer both good value and familiar food.

A word about geographic locations: Wherever you are in the Palm Springs area, you're never far from a good selection of dining spots. The layout of the valley, with Palm Canyon Drive (also known as Highway 111) running right through the middle of each city, means that most large shopping, dining, and entertainment clusters are right there, taking advantage of the nonstop traffic. So, in Palm Springs, you'll find most restaurants along Palm Canyon Drive downtown and in the half mile or so around the downtown core.

Restaurants in Cathedral City follow this rule as well, with a collection of fast-food places on the western city limits and

Some say that the Early Bird is the official bird of the Palm Springs area. With the exception of fast-food places and very upscale dining spots, most every restaurant features "early-bird specials" at some time during the year. Choices are limited and you'll have to eat early, often before 6:30 P.M., but the value is great.

more upscale places to the east. In Rancho Mirage the stretch of highway known as Restaurant Row stretches from Shame on the Moon and the Café at The Lodge on the western city limits to Wally's Desert Turtle on the east. In between these two elegant signposts is The River, the desert's most popular eating/entertainment area. A number of Southern California chains, such as P.F. Chang's, Johnny Rocket's, and the Cheesecake Factory, are here, as well as a fine selection of dining and drinking places, from the ubiquitous Starbucks to Baja Fresh, the Yardhouse, Acqua Pazza, and Fleming's Steakhouse, which also has a place in Palm Springs.

In Palm Desert, restaurants are concentrated both on Highway 111 and along El Paseo Drive, which parallels Highway 111 for several blocks. Here you'll find eating choices that range from fast-food outlets, to high-quality chains such as California Pizza Kitchen, to the haute cuisine spots that attract the country club set. As Palm Desert fades into Indian Wells on the east, the best restaurants are found in major hotels, from the Miramonte's Brissago to the Esmeralda's Sirocco, two of the finest Italian restaurants in the desert.

La Quinta also has its share of fine dining, with restaurants scattered all over the city, from the old downtown to small shopping malls and the La Quinta Resort.

Restaurants in Indio are more down-to-earth, with the full complement of fast-food eateries as well as a number of moderately priced Mexican and American places.

Choosing where to eat in the Palm Springs area is often a matter of deciding how far you want to drive and where you want to be at the end of the evening. And if you're suddenly starving at the end of the day, just head to Highway 111/Palm Canyon Drive—good food is always just a few minutes away. Restaurants come and go, and one that's been a mainstay for 20 years may have moved, closed, or been renamed by the time you are using this guide. Also, hours change with the seasons. A place that requires reservations in February may be happy to take walk-ins during the summer. Always call ahead to avoid disappointment. The same holds true for days of operation. During high season, most restaurants are open seven days a week. There is no consistent day of closing for six-day restaurants, though Monday and Tuesday are most common. Again, call ahead.

PRICE CODE

Prices vary as much as the type of food and the atmosphere, and there is a great deal of difference between high and low season in many places. The following price categories are indicative of high-season prices and approximate the cost of an average dinner for two, without cocktails or additional side dishes and desserts.

$	$10 to $24
$$	$25 to $49
$$$	$50 to $100

Readers should assume that all the establishments listed accept major credit cards unless otherwise noted. Unless otherwise noted, alcohol is served. All listings are in Palm Springs, unless otherwise noted.

All restaurants in California have a no-smoking policy, even in the bar areas. Some restaurants have separate outside patios where they may or may not allow smoking.

FAMILY FARE

Big Fish Grille & Oyster Bar $$
74225 Highway 111, Palm Desert
(760) 779-1988
www.restaurantsofpalmsprings.com
A good place for the family's special dinner, this is truly fish central, with a huge menu that changes daily according to the fresh fish available. The oyster bar features a large selection of oysters, clams, assorted other shellfish, and fresh fish in a more casual atmosphere. Diners can choose from a quiet indoor dining spot, the lively bar, or outside patio seating by

the waterfall. Prices are good, and each fish selection can be prepared in a variety of ways, all to order. Desserts include such classics as fresh fruit sorbet, hot fudge sundae, and cheesecake. The restaurant is open for dinner only.

Billy Reed's Restaurant $-$$
1800 North Palm Canyon Drive
(760) 325-1946

This is a Palm Springs institution, as popular for breakfast and lunch as it is for dinner. It's a bustling spot with several dining areas, including cozy tables, booths, a counter, and a separate bar/lounge area. You'll find all ages and income levels here, all coming for the yummy pot roast, meat loaf, fried chicken, enormous salads, and fresh, multilayered chocolate cake. It's all home-style cooking, with generous portions and very reasonable prices. The wait staff has been here for at least a thousand years, and they know how to make everyone feel at home.

Bit of Country $
418 South Indian Canyon Drive
(760) 325-5154

A local favorite for old-fashioned (forget the "heart-healthy" dishes—you won't find them here) trucker-style breakfasts and burgers. Try the scrambled eggs mixed with bits of ham and order it with the hot biscuits and country-style gravy. It's a tiny place, with a handful of tables outside on busy Indian Canyon Drive, and no more than a dozen booths inside. The wait is worth it. Open for breakfast and lunch only. No alcohol.

All of California is a no-smoking zone, although some establishments do offer small outside areas where you can light up, and the "cigar zone" seems to come and go in different places. The glaring exceptions are in the Indian-owned casinos, although these places have wisely made their dining rooms nonsmoking.

Café des Beaux-Arts $
73640 El Paseo Drive, Palm Desert
(760) 346-0669
www.cafedesbeauxarts.com

Right across from The Gardens shopping complex on El Paseo Drive, this is a great place to people-watch while you're refueling during a hard day of browsing art galleries, jewelry stores, and gift boutiques. Sidewalk seating is at a premium, and changing exhibits of fine art from neighboring galleries provide color. The menu features sandwiches and soups with a Mediterranean-French flair, classics such as coq au vin, and a great children's menu with a twist—ham-and-cheese crepes instead of a standard grilled cheese. There's a standard prix fixe, three-course dinner, with a good selection of French and Californian wines. Open for breakfast on the weekends and for lunch and dinner daily.

Cedar Creek Inn $
1555 South Palm Canyon Drive
(760) 325-7300

This is a lovely spot, with rather ordinary food that never strays too far from the basics you would find anywhere in middle America—burgers, Cobb salad, pot pies, and so on. A big advantage is that it's open seven days a week, all year, serving breakfast, lunch, and dinner. There are always early-bird specials and a nightly happy hour with live entertainment in the adjacent bar area.

Don & Sweet Sue's Café $
68955 Ramon Road, Cathedral City
(760) 770-2760

The cafe has delicious burgers, sandwiches, and salads, but breakfast is the all-star production here—massive waffles and pancakes, plates overflowing with ham and eggs and bacon and biscuits and gravy, oh my! You can find some reasonably healthy fare with fruit on the side, but why bother? This is the best breakfast in the desert, bar none, so expect a bit of a line on weekends. It's also known for fast and faultless service, though, so chat up your neighbors and get ready for Paul

Bunyan–style portions. The restaurant serves breakfast (until 2:00 P.M.), lunch, and dinner. No alcohol.

El Gallito Restaurant $
68-820 Grove Street, Cathedral City
(760) 328-7794

This is the famous "hole-in-the-wall" Mexican restaurant you always want to find but hear about only after you've left town. If you yearn for fresh, simple, homemade Mexican food with salsa that sears every corner of your mouth, this is the place. Service is warm and friendly, prices are dirt-cheap, and portions are huge. Open for lunch and dinner only.

Elmer's $
1030 East Palm Canyon Drive
(760) 327-8419, (800) 325-5188
www.elmers-restaurants.com

A bustling pancake house that's been serving big, fluffy German pancakes and delicate crepes for decades, Elmer's is a diner close to the heart of many a local. Home-style pot roast, fried chicken, and roast turkey dinners are the best bet for dinner. Open for breakfast, lunch, and dinner. No alcohol.

Fisherman's Market & Grill $
235 South Indian Canyon Drive
(760) 327-1766

44250 Town Center Way, Palm Desert
(760) 776-6533

78575 Highway 111, La Quinta
(760) 777-1601

Because the company owns a commercial fishing operation, they can guarantee fresh deliveries every day. The prices are very affordable, and the atmosphere is strictly paper napkins and Formica tables. You order from the counter, and your food is cooked to order and delivered directly from the kitchen. The Palm Springs location has a funky little cocktail/oyster bar offering appetizers, beer, and wine from early evening. In Palm Desert and La Quinta, the restaurants are located in small shopping centers with plenty of parking. All three locations are open for lunch and dinner only.

La Casita Restaurants $
100 South Indian Canyon Drive
(760)-320-2267
www.lacasitarestaurants.com

This family-owned group of seven little Mexican restaurants is one of the best values around, although the atmosphere is basic and frill-free. Several of the restaurants offer seasonal all-you-can-eat buffets on different weeknights, with the typical enchiladas, tostadas, burritos, and beans and rice. Try the chile verde and order some fresh tortillas on the side. The price is right, and you can feed a whole family for very little. Call the Palm Springs restaurant for hours and specials at the other ones throughout the valley. Open for lunch and dinner only.

Las Casuelas Café $
73-703 Highway 111, Palm Desert
(760) 568-0011

Las Casuelas—The Original
366 North Palm Canyon Drive
(760) 325-3213

Las Casuelas Nuevas
70-050 Highway 111, Rancho Mirage
(760) 328-8844
www.lascasuelasnuevas.com

Las Casuelas Quinta
78-480 Highway 111, La Quinta
(760) 777-7715
www.lascasuelasquinta.com

Las Casuelas Terraza
222 South Palm Canyon Drive
(760) 325-2794

The Casuelas restaurants are a desert legend and wildly popular with locals and visitors. All feature excellent, well-priced Mexican food, and each has its own specialties. Las Casuelas, the original family cafe, offers an unchanging menu of well-loved Mexican dishes, such as enormous burritos and enchiladas. Terraza builds on that base with heart-healthy items and a substantial children's menu. Nuevas brings

Las Casuelas

In 1958 Maria Hernandez de Delgado and her husband, Florencio Delgado, opened the first Las Casuelas on Palm Canyon Drive in downtown Palm Springs. The two had met and married in Jerome, Arizona, where they operated the town's favorite Mexican restaurant, Armida's. Las Casuelas instantly became a hangout for everyone from Hollywood stars to local laborers.

All of the Delgado children grew up working in Las Casuelas—busing tables, serving, working the cash register, and learning in the kitchen. As the family grew, so did their restaurant business. Son Joaquin and his wife Sharon now operate the original Las Casuelas, known locally as "little Casuelas."

Some years later the Delgados opened Las Casuelas Terraza a few blocks south of the original on Palm Canyon Drive; it is now operated by daughter Patty, who is the eldest of the third generation. *Hispanic Magazine* has ranked Terraza among the "Top 50 Best Hispanic Restaurants in America" two years in a row. Numerous other awards and long lines waiting for tables year-round are testaments to the restaurant's popularity. Most locals refer to Terraza as "Las Cas," and no visit to Palm Springs is complete without a meal and a margarita here.

Named "Businessperson of the Year" and "Small Business Owner of the Year," Patty carries on the family tradition of community involvement, serving on the boards of the Desert Regional Medical Center, Agua Caliente Cultural Museum, Shelter from the Storm, and United Way of the Desert. As Patty says, "Part of what we've done at Terraza is to create a learning experience for those unacquainted with Mexican culture. The image of the comic-book Mexican lying under a cactus is so prevalent that we delight in dispelling it."

In 1973 daughter Florence and her husband Rick went on to open Las Casuelas Nuevas on Rancho Mirage's Restaurant Row. Patterned after a colonial hacienda in Mexico, this is the most elaborate of all the Casuelas establishments, and its central location draws diners from all points of the valley.

Designed by local architect David Christian, Nuevas fills the two requirements Maria and Florencio had: "Make it beautiful, and make it Mexican." The design takes the hole-in-the-wall stereotype of a Mexican restaurant and runs it out of town. Huge mahogany doors imported from Mexico, handmade *saltillo* and Talavera tiles, and wrought-iron chan-

more salads into the mix; Quinta spotlights pasta, rotisserie, and barbecue; and Café features breakfast fare. All have a soft spot in their hearts for children and lots of seating options. All of the restaurants serve lunch and dinner.

Manhattan in the Desert $
2665 East Palm Canyon Drive
(760) 322-3354
This spot has gone through a lot of different incarnations, and it seems as if the current one may stick. It's a consistently

Las Casuelas Terraza is a visitor and local "must-do" in downtown Palm Springs. PHOTO BY TAYLOR SHERRILL, COURTESY OF LAS CASUELAS NUEVAS.

deliers, lanterns, and arches lend an air of old-world elegance and style. Like its cousin Terraza, the restaurant rambles from patio to dining room to bar to more dining rooms, making a very large building seem intimate and cozy.

Kitchen design and efficient service are two Casuelas hallmarks, and the restaurants have set the standard for both in the desert. Every meal feels relaxed and intimate, even though each restaurant often serves as many as 1,000 a day. Newer additions to the restaurant family include Las Casuelas Quinta and Las Casuelas Café, both of which continue the Delgado tradition of presenting traditional Mexican fare in beautiful surroundings.

With almost 30 years in the desert, Las Casuelas is an intimate part of the community, and a good place to get a true feeling for the personality of Palm Springs—an ambitious and hardworking heart beneath a beautiful, relaxed face.

good place for breakfast, lunch, and casual dinner, with affordable prices and a menu that offers more than 100 different sandwiches, salads, and entrees. There's a full bakery and deli here, as well as a limited selection of wines and beers.

More Than A Mouthful Cafe $
134 East Tahquitz Canyon Way
(760) 322-3776
Culinary Institute graduates run this high-quality breakfast and lunch spot in the heart of downtown Palm Springs. Every-

thing is fresh, and made on the spot. The menu changes constantly, and the chefs-in-training use a lot of imagination in the preparation and presentation. Service can be a little rough, and the more inventive creations may not always be successful—but it's a lively place and a nice change from the more predictable sandwich and soup spot. Plus, you may be one of the first to sample fare from Southern California's next big celebrity chef. No alcohol.

Native Foods $
1775 East Palm Canyon Drive
(760) 416-0070

73890 El Paseo Drive, Palm Desert
(760) 836-9396
This is the one consistently good "health food" place in the desert, and if you're lucky enough to get there in time on most Fridays, ask for the tamales, a specialty of the Palm Canyon Drive place. Tofu, tempeh, beans, and veggies are the mainstays, and the cuisine leans to Mexican and South American tastes. Open for lunch only. No alcohol.

Sammy's Woodfired Pizza $$
73595 El Paseo Drive in The Gardens on El Paseo, Palm Desert
(760) 836-0500
Generous portions of salads, fresh pizzas, and simple entrees, plus a tapas bar and casual outdoor dining make this a good place to rest up after your shopping spree in The Gardens. The service is consistently good, and the food is fresh. It's right next door to Tommy Bahamas, so if island-style cuisine isn't to your liking, this is a good alternative. Open for lunch and dinner only.

If you're having trouble getting into the newest, hottest restaurant, try asking the concierge at your hotel. These men and women are often very "plugged in" and can make the right call to get a reservation.

Sherman's Deli & Bakery $$
401 East Tahquitz Canyon Way
(760) 325-1199

Plaza de Monterey Shopping Center on Country Club Drive, Palm Desert
(760) 568-1350
A real Jewish deli with house-baked breads and desserts, scratch matzo-ball soup, and dozens of different sandwich combinations, Sherman's is the place where old-time residents meet to catch up on local gossip. The Palm Springs Sherman's is also a good place to spot Hollywood movers and shakers during the annual Palm Springs International Film Festival each January. The best values are the combination dinners—ordering a la carte can be a bit pricey. Open for breakfast, lunch, and dinner. No alcohol.

Simba's Rib House $
190 North Sunrise Way
(760) 778-7630
This is the place to abandon all thought of healthy, calorie-conscious eating and just dig in to amazing soul food—collard greens, hush puppies, jambalaya, fried chicken, barbecued ribs—in a huge buffet surrounded by cafe-style tables and chairs. There are menus, but they're pointless when the real bounty is in that buffet. Simba's is open for dinner only and is closed in the summer. No alcohol.

Thai Smile Restaurant $
651 North Palm Canyon Drive
(760) 320-5503

42-476 Bob Hope Drive, Rancho Mirage
(760) 341-6565
These unpretentious little places serve excellent, affordable, and authentic Thai dishes using fresh veggies, fish, chicken, herbs, and native spices. They're local favorites for the reliably good Pad Tai, hot-and-sour soup, and other specialties. The Palm Springs restaurant is situated on Palm Canyon Drive right between the arts and antiques district and the heart of downtown, so it's a good spot to stop for

an inexpensive and filling meal while window-shopping. Open for lunch and dinner only. No alcohol.

Tyler's Burgers $
149 South Indian Canyon Drive
(760) 325-2990
Get there early, because the lines can be formidable at noon, when what seems like the entire downtown shows up for juicy burgers, crispy fries, and plates of little "sliders," baby-sized burgers or cheese-burgers. It's in the former home of an A&W drive-in, and there's only room for the kitchen, a small counter, and a couple of seats inside. Outside, you can find a bit of room under a canopy and watch the tourists shop in La Plaza, the original shopping area in Palm Springs. But the burgers are what will bring you back and keep you waiting in line. Open for lunch only. No alcohol.

CASUAL EATS

Al Dente Pasta $$
491 North Palm Canyon Drive
(760) 325-1160
The menu includes homemade pasta, grilled chicken, steaks, veal, and fresh seafood. The veal piccata is to die for, and the fresh bread is always warm from the oven. It's a small, intimate spot perfectly placed for the first or last stop on a stroll around Palm Canyon Drive. The restaurant features an extensive wine list and is open for lunch and dinner only.

Arnold Palmer's Restaurant $$
78164 Avenue 52, La Quinta
(760) 771-4653
www.arnoldpalmers.net
Only in Palm Springs—a restaurant with its own 50-yard, nine-hole putting course. Arnold Palmer's features a three-pronged menu, with unusual takes on comfort food (macaroni and cheese with lobster, mush-rooms, and white cheddar), broiler selec-tions including prime rib and hearty steaks, and a changing Chef's Menu that

Valet parking may be your only option at a hotel restaurant or on a busy street. These services have excellent reputa-tions, and damage or theft is extremely rare. For peace of mind, though, use everyday caution when you're out, leav-ing valuables behind or storing them out of sight in the trunk.

takes advantage of seasonal items and the chef's fertile imagination. Every Thurs-day there's a traditional Thanksgiving din-ner, and the bar (Arnie's Pub) has become a favorite for dancing from late afternoon until closing. Open for dinner only.

The Beer Hunter $
78-483 Highway 111, La Quinta
(760) 564-7442
www.thebeerhunter.com
This is the desert's best sports bar, with nine satellite receivers getting coverage from four different satellites and showing it all on 32 TVs. Bored with being a barstool potato? There's also pool, shuffle-board, foosball, darts, and video games. As befits its name, the place offers oceans of beer, both in bottles and on tap. The menu has a lot of variety, including vege-tarian dishes, but those in the know will go for the juicy burgers or fresh roasted turkey. There's no livelier place to be for Monday night football, playoffs of any kind, and even the Tour de France. Open for lunch and dinner only.

Black Angus Steakhouse $$
69640 Highway 111, Rancho Mirage
(760) 324-8407
www.blackangus.com
This traditional, well-priced steakhouse has been around for 40 years. Prime rib is served daily, along with signature hand-cut New York steaks, center-cut filets, and traditional surf and turf (a hefty lobster tail that can be combined with any of the steak entrees). The children's menu is extensive, and the staff is warm and

friendly—very experienced in serving families. There's a full bar and traditional desserts such as ice cream, cakes, and crème brûlée. Open for dinner only.

Blue Coyote $$
445 North Palm Canyon Drive
(760) 327-1196

72760 El Paseo Drive, Palm Desert
(760) 776-8855
This started out as a tiny cafe-cum-patio on North Palm Canyon Drive in the years before that area became known as the gallery and antiques section of town. It's been hugely successful, expanding several times and opening a second place in Palm Desert. Cooking is Yucatán-style, set off with black beans, homemade tortillas, and fresh tomatillo-laced salsa. It's always a popular spot for happy hour, with an eclectic crowd downing the oversized Wild Coyote margaritas, people watching on the patio, and enjoying the music. Open for lunch and dinner only.

Capri Italian Restaurant $$
12260 Palm Drive, Desert Hot Springs
(760) 329-6833
One of the best restaurants in the desert and certainly the best in Desert Hot Springs, this busy, casually elegant place is famous for its thick, juicy steaks—not the usual specialty in an Italian restaurant. Capri does a fine job with the more traditional fare, as well, including tender veal, pastas, and antipasto. The atmosphere is warm and noisy. You'll leave feeling like a very well-fed member of a large Italian

family. Open for lunch and dinner only.

City Wok $$
73040 El Paseo Drive, Palm Desert
(760) 346-2340

74970 Country Club Drive, Palm Desert
(760) 341-1511
The exhibition kitchen lets you see your meal being prepared, if you're so inclined. Everything is fresh and imaginative—you won't find American-style chop suey here, but do try the lettuce wraps with savory bits of pine nuts and chicken, the steamed potstickers, and the Buddha's Delight, a huge vegetarian dish that mixes several different vegetables and spices in a most delicious way. Voted "Best Chinese Restaurant" by the locals for several years in a row, City Wok is reliably tasty. Open for lunch and dinner only.

Cliffhouse Restaurant $$
78-250 Highway 111, La Quinta
(760) 360-5991
www.laquintacliffhouse.com
Dramatically perched halfway up historic Point Happy mountain on the western edge of La Quinta just off Highway 111, this place is famous for its happy hours—with good drinks and good prices. The menu is nothing special, with the same salads, steaks, and seafood found in dozens of other California-style restaurants; but the view is worth a visit. Open for lunch and dinner only.

Crazy Bones Barbecue $$
262 South Palm Canyon Drive
(760) 325-5200
www.restaurantsofpalmsprings.com
The feature here is authentic, slow-smoked barbecue done like it is in Kansas City, Texas, Memphis, and the Carolinas. Beef, pork, chicken, and catfish are on the menu, with a good selection of sauces made in-house. Prices are good, the feeling is casual, and the seating overlooks Palm Canyon Drive, for great people-watching. Open for lunch and dinner only.

Happy hour can be as good a value as the early-bird special, particularly if you like cocktails with your dinner. Fare varies from place to place and can't compare to a three-course meal, but it's usually plentiful. Some places also offer late-night happy hours, providing value-priced drinks and food after 9:00 or 10:00 P.M.

Haleiwa Joe's Seafood Grill $$
69-934 Highway 111, Rancho Mirage
(760) 324-5613
www.haleiwajoes.com

A casual, friendly, noisy place offering "island food"—seafood, steaks, and prime rib with fruit and fresh vegetable trappings—this is similar to an upscale American-style lunch place in Hawaii. The colorful atmosphere and island music are good for getting into the vacation mood. Open for lunch and dinner only.

Hog's Breath Inn La Quinta $$
78-065 Main Street, La Quinta
(760) 564-5556
www.restaurantsofpalmsprings.com

An offshoot of Clint Eastwood's popular Carmel bar and restaurant, the La Quinta version features a drop-dead view from the second story, murals inspired by Eastwood movies, lots of fireplaces, and indoor and outdoor saloons. A big-screen TV, piano bar, and wide array of tequilas and margaritas add to the atmosphere. The food is familiar—burgers, seafood, pasta, and homemade desserts. Open for lunch and dinner only.

Kaiser Grille Palm Springs $$
205 South Palm Canyon Drive
(760) 323-1003
www.restaurantsofpalmsprings.com

A standby favorite with locals and also very popular with visitors, Kaiser is known for its substantial happy-hour appetizers and drinks; a broad menu featuring prime rib, sandwiches, salads, and fresh seafood; and its generous house-made desserts. It's a busy, loud place with a full bar and patio seating right on Palm Canyon Drive in the middle of downtown. Open for lunch and dinner only.

Kobe Japanese Steak House $$
69-838 Highway 111, Rancho Mirage
(760) 324-1717
www.koberanchomirage.com

Kobe has been in the desert almost 30 years, and the dining here is as much about entertainment as it is about food.

Guests are seated family-style around the teppan grills, and all the food is prepared on the spot—steak, seafood, vegetables, and rice. It's a good bargain and a fun night out. Open for dinner only.

LG's Prime Steakhouses $$$
74-225 Highway 111, Palm Desert
(760) 779-9799

255 South Palm Canyon Drive
(760) 416-1779

78525 Highway 111, La Quinta
(760) 771-9911
www.lgsprimesteakhouse.com

This is a traditional-style steakhouse specializing in enormous portions of beef, including a 20-ounce porterhouse. Rack of lamb, seafood, Caesar salad, and giant desserts round out the menu. The atmosphere is a bit harried, with servers pushing extras and trying to upsell at every opportunity. Open for dinner only.

Magie Ristorante Italiano $$
333 North Palm Canyon Drive
(760) 322-1234

Set in a sunken patio on North Palm Canyon Drive, Magie is a great place for people-watching while you savor a garlicky pasta, chicken, or veal dish. Everything's fresh, and the service is gracious. It's neither avant-garde nor contemporary—just good American-traditional Italian. Open for lunch and dinner only.

Matchbox Vintage Pizza Bistro $$
155 South Palm Canyon Drive
(760) 778-6000
www.matchboxpalmsprings.com

Visitors who remember Louise's Pantry, once a staple on Palm Canyon Drive famous for its pies and long lines, will find that times have changed indeed. Louise's is long gone, replaced by this cute little bistro-style spot serving wood-fired pizzas, creative salads, appetizers, and innovative entrees from snapper to New York strip steak. The lines are just as long as ever, so get there early if you want a bite to eat before catching a performance at the Fabulous Palm Springs Follies next door. Open for lunch and dinner only.

Midori's $$
36101 Bob Hope Drive, Rancho Mirage
(760) 202-8186
This desert old-timer has just moved into a fresh contemporary space with a spiffy granite-topped sushi and martini bar and a spacious dining room. Authentic Japanese foods also include noodle specialties, steamed dishes, tempuras, and boat dinners—samplers for two or more. Open for lunch and dinner only.

Oceans $$
67555 East Palm Canyon Drive
Cathedral City
(760) 324-1554

72286 Highway 111, Palm Desert
(760) 837-1516
Don't let the unprepossessing locations fool you—Oceans is one of the best places in the desert for fresh seafood and fish done simply and served with panache. The specials change according to the market, the bread is fresh, and the settings are quiet and warm. A local favorite. Open for lunch and dinner only.

Otani, A Garden Restaurant $$
266 Avenida Caballeros
(760) 327-6700
An architectural delight with teak trimmings and a soaring ceiling, Otani contains a small bar, bustling sushi bar, and busy dining area, plus private dining rooms where your party can take off their shoes and sit on the floor. Everything is fresh and very traditional Japanese, including tempura, yakitori, and bento. Service is always excellent and fast. Open for lunch and dinner only.

Palomino's $$
73101 Highway 111, Palm Desert
(760) 773-9091
Open-flame cooking techniques, fresh fish, beef, pizza, and a very popular happy hour keep this place busy into the

evening. It's known as a spot where the desert's youngish professionals go to unwind after the workday, and it's always a lively, entertaining scene. Open for lunch and dinner only.

Piero's Acqua Pazza $$
71800 Highway 111 in The River
Rancho Mirage
(760) 862-9800
A California-style bistro specializing in Mediterranean cuisine, this is a good place to relax and enjoy the bustle of The River from a beautiful patio spot right on the water. Pizza, pasta, and salads are the staples, and the kids' menu offers something more than the usual burger/dog/cheese-pizza choice. There's a fun tapas bar on the patio and live entertainment in the evenings. Open for lunch and dinner only.

Pincanha Churrascaria Brazilian Grill & Bar $$
73399 El Paseo Drive, Palm Desert
(760) 674-3434
Dinner as theater—hunky young men dressed as Brazilian gauchos, complete with blousy pants tucked into black boots, serve up your beef skewered on a sword, knives flashing as they carve it at the table. With flame-broiled meats, a high noise level, salad bar, buffet, and inexpensive martinis flowing, this is a great place for all your rowdy friends. Open for lunch and dinner only.

Pomme Frite $$
256 South Palm Canyon Drive
(760) 778-3727
Set off busy Palm Canyon Drive, this is a real find, a cozy European-style bistro with French-Belgian specialties such as steamed black mussels, beef stew, bouillabaisse, and lots of Belgian beers. The tables are close enough to hear your neighbors' conversations, and the service is almost too attentive, so don't book this if you're hoping for a romantic, private meal. Open for lunch and dinner only.

The Red Tomato
68-784 East Palm Canyon Drive
Cathedral City
(760) 328-7518

The Red Tomato and its next-door brother, House of Lamb, have been serving great food and big attitude for almost 35 years. The Tomato has won many local awards for its food and civic spirit, and it should be getting one any day for its unchanging decor, reminiscent of a 1950s mom-and-pop Italian joint in New York. Both places have some of the desert's smartest-talking waiters and some of the area's best no-nonsense traditional food—Balkan-style lamb dishes at House of Lamb and fresh pastas and pizzas at the Red Tomato. Open for dinner only.

Ristorante Brissago at Miramonte Resort & Spa　$$-$$$
76-477 Highway 111, Indian Wells
(760) 341-7200
www.miramonteresort.com

A comfortable, casual restaurant just off the hotel's lobby, Brissago serves upscale northern-Italian cuisine and features fresh seasonal produce and fish, chicken, and game dishes with a healthy California influence. Go early in the evening to watch the sun fade over Eisenhower Mountain and enjoy a romantic dinner on the candlelit patio. Open for breakfast, lunch, and dinner.

Spencer's Restaurant　$$$
701 West Baristo Road
(760) 327-3446

Located in the historic Tennis Club area right up against the foothills west of downtown Palm Springs, Spencer's is a favorite for business breakfasts, long lunches, Sunday brunch, and romantic dinners. Not many restaurants fit all of these specs, and Spencer's has the right combination of reasonable price, attentive servers, a great location, and crowd-pleasing food. Prime rib is a specialty, as are the breakfast egg dishes, huge sandwiches on fresh-baked bread, and gooey desserts.

Sullivan's Steakhouse　$$$
73-505 El Paseo Drive, Palm Desert
(760) 341-3560
www.sullivansteakhouse.com

This bluesy, boozy, big-city-style steakhouse specializes in classic beef and seafood dishes. The real attraction here is the bar, with live jump blues and swing music most nights. The knowledgeable bartenders pour a wide selection of top-shelf martinis, single-malt scotches, fine bourbons, and interesting wines. There's also a cigar-smoking area for those who just want that perfectly decadent end to a healthy day of golf and swimming. Open for dinner only.

Tommy Bahama's　$$
The Gardens on El Paseo Drive
Palm Desert
(760) 836-0188

A fun place with island-inspired decor and dishes, this is both a restaurant and a retail shop. Load up on their signature flower-print silk clothes and home knick-knacks downstairs, then go up to the second floor for appetizers, fresh fish, salads, and sandwiches. Make sure you get one of their tropical cocktails—nothing says "vacation" like an ice-filled drink topped with a little paper umbrella. Open for lunch and dinner only.

Yard House　$$
71800 Highway 111 at The River
Rancho Mirage
(760) 779-1415

The specialty of the house is the "yard of beer," one of several draft beers poured into yard-long glasses. It's a big, noisy,

---

If you're stuck at the hotel and don't have the option of room service, call the front desk and ask for menus from the local restaurant delivery service. This is becoming more popular in the desert, with a good variety of restaurants participating, offering their most popular dishes delivered to your door.

rock 'n' roll kind of place that draws tourists and the 20–30-something crowd. The food is pretty standard—salads, steaks, chicken, and seafood—and consistently good. Open for lunch and dinner only.

FINE DINING

Augusta at Plaza Roberge $$$
73951 El Paseo Drive, Palm Desert
(760) 779-9200
www.deniseroberge.com
Augusta is part of the Roberge complex on swanky El Paseo Drive—adjacent enterprises include Denise Roberge Jewelry, Roberge Gallery (fine art), gardens, and penthouse condos. The restaurant is architecturally impressive, with a loft-style dining room overlooking the large lower dining room and exhibition kitchen. The walls feature a changing selection of art from the gallery. The food is elegant and continental/American, with such items as Veal Oscar, roasted Peking duck with crunchy vegetables, and the signature dessert, a Granny Smith apple dumpling with vanilla bean ice cream. Open for lunch and dinner only.

Azur at La Quinta Resort & Club $$$
49499 Eisenhower Drive, La Quinta
(760) 564-7600, (800) 598-3828
Chef Eric Wadlund, who's had the honor of preparing a James Beard Foundation dinner, favors a menu starring fresh

regional and organic foods with an emphasis on fresh fish. He uses French cooking methods to prepare such dishes as prime tenderloin rubbed with espresso-cocoa, coconut butter-poached Maine lobster, pan-roasted Sonoma foie gras, and an appetizer that layers crab, tomato, avocado, and lemon-vodka-tomato cocktail sauce. The restaurant is in the remodeled original lobby of the 80-year-old resort and has a casual, contemporary feel. Open for dinner only.

Bangkok Five $$$
70026 Highway 111, Rancho Mirage
(760) 770-9508
www.bangkok5.com
A sophisticated place for authentic Thai cuisine, this spot features fresh, original creations as well as perfectly replicated traditional dishes such as Pad Thai and Pa Duk, a crisp whole catfish with spicy chili sauce. Dishes are prepared to order on a heat scale of 1 to 10. The space—a spare, elegant area with rice paper and wood lanterns, softly colored walls, and simple flower arrangements—can be broken into one or several private dining areas. There's a full bar with a good selection of exotic specialty drinks. This spot may close for the summer. Open for dinner only.

Café at The Lodge at Rancho Mirage $$$
68900 Frank Sinatra Drive
Rancho Mirage
(760) 321-8282
The Lodge at Rancho Mirage is currently closed for renovations and is not scheduled to December 2007.
The café has one of the best views in the entire desert and has been a favorite for elegant breakfasts, lunches, and dinners since its original days as part of the Ritz-Carlton. The chefs pride themselves on creative use of local ingredients at the peak of seasonal freshness. Dates, asparagus, artichokes, organic greens, top-grade beef, poultry, and fish make their appearance in gorgeously arranged dishes served with flair. With its own pastry chef, the

---

"Jackets not required"—that's the time-honored dress code in the desert, where the weather and the laid-back atmosphere give everyone the chance to relax. Keep in mind the type of restaurant, though, and never wear jeans or shorts to a Fine Dining establishment. Cocktail dresses, nice slacks, and dressy shirts are appropriate there.

Café is also no slouch for dessert. Sunday champagne brunch in season is downright decadent. Check with the staff to find out about promotions such as the Friday night seafood buffet, a true bargain.

Castelli's $$$
73-098 Highway 111, Palm Desert
(760) 773-3365
www.castellis.cc
With almost 20 years in the desert, this spot has a well-established reputation for personal service and classic Italian cuisine. House specialties include fettuccine Alfredo, osso buco, and lots of beef, lamb, veal, seafood, and pasta dishes. It's a cozy, intimate space reminiscent of a romantic Tuscany bistro. Open for dinner only.

Charlotte's $$
6 La Plaza
(760) 327-9066
Born in the Philippines and raised in Palm Springs, Charlotte brings an international flair to her cooking, serving up such dishes as Cuban-style roast pork rack, veal piccata, New Zealand lamb, French onion soup, and poached fresh salmon. Dining is in several little cottages just off the historic La Plaza in downtown Palm Springs. The decor is charming, with tiny fireplaces, soft hues on the plastered walls, and fresh flowers everywhere. Afternoon tea is a special treat, with delicate little sandwiches and pastries. Open for lunch and dinner. Afternoon tea by reservation.

Chop House $$$
262 North Palm Canyon Drive
(760) 320-4500

74040 Highway 111, Palm Desert
(760) 779-9888
www.restaurantsofpalmsprings.com
A venture of the Morcus family, who also operate the Hog's Breath Inn in La Quinta and Crazy Bones Barbecue upstairs from the Palm Springs Chop House, these spots specialize in top-quality steaks, chops, and seafood. All the beef is aged and cut on the premises, the service is spot-on, and

the atmosphere is sophisticated but not stuffy. Ask for your filet or New York steak cooked "bone-in" for an amazingly savory taste. Add a classic iceberg lettuce wedge with blue cheese dressing and some French-cut green beans, plus a scoop of homemade ice cream and an after-dinner port, and you've got the best of American cooking. Open for dinner only.

Citron at Viceroy Palm Springs $$$
415 South Belardo Road
(760) 318-3005
With its sunny yellow and white decor, white marble floors, and abundance of mirrors, this place evokes the 1950s glamour of a Rock Hudson–Doris Day set. Just off downtown Palm Canyon Drive, it's a good place to enjoy a traditional or "spa cuisine" breakfast, stop in for a cool-down at lunch, or linger for a romantic dinner. A covered patio and tables poolside are good choices when the weather is mild. The food is what the chefs call "California modern," featuring grilled lamb rack, steak frites, fresh halibut, and monkfish filet. If you dine elsewhere, save your dessert calories for the droolworthy Valrhona molten chocolate cake with vanilla bean ice cream.

Cuistot $$$
72-595 El Paseo Drive, Palm Desert
(760) 340-1000
Designed with a contemporary interpretation of a grand French farmhouse, this spot features a huge stove island surrounding the open kitchen so diners can see the chefs at work. There's also a spacious patio with an outdoor fireplace and waterfall, as well as a wine room for private parties. Chef Bernard Dervieux has been at the helm for almost 20 years and has won numerous awards for his creative, consistently high-quality cuisine. Open for lunch and dinner only.

The Desert Sage $$–$$$
78085 Avenida La Fonda, La Quinta
(760) 564-8744
This is an absolutely stunning little jewel-box restaurant, with a lively bar and several

separate dining rooms. The wine list is extensive—the owners have their own vineyard in Northern California and pride themselves on their selection of small-production boutique wines. The food is an imaginative blend of fresh ingredients and classical preparation— seafood, game, lamb, and beef along with just-picked fruit and vegetables, elegant sauces, and fresh baked goods. Open for lunch and dinner only.

Europa Restaurant at
Villa Royale Inn $$$
1620 Indian Trail
(760) 327-2314, (800) 245-2314
www.villaroyale.com
Almost 20 years ago, a Palm Springs city councilman who had been a pretty good Hollywood set decorator before moving to Palm Springs bought this historic com-pound and turned it into one of the most eclectic and charming inns in the valley. A big part of the charm is the cozy, wildly romantic Europa and its award-winning cuisine. Like the inn, which decorates each room in the style of a different European country, the menu may feature German schnitzel one night, Parisian duck the next, and Italian veal on another. Reservations are a premium, so call early. Open for lunch and dinner only.

The Falls Prime Steakhouse
& Martini Bar $$$
155 South Palm Canyon Drive
(760) 416-8664

The Falls Prime Steakhouse, Martini
Dome and Water FX
78-430 Highway 111, La Quinta
(760) 777-9999
www.thefallsprimesteakhouse.com
These flashy, highly visual restaurants fea-ture stunning water effects and more than a dozen different martinis served in stems the size of a Buick. The atmosphere harks back to the excessive '80s, with lots of glit-ter, glamour, and well-dressed folks on the prowl. The food may seem like an after-thought, but it's extremely well done—

steaks and sides in elegant rooms just far enough from the bar to see the action and still have a quiet conversation. Open for dinner only.

Fleming's Prime Steakhouse
and Wine Bar $$-$$$
71800 Highway 111 at The River
at Rancho Mirage
(760) 776-6685
www.flemingssteakhouse.com
This is one of the best of the valley's many steakhouses, with an interior that can pack in a lot of people and still retain its special-night-out feeling. Prime beef, a variety of chops, fish, and chicken are done simply and served with style. The wine list is one of the best in the area, and because more than 100 wines are offered by the glass, you can taste a great variety without committing to the entire bottle. Open for dinner only.

Jillian's $$$
74155 El Paseo Drive, Palm Desert
(760) 776-8247
This romantic, unpretentious spot—filled with antiques, old-world paintings, and fresh flowers—features four dining rooms connecting to a garden courtyard. Jillian's has been in the desert since 1986, and most of their staff has been with them since the beginning. Winner of awards from *Wine Spectator* magazine since 1994, this is a local favorite, and reservations are at a premium. The eclectic cuisine features fresh fish, lamb, and house-made pastas, breads, and desserts. Open for dinner only.

Johanna's Restaurant $$$
196 South Indian Canyon Drive
(760) 778-0017
Johanna's is perhaps the hautest of the haute cuisine restaurants in the desert. Every item is a complex and imaginative blend of ingredients and a visual treat that obviously took a lot of time to build. At times it can be just too-too refined, with minuscule portions and monumental prices. It's one of the loveliest spots in the area, however, with ingenious lighting that

turns everyone in the room into a movie star. Open for dinner, only.

John Henry's Café $$-$$$
1785 East Tahquitz Canyon Way
(760) 327-7667

This is a must when you're in Palm Springs; so call ahead because reservations are very difficult to get on a moment's notice. You'll find elegant variations on American standards such as pot roast, steak, and chicken. In fact, calling this delicious, melt-in-your-mouth concoction of beef and vegetables "pot roast" seems just silly. The food is always delicious, and the atmosphere is a clubby, intimate one that makes you feel as if you're in a special club, the one that was lucky enough to have dinner at John Henry's. Open for dinner only; closed in the summer.

Le St. Germain $$$
74985 Highway 111, Indian Wells
(760) 773-6511

Private rooms can accommodate groups of up to 300. Continental-Mediterranean seafood is the specialty, with an extensive wine list and elaborately prepared desserts. One of the desert's first French-classic restaurants, this is still a favorite, though the quality of the food and presentation have become unpredictable in recent years. Open for dinner only.

Le Vallauris $$-$$$
385 West Tahquitz Canyon Way
(760) 325-5059

A Palm Springs institution for decades, Le Vallauris is the place to go to impress your date, your boss, and yourself. This is old Palm Springs money combined with old Palm Springs warmth. When the Gabor sisters were all alive, this was their favorite luncheon spot, and it is still the favored place for wealthy, stylish ladies who lunch. The walled, tree-shaded patio is misted in the summer and heated in the winter. Inside, the bar and several dining rooms ooze casual elegance. The food is classic French, always fresh, and surprisingly reasonable. The service is impeccable. Open for lunch and dinner only.

Lord Fletcher's $$
70385 Highway 111, Rancho Mirage
(760) 328-1161

After almost 40 years, this is still a desert favorite, with affordable prices and generous portions of such comfort food as roast chicken and meat loaf, as well as lamb, ribs, and fresh fish. English rice pudding is a staple dessert, made fresh daily and served with whipped cream. The pub, main dining room, and Shakespeare Room are stuffed with interesting bits and pieces of British bric-a-brac, and the service is always warm and unpretentious. Open for dinner only.

Lyons English Grille $$
233 East Palm Canyon Drive
(760) 327-1551

This family-owned restaurant is a desert landmark, serving English food for almost 25 years. The atmosphere is dark and cozy, somewhat like a 19th-century London inn. The food is substantial and traditional—prime ribs and steaks, chicken in the pot, steak and kidney pie, rack of lamb, and roast duck..The one dessert is English trifle. Open for dinner only; closed in the summer.

Melvyn's at the Ingleside Inn $$$
200 West Ramon Road
(760) 325-2323

This is the place where you're guaranteed to get a feeling of the old Palm Springs, when movie stars and their hangers-on gathered around the piano and tippled expensive scotch at the bar. Melvyn's maître d', Brian, is famous all over Southern California for his gracious manners and unbeatable memory for names and faces. Owner Mel Haber is often there—if you can get him to sit still long enough, he'll share some bad jokes and real insider stories about the hundreds of famous people who've spent time here. Sunday brunch by the pool is a must. Open for breakfast, lunch, and dinner.

Pacifica Seafood Restaurant $$$
The Gardens at El Paseo Drive, Palm Desert
(760) 674-8666
www.pacificainthedesert.com

The first upscale restaurant to open at The Gardens, Pacifica has retained its quality edge for several years. As the name says, seafood is the main attraction. Specials change daily according to the catch on the coast. Steaks, pasta, and salads are also available. This is a locals' favorite for happy hour and late-night cocktails. Open for dinner and Sunday brunch.

Ristorante Mamma Gina $$$
73705 El Paseo Drive, Palm Desert
(760) 568-9898
www.mammagina.com

A desert favorite for 20 years, this may become your favorite night-out spot—a place with the right amount of candles and white linen to give everyone a glow, and a staff that knows how to give professional service without being overbearing. The location, looking out on El Paseo Drive, is ideal for people-watching. An extensive wine list, homemade pastas, fresh fish, veal, and chicken are the basics. Desserts and new vegetarian dishes are also standouts. Open for lunch and dinner only.

St. James at the Vineyard $$$
265 South Palm Canyon Drive
(760) 320-8041
www.stjamesrestaurant.com

With an elegant, beautifully done interior that mixes Southwestern and Asian styles, St. James serves up equally complex dishes that include curries, bouillabaisse, pastas, seafood, lamb, steaks, veal, and vegetarian entrees. The little bar features jazz music and a cozy dance floor. It's also a good place to stop in for dessert and an after-dinner drink. Open for dinner only.

Shame on the Moon $$$
69950 Highway 111, Rancho Mirage
(760) 324-5515

This popular restaurant began life as a humble cafe on Palm Canyon Drive in Cathedral City. In the new, elegant setting, the food is so good—continental with fresh local notes—and the service so warm and accommodating, that it's become wildly popular with locals. Reservations are required, and it's often booked weeks in advance during season. Open for dinner only.

Sirocco at Renaissance Esmeralda Resort and Spa $$$
44-400 Indian Wells Lane, Indian Wells
(760) 773-4666, (800) 552-4386

Sirocco is considered one of the finest of the desert's many Italian restaurants. The Massignani family runs this dark, sleekly simple restaurant with impeccable graciousness and can be counted on to bring authentic Italian cuisine to the table. Their surf and turf may not be old-world Italian, but the succulent lobster and tender steak, served with crunchy fresh vegetables and hot Italian bread, is delightful. Open for dinner only.

Vicky's of Santa Fe $$-$$$
45100 Club Drive, Indian Wells
(760) 345-9770

Steaks, filet mignon, prime rib, poultry, and seafood are the stars here, prepared in classic continental style and served in an atmosphere that can be festive or elegant, depending on where you sit. It's a desert favorite for consistently good food and service, and the bar is known for its laid-back, congenial atmosphere. Open for dinner only.

Wally's Desert Turtle $$$
71775 Highway 111, Rancho Mirage
(760) 568–9321
www.wallys-desert-turtle.com
Long before the influx of restaurants featuring California cuisine, Wally's set the standard for opulent dining. With its fine French-continental food and showy elegance, it's still a favorite for the ladies who lunch and for "occasion" dinners. Lunchtime fashion shows are a staple during high season. At night, with flickering candles reflected in mirrored walls and polished silver, fresh flowers everywhere, and extremely attentive service, it's a "rich and famous" ambience you've got to love. Open for lunch and dinner only; closed in the summer.

NIGHTLIFE ♉

As recently as 20 years ago, the concept of "nightlife" in Palm Springs was limited to a handful of lounges with deejays or the occasional live group, playing tunes for two different crowds—the early 20-somethings or the late 60-somethings. Antiquated "cabaret" ordinances in the city of Palm Springs, which has the valley's only real downtown, banned outdoor dining and made it mandatory that neighborhoods around the downtown area were quiet after 9:00 P.M. This put a severe crimp on any high-stepping, hip-shaking, hollering fun. When the sun went down in the desert, people had dinner and went to bed early, all the better to get up for a dawn tee time or a few laps around the pool.

The economy changed all that in the late 1980s when Palm Springs created the Thursday night VillageFest to attract locals to the downtown area and encourage visitors to come early for the weekend.

VillageFest turned the sleepy downtown into a vibrant, crowded party where shops, restaurants, and bars stayed open late to entice business from the street fair. At about the same time, The Fabulous Palm Springs Follies opened downtown, followed by several new nightclubs and restaurants with live music. Cafes put tables and chairs out on the sidewalks. People started going to bed a little later and playing golf a little later the next morning.

In the large resort hotels, nightclubs and dance spots opened to entertain guests and became favorite local hangouts. Then the casinos came along and stepped up the pace once again.

Desert nights have changed considerably in the past 20 years, but the variety and quality of entertainment is still nowhere near what you will find in Los Angeles, San Diego, or the beach communities in Southern California.

Sometimes there are too many fun things happening to get to all of them in one visit. The next time you come, you may find nothing but a few bars with recorded music. If that happens, do what the locals do—go to bed early and pop up the next morning for another day of brilliant sunshine.

One benefit of the desert's laid-back attitude is the rarity of cover charges. Only a few nightclubs routinely charge at the door, and those that do will rarely have a cover charge on Sunday through Thursday nights. We have noted those establishments with a cover charge policy. It is always a good idea to call ahead to verify this, particularly on weekend nights in season. One thing to keep in mind is the age requirement for entering casinos—it's 21, though families can bring their children to eat in the casino restaurants.

All listings are in Palm Springs, unless otherwise noted.

CASINOS

Agua Caliente Casino
32250 Bob Hope Drive, Rancho Mirage
(760) 321-2000, (888) 999-1995
www.hotwatercasino.com
A beautifully designed, lavish facility, this is the second venture of the Agua Calientes, who were responsible for starting the high-end gaming business in Southern California. There are 50 table games, a 10-table poker room, a high-limit room, more than 1,000 slots, and bingo six days a week. Restaurants include Maraskino, an elegant continental-cuisine dining spot; the Prime 10 Steakhouse; Grand Palms Buffet; and a food court. The showroom and lounge feature live entertainment from the Vegas circuit and dancing to live local and regional groups.

Augustine Casino
84001 Avenue 54, Coachella
(760) 391-9500
www.augustinecasino.com

More casual and low-key than the big desert casinos, Augustine is the latecomer to the valley lineup. Its location, at the far eastern end of Indio, may keep it less popular and make it harder to attract the big crowds, but it's still a casino, and gamblers are there playing the machines every day. Two restaurants offer moderately priced fare.

Fantasy Springs Resort Casino
84-245 Indio Springs Parkway, Indio
(760) 342-5000, (800) 827-2946
www.fantasyspringsresort.com

This is the valley's biggest casino and the biggest permanent entertainment venue. Regular special events include top concerts, rodeos, sporting events, and pow-wows sponsored by the Cabazon Band of Mission Indians, the casino's owners. In the 80,000 square feet of gaming, there are almost 2,000 slots, blackjack, poker, bingo, and off-track satellite horse wagering. The Springs cocktail bar also has 44 bar-top slots and 10 plasma TVs. Players' clubs and VIP rooms accommodate regular gamblers and high rollers. The 750-seat bingo hall runs seven days a week.

For entertainment, the Fantasy Lounge is a 400-seat concert-style venue with mezzanine VIP seating and a weekly "Wild West Wednesday" for country dance fans. The sky bar on the top of the recently constructed 12-story hotel offers one of the valley's highest man-made viewing spots, with an open balcony and nightly live music. Players Steakhouse features prime beef, seafood, and an extensive wine list. The Café serves casual meals round the clock, the Fresh Grill Buffet features international foods with "action cooking stations," and the Bistro is an indoor/outdoor place with light California food and another long wine list. The Fantasy Lanes Bowling Center is located adjacent to the casino.

Augustine's machines use no coins, so you won't hear that magical "ching, ching, ching" when a slot pays off. You'll be using a paper ticket and can transfer your winnings from one slot to another electronically. It takes some getting used to.

Morongo Casino, Resort & Spa
I-10 at Seminole Drive, Cabazon
(951) 849-3188
www.morongocasinoresort.com

The Morongo Casino offers nearly 150,000 square feet of gaming—one of the largest gaming floors on the West Coast and west of Vegas. There are 2,000 slots, 100 table games, a private poker room, and the usual assortment of clubs and tournaments. With its location right on I-10 to the west of Palm Springs, Morongo attracts primarily dedicated gamblers, as well as the many truckers passing through and shoppers taking a break from the different crowds at the nearby outlets.

Viewbar on the 26th floor of the casino hotel has a fabulous 360-degree view of the desert, with dramatic floor-to-ceiling windows. This is a full bar with deejay music and dancing nightly. There's also a full-service spa and a major hotel attached to the casino, should you feel in need of a nap and a facial before hitting the club. The entire complex is adjacent to the Desert Hills Premium Outlets shopping area. Mystique Lounge features live entertainment on the weekends, plus Sunday- and Monday-night football.

Spa Resort Casino
401 East Amado Road
(888) 999-1995
www.sparesortcasino.com

The desert's first casino and the only one in downtown Palm Springs, Spa Resort Casino offers 1,000 slots, 30 table games, a high-roller room, and continual promotions. Just across the street from the Spa Hotel, the casino takes up an entire city

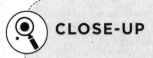

Casinos

When the U.S. Indian Gaming Regulatory Act passed in 1988, it set in motion a cascading series of political maneuvers that have created the biggest change in the Palm Springs area since the arrival of air-conditioning. The act's intention was to make it legal for Indian tribes to offer the same types of gaming that were already legal in each state. That sounds simple on its face, but given the scale of gaming revenues and the fact that neither the states nor the federal government can tax these revenues (each Indian tribe is a sovereign nation), the game gets much more complex. In California it took years of lobbying and a series of referendums before the tribes could actually move on this new initiative.

In Palm Springs the Agua Caliente Band of Cahuilla Indians, owners of the Spa Hotel, had gone through all the required hoops to open a casino in that hotel. All, that is, with the exception of one odd regulation that made it illegal to transport slot machines within the state. They had purchased hundreds of the slots and were ready to install them for a planned grand opening. What to do? In a masterful move akin to cutting the Gordian knot, the tribe simply moved the machines in overnight, avoiding the watchful eyes of the regulatory commission staff, and the next morning they were open for business.

Because tribes do not report their revenues to local, state, or federal governments, the exact amount of their gaming

revenue is a closely held secret. By any standards, though, the amount is stunning. Since opening the Spa Resort Casino in Palm Springs, the Agua Calientes have set up health and education funds for all their tribal members, donated impressive sums to local charities, built an elaborate new casino—the Agua Caliente—just off I-10 in Rancho Mirage, purchased their own bank, funded their Cultural Museum, and embarked on many other successful ventures.

The state of California, which fought so hard (with urging from Las Vegas lobbyists) to prevent Indian gaming, is now working just as hard to get a share of the gaming money. The state's power to negotiate compacts with tribes and approve additional slots, tables, and locations is their ace in the hole. Southern California is the fastest-growing gaming market in the country right now. Since the state can't tax the tribes, the governor is working on deals that would have the tribes pay "fees" for the gaming franchise, adding an additional "fee" for each machine they add.

In the Palm Springs area, the casinos have done much to change the sleepy, somewhat elitist feeling of the valley, drawing thousands of day-trippers from all over Southern California. They are also the main draw for big-name entertainers, many of whom spend their lives on the road traveling from casino to casino across the country. You'll find many of the same stars that headline Vegas here, as well as a constantly changing lineup

Casino gaming is one of the major indoor activities in the desert. PHOTO BY JACK HOLLINGSWORTH, COURTESY OF THE PALM SPRINGS DESERT RESORTS CONVENTION AND VISITORS AUTHORITY

of midlevel performers. The casinos' restaurants are among the best in the valley, and the prices are extremely good. After all, the dollars you leave at the table or slot machine on your way out the door after dinner will more than compensate for the pennies the kitchen gave up to serve prime rib at the best price within a hundred miles.

With their newfound financial suc-cess, the desert tribes have been excel-lent neighbors, contributing to valley charities and making sure that all their tribal members share in the bounty. Many desert old-timers feel that if the casino explosion has a downside for the valley, it has to do with the slight but growing loss of the small-town atmosphere and the influx of day visitors who come just for the gaming.

Like other casinos across the county, the ones in the desert allow smoking, even though it is verboten in every other California club, bar, and restaurant. Many casino restaurants are nonsmoking or have nonsmoking sections, however, so make your dinner reservations without worry.

block and is within easy walking distance from almost all of the city's major hotels.

The Cascade Lounge draws a lot of locals to dance and drink and is one of the most popular downtown spots for visitors as well. Restaurants include the Asian fusion Roppongi, the Noodle Bar, the Stage Deli & Café, and the Oasis Buffet.

Spotlight 29 Casino
46200 Harrison Place, Coachella
(760) 775-5566, (866) 878-6729
www.spotlight29.com
Owned by the small Twenty-Nine Palms Band of Mission Indians, Spotlight made gaming history this year when it met the goals set out by the Indian Gaming Regulatory Act and bought out the Trump Casino management contract. To celebrate, the band renamed the casino, retiring the "Trump 29" moniker.

This casino is also a big draw for top entertainment in the valley. On the gaming floor there are 2,000 slots, 30 table games, a poker room, and a host of daily tournaments. Spotlight is known for having the most penny slots in the valley and also has hundreds of nickel and quarter games.

The Blue Bar features live dance music on the weekends, plus country deejay music on Wednesday, salsa on Thursday, and Sunday-afternoon and Monday-night football.

GAY NIGHTLIFE

Palm Springs is known around the country as having one of the hottest nightlife

scenes for gay men. In addition to the annual White Party (see Annual Festivals and Events), there are a number of bars, dance spots, and lounges catering to gay men.

Badlands
200 South Indian Canyon Avenue
(760) 778-4326
This is a friendly neighborhood bar with lots of pool tables. It's often the spot where guys start the evening with a few beers, then wind up after dinner for a game of pool and a nightcap.

Barracks
67625 East Palm Canyon Drive
Cathedral City
(760) 321-9688
www.thebarracksbar.com
This is just about as wild as it gets in the gay nightclub scene. Barracks is a leather/fetish place, so be prepared for just about anything on busy weekend nights.

Blame It on Midnight
777 East Tahquitz Canyon Way
(760) 323-1200
Set in the lower level of the building that houses one of the city's movie complexes, this has become a very dressy, ultra-chic spot to have dinner and check out the competition. The food is excellent, the waiters are always good-looking, and the drinks are strong.

Headhunters Dance Haus
611 South Palm Canyon Drive
(760) 416-0950
This place is almost all dance floor, with a wild light system and a pounding selection of techno and disco. It seems to attract every gay man in Southern California at one time or another and is especially busy during White Party and Pride Weekend.

Hunter's Video Bar
302 East Arenas Road
(760) 323-0700
www.huntersnightclubs.com
One of the city's oldest gay spots,

Hunter's is in the middle of the predominantly gay section of Arenas Road just off Indian Canyon.

Oscar's
440 El Cielo Road
(760) 325-7072
This unpretentious spot near the airport is popular with those who want a casual dinner and drinks.

Rainbow Cactus Cafe
212 South Indian Canyon Avenue
(760) 325-3868
A lively piano bar and good food make this a popular spot for lunch and dinner. It's right off the heart of downtown at the beginning of a section of Andreas Road that has become known as the "gay street" in Palm Springs.

Spike's Wonder Bar & Grill
241 East Tahquitz Canyon Way
(760) 322-5280
A regular bar—just drinks, bar food, and a casual crowd—that welcomes a regular crowd looking for a friendly spot to meet, have a beer and a burger, and make plans for the evening.

Tool Shed
600 Sunny Dunes Road
(760) 320-3299
www.toolshed-ps.com
Billing itself as "Palm Springs' only leather and Levis cruise bar," this is a no-frills corner bar known as a popular place to meet the burly, bearded guys who refer to themselves as "bears." Pounding recorded music and typical bar food set the stage for crowds every weekend.

Toucans Tiki Lounge
2100 North Palm Canyon Drive
(760) 416-7584
The decor is faux rain forest, with tropical touches, festive drinks, and "optional sarongs." This is one of the campiest spots on the gay scene, always a lot of fun and never serious.

Gay men's clubs and bars in the desert offer a Sunday-night "beer bash," where inexpensive pitchers and an open-house atmosphere welcome men to move from club to club and catch up with friends.

MORE DANCING AND NIGHTLIFE

Arnold Palmer's Restaurant
78164 Avenue 52, La Quinta
(760) 771-4653
www.arnoldpalmers.net
Live entertainment nightly except Monday in the bar featuring desert favorite Kevin Henry and a tasty bar menu. The crowd is mostly middle-aged and country-clubby—men who spent the day on the golf course and women who took a lot of time with their nails and hair before slipping in for a drink.

Azur at La Quinta Resort & Club
49499 Eisenhower Drive, La Quinta
(760) 777-4835
Azur is elegant and unpretentious at the same time. It offers live jazz with desert favorites, a bar menu, and a vast wine list. It's a good spot to enjoy a delicious dinner and linger over cocktails. The crowd is often made up of hotel guests, with an occasional local stopping in for a look and listen.

Blue Guitar
120 South Palm Canyon Drive
(760) 327-1549
www.blueguitar.com
An anomaly in the desert, this little upstairs spot pumps out blistering soul,

Gay bars and restaurants change names, locations, and owners frequently. For the most up-to-date information, pick up a copy of the local gay newspaper, **The Bottom Line.**

blues, and jazz with front man Kal David, singer Laurie Bono, and the Real Deal band. The cover is $10 and the space is quite tight, but the outdoor balcony gives a great view of the street action below on Palm Canyon, and the music is a shot of energy every time.

Casablanca Lounge
Melvyn's at the Ingleside Inn
200 West Ramon Road
(760) 325-2323
This is the place to go for real '50s-style piano bar music and sing-alongs in a tight little bar that clings to the aura of days gone by. Go early in the evening for a cocktail and some gossip. Late nights here tend to attract the over-60 crowd looking for the old Rat Pack atmosphere.

Castelli's
73-098 Highway 111, Palm Desert
(760) 773-3365
www.castellis.cc
Castelli's has been one of the desert's most popular Italian restaurants for almost 20 years. Decorated to resemble a Tuscan bistro, it features traditional beef, veal, and seafood dishes. The "Celebrity Room," with autographed glossies of stars, provides a Southern California touch. Pianist Joe Jaggi entertains in the bar every evening and this is a popular place to visit for after-dinner drinks and nostalgic tunes.

Costas at Desert Springs JW Marriott Resort & Spa
74855 Country Club Drive, Palm Desert
(760) 341-1795

This is a high-energy nightclub with deejays and dance bands, and a frenetic atmosphere that harks back to the 1980s. Costas almost always charges a cover, and it's stuffed with great-looking 20-somethings mixing with older couples or singles staying at the hotel on convention business.

Hog's Breath Inn La Quinta
78-065 Main Street, La Quinta
(760) 564-5556
www.restaurantsofpalmsprings.com
A cousin to Clint Eastwood's famous Carmel bar, this is a rowdy but cleaner version of an old-time saloon, with Hollywood memorabilia, a wide selection of tequilas and bottled beers, and a good bar menu. A piano bar provides entertainment on weekends.

Jillian's
74155 El Paseo Drive, Palm Desert
(760) 776-8242
Piano entertainment Monday through Saturday is a good accompaniment to drinks after dinner. Jillian's is a romantic little spot and very low-key—no dancing or wild parties here.

McCormick's
74360 Highway 111, Palm Desert
(760) 340-0553
Sad to say, this may be the desert's best offering for dancers between 30 and 60, though that upper limit is a bit flexible. Live rock 'n' roll brings out the hopefuls most nights of the week. There is usually a cover charge on weekend nights.

The Nest
75188 Highway 111, Indian Wells
(760) 346-2314
The Nest has been known as a pickup spot for out-of-towners for decades. The food is good, and the piano bar often brings in celebrity guests. There's also a small dance floor, which is often packed as the hour gets later.

St. James at the Vineyard
265 South Palm Canyon Drive
(760) 320-8041
www.stjamesrestaurant.com

This is a lovely little restaurant with a stylish dance floor and good tunes right in the middle of downtown Palm Springs. The food at the restaurant is some of the best and most elegantly presented in town, and the staff is always accommodating and friendly.

Sullivan's Steakhouse
73-505 El Paseo Drive, Palm Desert
(760) 341-3560
www.sullivansteakhouse.com

This is a jumping spot for live jump blues, swing, and jazz. Martinis, wines, and cigars are the specialties from the bar. There can be a cover charge on weekend nights, especially during high season.

The desert dress code is casual, but that doesn't mean jeans or shorts and T-shirts in nightclubs or restaurants. Do your fellow clubbers a favor and buff up your look for the evening.

Village Pub
266 South Palm Canyon Drive
(760) 323-3265

The Village Pub, in downtown Palm Springs, features nightly entertainment, three full bars, a cigar bar upstairs, and a large tented patio. This is a rowdy, college-age crowd that often spills out onto the sidewalk and gets downright crazy on weekends. Open until 2:00 A.M.

SPAS

aken from the name of a celebrated watering hole in Belgium, "spa" technically refers to a mineral spring or any place with a mineral spring. The European spas that became enormously popular in the early 20th century were elaborate resorts where people came to "take the waters," sipping and bathing in natural hot mineral springs for a variety of health objectives. A hundred years later, the word has evolved dramatically—today it's not unusual to find hotels with no more than a hot tub and a sauna advertising their "spa."

To help you find exactly what you're looking for—from a simple soak in a natural hot mineral spring, to pampering massages and facials, to the most comprehensive health and fitness evaluations in an atmosphere of extreme pampering—we've compiled a comprehensive listing of the desert's many excellent spas, along with some tips on getting value for your vacation dollar. To qualify as a spa for our listings, the establishment must either offer a variety of body and skin treatments that go well beyond what one would find in a typical beauty salon or feature a genuine hot mineral springs pool for soaking. In the desert the most luxurious spas generally are located within large resort hotels, and they offer everything from medical screening to fitness classes and exotic body treatments.

To help you choose a favorite from the Palm Springs area's many options, we've grouped spas in two categories: Resort Spas and Hot Mineral Spring Spas.

Resort Spas are located within full-service hotels or resorts and offer a complete range of body and face treatments, as well as use of swimming pools, saunas and/or steam rooms, and fitness centers.

Hot Mineral Springs Spas, as the name states, have a natural mineral spring to supply water for the soaking/swimming pools. Hot mineral springs abound in the nearby city of Desert Hot Springs, and many small to midsize hotels are built around one or two pools that are filled with hot mineral water from the hotel's own underground wells. In this group there are midsize hotels with moderate prices and amenities, as well as those hotels whose only claim to spa fame is the water itself. These hotels can offer excellent value for long-stay visitors who enjoy simplicity and the reputed healing properties of the water.

Just like rates for hotel rooms, prices for spa services vary with the seasons, and visitors can get the best values in the hot summer months. If you're staying at a resort with a spa, use of the spa may be included in your room rate—always ask when you make reservations.

Prices for standard services such as a basic massage and facial do not vary much among the larger resorts, which are all in competition for the same customer—it's not unusual for a resort spa to have at least 30 percent of its clients come from the local population or from other hotels without spas. You can count on paying top dollar for the spas with the most elaborate facilities, such as large fitness centers, on-site medical services, and top beauty salons. That said, these places may offer the best value if you are going to get a great many services at one visit. Always ask for the package prices. Prices for standard facials will run around $80 to $95, a half-hour massage will cost from $50 to $65, and a one-hour massage will cost from $95 to $125.

If you want just a basic massage, facial, or nail service, you will probably get the best deal by booking your appointment at a stand-alone day spa or beauty salon that doesn't offer the extra luxury of soaking tubs, saunas, pools, and a fitness center. A good source of recommendations is your

Spa Etiquette for First-Timers

- Reservations are de rigueur for all but some express services in some spas.
- Most spas limit their services to guests who are 18 years or older.
- You can request either a male or a female massage therapist.
- Leave your cell phone and pager behind—this is quiet time for everyone.

- Always tell your therapist if something makes you uncomfortable, so he or she can make the proper adjustments.
- Keep your appointment and be on time. Many spas will charge full price for skipped appointments. If you are 10 minutes late, expect your service to be 10 minutes shorter, in order to accommodate the guest following you.

hotel's concierge or front-desk staff. If the hotel has a spa, they'll certainly tell you about it and will also give you tips on where else to go.

Unless otherwise noted, the resort spas and mineral springs spas offer their services to non-hotel guests and include use of the adjacent fitness facilities, sauna, and other amenities when a service is purchased. Depending on whether the hotel has a "full house," some also offer day rates for use of the pool and fitness facilities without purchasing a service. Make sure to call ahead, because these policies are subject to change.

A note on "day spas": These facilities, often part of a beauty salon, do not offer lodging or such amenities as a fitness center, sauna/steam room, or swimming pool. They vary widely in scope and quality of service, and because most offer only basic massage and facial treatments, we have not included these in the listings below.

Readers should assume that all of the establishments listed accept major credit cards, unless otherwise noted. All listings are in Palm Springs, unless otherwise noted.

RESORT SPAS

Resort spas offer all the amenities of a traditional vacation destination, including

a complete selection of spa services, programs, and dining.

**Desert Springs
JW Marriott Resort & Spa
74855 Country Club Drive, Palm Desert
(760) 341-2211, (800) 808-7727
www.desertspringsresort.com**
One of the biggest convention and business hotels in the Southwest, Desert Springs is all about the numbers—450 acres, 884 rooms, two championship 18-hole golf courses, 20 tennis courts, 13 restaurants and lounges, 17 gift shops, and a 30,000-square-foot stand-alone fitness center/spa. The fitness center is really the highlight of the facility, with lots of classes, a good selection of equipment and free weights, a heated lap pool with a stunning view of the mountains, and several personalized options, such as a computerized body composition analysis, fitness counseling, private instruction, and personal training sessions.

There's a good selection of body treatments, facials, and massages, and though the facilities are showing their age a bit (the hotel was built in 1987), the overall ambience is quiet and professional. The spa specializes in Ayurvedic treatments, personalizing the particular herb, oil, and so on to the individual's "dosha," or energy pattern. For total relaxation, try the Bindi

Treatment, a full-body mask using warm crushed herbs to cleanse and exfoliate, followed by an application of herb-infused oil. To really get your dosha tuned, add on the Shirodhara, which features a stream of warm oil poured on the forehead to encourage relaxation. A scalp massage, light facial, and hand and foot treatment are also included.

The beauty salon adjacent to the spa is operated separately. The basic hair and nail services are not up to the standards set by the spa.

Doral Desert Princess Resort
67-967 Vista Chino, Cathedral City
(760) 322-7000, (888) 386-4677
www.doralpalmsprings.com

A vacation condominium/hotel development, the Desert Princess has a 27-hole golf course and a beautiful location on the north side of Cathedral City near its border with Palm Springs.

The Body Center'd Spa here is a small, well-kept facility with a limited array of massage and body treatments, plus basic salon services for hair and nails. Women's and men's saunas and a coed hot tub and lap pool are also available. The resort's small fitness center is located separately.

Hyatt Grand Champions Resort:
Agua Serena Spa
44-600 Indian Wells Lane, Indian Wells
(760) 341-1000, (800) 554-9288
www.aguaserenaspa.com

Also located within or adjacent to the Agua Serena Spa are:
Loran Loran Atelier Salon
44-600 Indian Wells Lane, Indian Wells
(760) 675-4160

The Medical and Skin Spa
44-600 Indian Wells Lane, Indian Wells
(760) 674-4106
www.medicalandskinspa.com

When the Pacific Life Open (formerly the Newsweek Champions) tennis tournament grew too large for the stadium at the Hyatt Grand Champions, Hyatt embarked on a major remodeling, updating rooms,

enlarging their meeting space, and creating the remarkable Agua Serena Spa. This is one of the desert's top spas, in terms of both aesthetics and the variety of services they offer.

The 30,000-square-foot facility includes a spacious fitness center with modern equipment and free weights, personal training, and classes in yoga, aerobics, and Pilates. Every resort guest and spa patron gets to enjoy the center, as well as the steam room, sauna, and whirlpool adjoining the private locker rooms. The men's retreat area features a cold plunge pool, and the women's area has a private entrance to the realm of the Medical and Skin Spa. There is also an exceptional beauty salon.

The retreat, or relaxation, areas are much more than just a place to wait for a massage. Carrying out the decorating theme of rich wood, sleek tile and glass, and smooth stone, these lounges have indoor and outdoor areas with reclining teak chairs, reflecting pools, and aromatic herb gardens filled with the spa's signature scents of grapefruit and sage. If you have to check your e-mail, this is a very calming place to do it.

Each of the spa's treatment rooms has a walled terrace and floor-to-ceiling windows overlooking beautiful garden areas and allowing each guest to have as much fresh air and natural light as desired. Eight of the treatment rooms also have private outdoor showers. There are also outdoor treatment rooms, a couples massage room, and a Vichy shower room.

The Desert Sage and Date Sugar Scrub is one of the spa's signature treatments, using organically grown Medjool dates from the date grove down the road, along with sage, juniper, grapefruit, and date sugar. These edible treats are whipped into shea, cocoa, mango, and kukui nut butters for a super-rich exfoliating and moisturizing treat.

Other original treatments include the Stone Facial, using smooth basalt stones, warm mud, and botanicals, and Fit2Golf, which combines a fitness consultation and training session, 18 holes of golf with swing analysis, and a one-hour sports massage.

The Loran Loran Atelier Salon at the spa is one of the desert's best, with top stylists who can be counted on for hair color and cuts, as well as nail and makeup services. The salon also has a spacious suite for bridal and special-event groups.

The Medical and Skin Spa is a true medical office with all the luxurious trimmings and atmosphere of the spa next door. Specialties here are many of the most currently popular cosmetic procedures, such as Botox and Restylane, which are performed by the spa's founder and medical director, Dr. Richard M. Foxx. All clients have a personal consultation with the doctor, who also supervises the laser treatments for skin rejuvenation, hair removal, and spider veins. Microdermabrasion and all types of medical peels are on the menu, as well as comprehensive health and lifestyle evaluations, hormone evaluations, and diet and vitamin analyses.

La Quinta Resort & Club: Spa La Quinta
49-499 Eisenhower Drive, La Quinta
(760) 564–4111, (800) 598–3828
www.laquintaresort.com
The granddaddy of the desert resorts, La Quinta Resort & Club opened in 1926 and has grown into a true destination, with sprawling, beautifully manicured grounds that contain both hotel rooms and plush casita-style lodging, five golf courses, 23 tennis courts, 41 swimming pools, and 53 hot tubs, plus three full-service restaurants, a fitness center, and the 23,000-square-foot Spa La Quinta, which was added in 2002. The Yamaguchi Salon (760-777-4800) and the WellMax Center for Preventive Medicine (800-621-5263; www.wellmax.com) are both part of the spa facility (see below).

One of the highlights of the spa is its outdoor Sanctuary Courtyard, a lushly landscaped extension of the spa itself. Here, guests can sign up for the Celestial Shower, a private open-air Swiss shower treatment with sprays of varying strength; soak in a private tub; or have a massage

alfresco before or after a delicious health-conscious lunch. The soaking baths include the Seawater Soak, Citrus Soak, and Desert Rose Bath, all nice by themselves or as a prelude to a massage or one of the exotic body treatments, such as the cleansing/moisturizing Orange Blossom Special Body Facial. Men's facials and sports massages that target the specific muscles used in golf or tennis are also a specialty.

Adjacent to the spa is the Yamaguchi Salon, a top-notch hair and makeup spot, featuring hair and nail treatments based on each person's feng shui element, as well as makeup applications and lessons.

The WellMax Center for Preventive Medicine is a one-stop medical testing and evaluation office that offers extensive physical examinations, including such components as CT scans of the lungs, conventional or virtual colonoscopy, hormone level testing, and on and on. Staff physicians are also on staff at Eisenhower Medical Center, the desert's largest and most respected hospital and research facility.

The services are expensive, and most are not paid for by insurance, since they're regarded as preventive rather than medically necessary. The center does offer packages and often runs summer specials that can help with the cost.

Another feature is the "24/7Access" program, which copies and encrypts a client's medical data to one CD. This information is available to the client and his or her medical professionals on a 24-hour basis.

WellMax clients can spend as little as a half day and as much as four days getting all the tests and evaluations, and that's

---

The rule of thumb on tipping is the same as it is for dining out: A 15 to 20 percent gratuity that reflects your satisfaction for the service is considered appropriate. Some resort spas automatically add a gratuity to the bill.

---

where the benefit of a spa next door is really seen. Somehow, having your blood drawn is a little more palatable when it's followed by a massage and facial.

Le Parker Meridien Palm Springs: Palm Springs Yacht Club
4200 East Palm Canyon Drive
(760) 770-5000, (800) 543-4300
www.parkermeridien.com
Ranked by *Condé Nast Traveler* as one of the top 10 spas in America for four years running, the Parker's spa began its life when the former Autry Hotel became the Givenchy Resort & Spa. Now under new ownership, the hotel has undergone a complete transformation. What was once a kitschy Versailles look-alike is now a popular and trendy retro hideout, complete with croquet and bocci ball courts, Joseph Adler–designed furniture and decor, and a tongue-in-cheek attitude. This, plus great service, is also the reigning atmosphere at the new spa, the Palm Springs Yacht Club (PSYC), which has shed its French frosting look for a trim, nautical theme.

How's this for a signature treatment? The Ultimate Parker Experience features real gold in every step, including a golden moisturizing scrub, a body masque laced with gold, a frothy golden milk bath, a rubdown with bronzed dry oil, and a light dusting with gold flecks. Now that's proper tongue-in-cheek decadence. Around the World gets you a 90-minute massage that alternates among Lomi Lomi, Shiatsu, Plantar Reflexology, and European Lymph Drainage techniques, targeting virtually every muscle in the body.

One innovation at the PSYC is the pricing structure for massage. No matter the type of therapy, all massages are charged by the half hour, hour, or 90 minutes. Wraps, scrubs, facials, and waxing round out the spa offerings. An on-site beauty salon provides full hair and nail services.

Men's and women's areas are completely separate and clothing-optional. Each side has its own indoor swimming pools, Jacuzzi, and steam and sauna rooms. The 24-hour fitness center is also in the spa building and has a good selection of weights, machines, and classes—yoga, tai chi, chi gong, Pilates, bocci ball, and croquet classes are available throughout the day, both indoors and outdoors.

The Lodge at Rancho Mirage: Avanyu Spa
68-900 Frank Sinatra Drive
Rancho Mirage
(760) 321-8282, (866) 518-6870
www.lodgeatranchomirage.com
Originally built as a Ritz-Carlton and in possession of the desert's most spectacular hotel view, The Lodge is now a Rock Resort and is currently closed for renova-

Massage Schools

Many locals indulge in frequent massages by taking advantage of the bargains offered by student therapists. The area's two licensed massage schools offer top value for professional service—$30 for a one-hour Swedish massage. Desert Resorts School of Somatherapy (2100 North Palm Canyon Drive, C100, Palm Springs; 760-323-5806, 800-270-1175; www.somatherapy.com) offers massages at a separate Palm Desert location on Wednesdays, Thursdays, and Saturdays. Academy of Professional Careers (45-691 Monroe Avenue, Indio; 760-347-5000; www.academyofhealthcareers.com), the desert's oldest massage school, offers services at varying times. Call for availability.

tions until December 2007. The Avanyu Spa will also be closed during this time. Past offerings at Avanyu have included a fitness center with cardio equipment, free weights, and aerobic and yoga classes for all ages and fitness levels. Outdoor massage cabanas have taken advantage of the view and fresh air.

The spa is an elegant, clean-lined space, and the staff is extremely professional. This has been one of the best places in town to really get a pampering, with a variety of treatments that rely on products indigenous to the desert, such as desert clay, lavender, and citrus.

Packages have been a good value here and have been well thought out. For example Desert Avanyu has included a half-hour massage or wrap of choice, an hourlong facial, lunch on the terrace, and a finishing manicure and pedicure.

Another specialty has been the Abhyanga Massage, a four-handed massage with two therapists working on every muscle from head to toe. The hour and a half has included a scrub or wrap and, of course, has cost about twice as much as a traditional one-therapist massage.

Rancho Las Palmas Resort and Spa: Spa Las Palmas
41-000 Bob Hope Drive, Rancho Mirage
(760) 836-3106, (800) 458-8786
www.rancholaspalmas.com
A 20,000-square-foot facility with 23 treatment rooms, Spa Las Palmas has its own outdoor lap pool and a serviceable fitness center that offers free weights, machines, personal training, and fitness counseling. The hotel is located across the street from The River, the area's newest and largest dining/entertainment/shopping complex, and, primarily because of its location, is a favorite with locals.

The selection of body scrubs, wraps, massages, and facials is changing at this time, and the Web site is notably lacking in specific information, so it's a good idea to call ahead and talk with the staff if you're planning your vacation and want to make sure you get the full selection.

Part of the spa experience here, as in many of the larger hotels, includes men's and women's steam rooms and therapy baths. Several different daily classes in the fitness center are also on the menu. A separately owned, adjacent beauty salon offers waxing and hair and nail services.

Miramonte Resort & Spa: The Well Spa
45-000 Indian Wells Lane, Indian Wells
(760) 837-1652, (800) 237-2926
www.miramonteresort.com
A luxurious, midsize resort hotel with a Tuscan theme and 11 acres of winding gardens, Miramonte added The Well Spa in 2004. Right in step with the current trend of indoor/outdoor treatments, The Well Spa has a Watsu pool and a Vichy shower with tables made from 100-year-old acacia cedar. In the shallow spa pool, smooth stone benches make for "natural chaise lounges" and encourage lingering.

There are nine indoor and 10 outdoor treatment rooms; men's and women's steam, sauna, and locker facilities; a swimming pool and whirlpool; as well as a full-service beauty salon and 24-hour fitness center. The fitness center offers two outdoor pools with hot tubs, machines, free weights, and fitness classes. Personal trainers are available by appointment. Waxing is available in the spa, and nail services are also offered.

One of the spa's signature services is the Pittura Fiesta, or mud-painting party. Guests paint themselves or their partners with colored mud and clays, then let the sun bake the mud dry while aestheticians deliver a scalp massage and personalized pressure-point facial. A Swiss shower is the finale, rinsing off the detoxifying mud and leaving the skin soft and refreshed.

Italian-themed treatments are the signature here and include such services as the Wine Bath Cobblestone Massage, Mediterranean Veggie Organic Wrap, and Monticelli Mud Wrap.

Renaissance Esmeralda Resort and Spa
44-400 Indian Wells Lane, Indian Wells
(760) 773-4444, (800) 552-4386
www.renaissanceesmeralda.com
Completed in 2002, this medium-size spa
has 14 indoor treatment rooms and eight
private cabanas outside in the "tranquillity
garden," a relaxing landscaped area with
waterfall soaking pools. One of the signature treatments is the Botanical Bliss, featuring a bath with Dead Sea salts, a scrub
using a combination of shea, mango,
kukui, and cocoa butters, and a massage
with a choice of aromatherapy oils. The
Caviar Facial and Caviar Eye Treatment
use real caviar, an antioxidant cocktail, and
marine extracts to rev up circulation and
bring a glow to skin that may have lost its
luster in the dry desert air.

Other specialties include the Spa Trios,
which combine an herbal with a wrap or
scrub and a massage. Reflexology and
special pregnancy massages for the second and third trimesters of pregnancy,
men's facials, and golf massages are also
popular.

Waxing is available in the spa, and a
full-service beauty salon offers hair, nail,
and makeup services.

The Westin Mission Hills Resort and Spa
71333 Dinah Shore Drive
Rancho Mirage
(760) 328-5955, (800) 228-3000
www.westin.com
The new spa in this Spanish-Moorish
theme resort is medium-size (13,000
square feet) with an intimate, cozy boutique atmosphere. All of the treatments
are indoors, and guests have the use of

---

*Some of the best values are at spas
where one service entitles you to use
the facilities all day. You can spend the
day soaking, steaming, using the gym,
eating lunch, and hanging out by the
pool, all for the price of the one service
you were going to pay for anyway.*

---

steam rooms, hydrotherapy rooms, lockers, Jacuzzi, and a full fitness center.
Classes include yoga, the trademark
WestinWORKOUT, cardio fitness,
weightlifting, and personal training.

The ample treatment menu includes
clay and aloe wraps, several scrubs and
facials, and a variety of massages. One of
the signature massages is the Sole Stone,
a reflexology treatment that combines hot
stone massage techniques with foot reflexology.

The beauty salon offers makeup, waxing, and nail services and features local
celebrity hairstylist Agim and his crack
team of colorists and cutters.

And, befitting the area's reputation as
a plastic surgery hot spot, the Westin's signature facial is the Pre/Post Lift and Laser
Facial, a three-treatment regime said to
enhance the effects of facial surgery.

HOT MINERAL SPRINGS SPAS

Hot mineral water has been sought out by
health enthusiasts the world over. Europeans have gone to the hot baths since
ancient days. Traditionally these waters
have been used to treat many physical ail-
ments. The mineral water found in all of
the Desert Hot Springs mineral springs is
odorless, tasteless, and colorless, a little
like the still mineral water you'd drink with
a nice lunch. Because of these qualities,
you can soak in it for hours without turning into a prune.

If you're looking for a soak in natural
hot mineral springs, DHS, as the locals call
it, is the place. Even the tap water is
exceptional here, having won several
awards in the annual International Water
Tasting competition in Berkeley Springs,
West Virginia. Knowing a good marketing
tool when they sip it, city officials have
gone into the bottling business, calling
their water "a business card you can taste."
The city's drinking water comes from a
cold-water underground aquifer. The hot
mineral springs well up from the hot-water

aquifer, often rising to the surface at temperatures as high as 180 degrees, then cooled for use in the hotel pools.

Few of the hotels listed here have full-service spas; many are modest accommodations built around the hot mineral springs, and their rates often reflect that fact.

Adobe Inn & Spa
66365 7th Street, Desert Hot Springs
(760) 329-7292, (877) 700-1772
www.adobespa.com

A recently remodeled 1960s adobe-style motel with 11 rooms and six detached cabins, the Adobe Inn has a quaint Mexican hacienda ambience and two nice pools—one for swimming and one for soaking. No spa services are provided.

It's located on a quiet residential street within a few blocks of downtown Desert Hot Springs and caters to guests wanting a simple accommodation and low rates.

Agua Caliente Hotel & Mineral Spa
14500 Palm Drive, Desert Hot Springs
(760) 329-4481, (800) 423-8109
www.aguacalientehotel.com

One of the best features of this little spot is the in-room mineral water Jacuzzis, although the outdoor pool is large and attractive as well. Many of the rooms have kitchens, and the hotel also offers monthly rates for retired individuals. The spa includes a fitness center with personal trainers; provides services such as massages, facials, wraps, and polishes; and has a beauty salon.

A fairly recent addition is the Desert Cruise Detox and Weight Loss Package, which includes lodging, meals, vitamin and mineral supplements, therapeutic treatments, detox baths, personal training, and nutritional classes.

Desert Hot Springs Spa Hotel
10805 Palm Drive, Desert Hot Springs
(760) 329-6000, (800) 808-7727
www.dhsspa.com

This medium-size hotel features eight natural hot mineral pools and is set up for family use, with a lot of locals coming for the day just to soak and take it easy. There are separate men's and women's saunas and lockers rooms. In the less busy low season, the hotel often offers a special day rate for rooms and spa admission. It's always a good idea to call for availability. There is no fitness center, steam room, or beauty salon.

Hope Springs
68075 Club Circle Drive
Desert Hot Springs
(760) 329-4003
www.hopespringsresort.com/

Ten rooms, three pools, and a determined-to-be-hip attitude have transformed this little old motel into a favored destination for Southern Californians looking for the next new thing. Clean, light, and retro-'50s in style, it offers three varieties of salt rubs, three different wraps, and nine types of massage. Meals can be arranged in advance and served poolside or in the rooms. Most rooms have kitchens.

The Last Resort
E-mail thelastresort@dc.rr.com for directions
(760) 322-8759
www.thelastresortcalifornia.com

This little jewel has just four one- and two-bedroom suites. All are tastefully decorated with high ceilings, polished concrete floors, and simple, colorful furniture. Each suite has a full kitchen, dining area, and patios off the dining room and bedroom. The single pool and two large hot tubs are the main entertainment at a spot known for its privacy and tranquillity. Long stays are a specialty here.

La Toscana Resort & Spa
11000 Palm Drive, Desert Hot Springs
(760) 329-6484, (800) 635-8660
www.latoscanaresorts.com

One of the older and larger mineral springs hotels in Desert Hot Springs, La Toscana has recently changed owners and is in the process of renovation. Central to the hotel is the courtyard with mineral pool, waterfalls, and Jacuzzis, flanked by the bar and patio dining area. This is not a private retreat atmosphere, but rather a somewhat boisterous, family-oriented experience.

Away from the main waterworks, guests can sign up for a variety of massages, body wraps, scrubs, facials, waxing, and nail services. The fitness center is a basic facility with men's and women's lockers, steam rooms, sauna, and a relaxation room with another waterfall.

Lido Palms Spa Resort
12801 Tamar Drive, Desert Hot Springs
(760) 329-6033
www.lidopalms.com

An immaculate little mineral springs motel, Lido Palms has 11 one-bedroom guest rooms and one two-bedroom, two-bath suite. All have full kitchens, large TVs, and recliners, but no phones. Children and pets are better left at home.

One large swimming pool, a 20-seat hot tub, and a smaller hot tub provide the mineral water. The larger hot tub is located inside a small area that also houses the exercise room and sauna. A variety of in-room massages are available from the staff therapists.

Living Waters Spa
13340 Mountain View Road
Desert Hot Springs
(760) 329-9988, (866) 329-9988

This was a custom-made "spa-tel" in the 1960s and has been completely renovated. The owners kept the original neon KISMET LODGE sign, and the nine guest rooms also show a retro flair, but with a modern twist and amenities such as free Wi-Fi. Seven of the rooms come with full kitchens.

Be warned—this is one of the desert's clothing-optional places, and most guests take the no-clothes option. The hotel is designed to cater to couples, and there are no facilities or provisions for children. It's also an excellent facility—Trip Advisor gave Living Waters the number-one hotel rating

in Desert Hot Springs for 2005. A covered soaking pool and outdoor swimming pool are, of course, full of hot mineral water. Lockers are available for day-use guests, who must bring their own towels.

Miracle Manor Spa Retreat
12589 Reposo Way, Desert Hot Springs
(760) 329-6641, (877) 329-6641
www.miraclemanor.com

A six-room jewel furnished in a "desert Zen from the '50s" style, Miracle Manor has been featured in just about every travel publication in the country. The privacy, ambience, and attention from the owners are unbeatable, the rooms are clean and stylish (many also have kitchens), and the water is hot. This little place books up very quickly, so it's wise to check on reservations early in your vacation planning.

A single hot mineral pool is the center of the inn, and there are two separate treatment rooms situated at the opposite end of the property, for maximum privacy and quiet. Several different types of massage and facials are on tap. The signature treatment, Back on Track, uses essential oils in a targeted spinal massage combined with craniosacral therapy to treat trauma and headaches.

Miracle Springs Resort & Spa
10625 Palm Drive, Desert Hot Springs
(760) 251-6000, (800) 856-3174
www.miraclesprings.com

The newest hotel in Desert Hot Springs, Miracle Springs features eight mineral pools and a full-service spa with a complete range of massages, facials, body scrubs, wraps, nail services, and waxing.

The specialty here is the great variety of packages. A favorite of locals and guests at other hotels is one that includes day use of a hotel room, brunch, a massage, facial, wrap, and manicure/pedicure. After all that, you may be so relaxed that you decide to spend the night in one of the quiet, simply furnished rooms.

Nurturing Nest
11149 Sunset Avenue, Desert Hot Springs
(760) 251-2583
www.nurturingnest.com

A little seven-room retreat newly renovated in the increasingly popular minimalist Zen style, Nurturing Nest is operated by its owners, holistic health practitioners Dr. Sandra and Ramesh Gune. Their specialty is three- to seven-day retreats tailored to each individual's needs and wants. A wide range of physical and counseling-oriented therapies, including energy healing, Ayurvedic treatments, yoga classes, and basic spa services, are on the menu for anyone taking the retreats or just staying for a few days. Breakfast is complimentary, and five of the rooms in the inn have full kitchens for those who want to prepare their own meals.

Sagewater Spa
12689 Eliseo Road, Desert Hot Springs
(760) 251-1668, (800) 600-1668
www.sagewaterspa.com

Originally built in 1954, the seven-room Sagewater has been beautifully restored and now offers top-of-the-line amenities such as European zillion-thread-count linens, DSL connections, flat-screen TVs, DVD players, and kitchens stocked with designer coffee and coffee cakes.

Guests can choose from a wide selection of massage and body treatments performed in their rooms, as well as Watsu massage in the outdoor mineral pool.

Sam's Family Spa
70875 Dillon Road, Desert Hot Springs
(760) 329-6457
www.samsfamilyspa.com

Built as a family park in 1971, Sam's has 50 acres available for tents, campers, travel trailers, and motor homes and also offers a small selection of motel rooms and mobile homes for rent. It's meant for long stays as well as those travelers who are just passing through and want to soak in the springs for a few days. The pools are fed from three wells on the property. This is the epitome of simple, laid-back, family-oriented vacationing.

Spa Resort Casino
100 North Indian Canyon Drive
(760) 778-1772, (888) 293-0180
www.sparesortcasino.com

It's a resort, it's a casino, and it's a spa. And it's also the desert's original spa and first casino. Located in the heart of downtown Palm Springs, the Spa Resort Casino has recently been completely remodeled to upgrade the spa and public areas.

The spa is built on top of the city's namesake hot springs, a sacred site to the Agua Caliente (hot water) Band of Cahuilla Indians, who are owners and operators of the resort and casino. An integral part of any visit to the spa is Taking of the Water, an hourlong experience that includes stops in the steam room, sauna, eucalyptus inhalation room, and mineral soaking tubs. An all-day pass to the spa includes this, as well as access to the fitness center, outdoor whirlpool, and swimming pool. Men's and women's spa areas are separate, and each includes these amenities as well as a number of treatment rooms. The fitness center offers machines, free weights, personal training, and a range of activity classes.

Spa treatments run the gamut of different massage therapies, facials, scrubs, wraps, and waxing. Packages are generally a good value, particularly if you can persuade a group of six or more to join you for a day or half day of pampering. A full-service beauty salon offers hair, makeup, and nail services.

The Spring
12699 Reposo Way, Desert Hot Springs
(760) 251-6700
www.thespringresortandspa.com

The Spring is one of the small treasures of Desert Hot Springs, with nine rooms and one suite opening onto a courtyard and three mineral pools. Hammocks, sunbathing spots, and a massage cabana ring the main pool. Six of the rooms have kitchens, and all have courtyards with privacy panels. Service is exceptional, including meal delivery from the area's top restaurants.

CLOSE-UP

The Spa Resort Casino

In Palm Springs there is no spot that has had a more pivotal role in the city's history and fame than the hot spring that now feeds the soaking tubs in the Spa Resort Casino. Considered a sacred place by the Agua Caliente Band of Cahuilla Indians, the spring was the heart of the tribe's winter social life for hundreds of years. When Dr. Welwood Murray built the town's first hotel in 1887, he made sure to erect it as close as possible to the hot spring, which was reputed to have considerable curative powers. The water came out of the ground at around 104 degrees and had a distinctly sulfurous smell, unlike the odorless waters of the hot mineral springs in Desert Hot Springs.

Murray leased the site from the tribe for $100 a year and built a bathhouse and dressing rooms directly over the spring. It stood there until the tribe razed the shabby wooden building in 1916 and built their own bathhouse, which in 1939 charged just 25 cents per visitor.

This bathhouse was an improvement over the older one, with the corners of four separate rooms intersecting over the spring, but it was still little more than a simple wooden building.

In 1957, as the tribe gained the authority to offer their property on long-term leases, developer Sam Banowit convinced the Tribal Council that he could build a hot springs bathhouse that would finally make a profit for them. As part of the agreement, he relocated the palm trees, sacred to the tribe, to another site on the property. Banowit later negotiated the first 99-year lease on Indian land and built the five-story Spa Hotel next to the bath-

A central lounge area serves breakfast and is a good spot to read or relax before spa treatments in the separate spa building, an elegantly simple facility decorated in cool neutral tones with lots of natural light. Services include a variety of massages, wraps, scrubs, and facials. Simple non-polish manicures and pedicures are offered poolside on weekends. A special seven-day fasting and cleansing retreat is offered at different times during the year.

Two Bunch Palms Resort & Spa
67425 Two Bunch Palms Trail, Desert Hot Springs
(760) 329-8791, (800) 472-4334
www.twobunchpalms.com
Two Bunch Palms has been a magnet for stressed-out celebrities and wealthy businesspeople almost since it first opened in the early 1920s. It's one of the few desert resorts that can truthfully say it's never advertised—word of mouth is just amazingly strong. And, despite its obsessive rules on guest privacy, the place has been featured in a number of movies. Readers of *Condé Nast Traveler* and *Travel &*

house. With a slick modern hotel and tile-lined spa, the bathhouse once again became a center of social life for the entire town.

In the 1980s and 1990s, as the tribe worked for financial independence, they were eventually able to buy back their land lease and become full owners of the most prominent piece of land in Palm Springs. Sitting in the heart of the city, the new Spa Resort Casino has undergone near-constant renovation and enlargement and is the centerpiece in the tribe's impressive economic engine. As part of their long-range plan to create financial stability for all their members, the Agua Caliente Band of Cahuilla Indians currently owns and operates multiple business ventures in the Palm Springs area, including a bank, golf course, the Indian Canyons, the Agua Caliente Casino in Palm Desert, the Spa Resort Casino, and the Indian Canyons Tours.

The recently renovated Spa Resort Casino, built around the city's original hot mineral springs, attracts locals and visitors alike.
PHOTO COURTESY OF THE SPA RESORT CASINO

Leisure Magazine have consistently rated it among the world's top 10 spas.

The facility is located behind private gates, and accommodations are a mixture of casitas, villas, spa suites, suites, and guest rooms spread out over 256 acres. Dedicated to destressing and pampering, this is an unusual place that emphasizes quiet and serenity. Guests are cautioned about using cell phones in public areas and asked to speak quietly to preserve the peace.

Among the more than 45 different treatments, one of the newest is Trager massage, a dry, nonintrusive treatment that aims to release tension by gently pressing, lengthening, and rocking the limbs and torso. Natural green clay is one of the resources on the property and is used in several of the treatments, particularly the Egyptian Clay Body treatment, which includes a dry brushing and essential oil massage.

Some of the more exotic treatments at Two Bunch include crystal sound therapy, Reiki energy work, and Color Therapy, which uses guided meditation and intense colored light to increase well-being and balance.

SHOPPING

S urvey after survey of American travelers tells us that there are three activities that are always at the top of the "must-do" list: dining out, shopping, and sightseeing. Even people who do little shop-hopping at other times feel the need to buy something when they're in a new place—a memento of their visit, a gift for people back home, a hard-to-find item at a great price, even vacation necessities such as flip-flops or swimsuits. Though Palm Springs doesn't measure up to such Southern California shopping meccas as Los Angeles, Santa Monica, or San Diego, it has its share of national stores, specialty boutiques, and places that are unique to the desert.

Jewelry is a big deal here, as is the type of bright, glittery, casual women's clothing known as resort wear. It's telling that the Eddie Bauer store closed its doors and vacated its prime spot on El Paseo after only a few years. Its style of simple, rugged sportswear and plethora of sweaters and coats in the winter always seemed out of place in the perpetual sunshine and highly groomed surroundings. On the other hand, St. John has a flagship store here, as does Tommy Bahama, and they sell lots and lots of clothing.

To help you in your hunting and gathering, we have included a brief rundown on the major shopping areas in the valley and the general type of merchandise you will find there. Otherwise, shopping options are presented by category of goods, making it easy for you to find

antiques, toys, books, and more. Chain stores are not listed in the individual categories, but we do note where they can be found.

MAJOR SHOPPING AREAS

Palm Springs

In the past five years or so, the city has developed its own antiques and art gallery section known as the **Uptown Heritage District.** Covering several blocks beginning in the 300 block of North Palm Canyon Drive, the area is a charming collection of historic buildings housing consignment stores, gift shops, galleries, restaurants, and home-decorating boutiques. This area really got its start when the midcentury modern craze hit Southern California. Suddenly, movie types and hipsters from Los Angeles discovered a few furniture consignment stores offering amazing bargains on well-preserved furniture and bric-a-brac from the 1940s and '50s. The bargains are no longer amazing, but they're pretty darn good, and spending the day wandering through the shops can be quite entertaining. This area also puts on a First Friday shopping event the first Friday of each month. Stores stay open until 9:00 P.M. and offer music, entertainment, snacks, and refreshments.

In the heart of downtown, the onceshuttered Desert Fashion Plaza is now the site of Cirque Dreams, a Cirque du Soleil–type production that opened in January 2006 and has had a highly successful season in its first five-month run. It's set to run again in the winter 2006/2007 season and has secured a $300,000 interest-free loan from the city, plus a three-year lease from Desert Fashion Plaza at $1.00 per year. The 1,000-seat theater has hopes of doing what the Fabulous Palm Springs

---

i *Palm Desert runs a free "Shopper Hopper" shuttle in a cute little trolley. It runs a continuous loop, with stops at most of the major hotels and shopping areas. For times call SunBus at (760) 343-3451.*

Follies did for downtown when that show first started in 1991—draw theater-goers into the central district and send them out on the street for dinner and clubbing after the show. In the long run, the city and local merchants hope the combination of both entertainment venues will attract upscale retailers and high-end boutiques to replace the myriad souvenir storefronts and T-shirt shops that line the street now.

The **Palm Springs Mall,** at the corner of Tahquitz Canyon Way and Farrell Drive, is geared to bargain shoppers, anchored by Ross Dress for Less and Harris-Gottschalks department store.

Cathedral City

This is car-shoppers' heaven, with several major car dealerships concentrated in one area just off Palm Canyon Drive/Highway 111. Other than that, the city's retail offerings consist mainly of a small shopping area with national chains such as Target and the discounter Tuesday Morning.

Rancho Mirage

Until **The River** opened a few years ago, Rancho Mirage was a retail wasteland. This new open-air shopping and dining complex is more geared to food and entertainment, but it does have some nifty shops, such as Cohiba Cigar (see the listing under Boutiques/Gift Shops/Specialty Shops) and Tulip Hill Winery (see the listing under Specialty Food Stores), as well as a spacious and well-stocked Borders Bookstore, a few boutiques, and the cosmetics giant Ulta.

Palm Desert

This city is the valley's undisputed retail king. **Westfield Shoppingtown** is a midlevel enclosed mall anchored by

Though the department stores, national retailers, and most of the merchants in Palm Springs stay open late at least one night a week—Friday—the shops on El Paseo Drive stubbornly close their doors at 5:30 or 6:00 P.M.

JCPenney, Sears, Macy's Robinsons-May, and a huge Barnes & Noble. Built in the early 1980s, it was the first enclosed mall in the desert and was the start of the retail boom for Palm Desert. There are around 150 of the usual small mall shops, kiosks, and food court stations, plus extras such as a shopping concierge, valet parking, parking services for pregnant women, package carry-out, and new covered parking areas to stash the car out of the heat.

El Paseo Drive has long been promoted as the "Rodeo Drive of the Desert" but is now growing into something even better, with a great variety of restaurants, art galleries, bistros, and boutiques. The street's contribution to "mall" shopping is The Garden on El Paseo, a two-story open-air complex with covered parking and a desert landscape. During the winter season there are free weekend jazz concerts and frequent wine-and-cheese benefits for local charities. It's anchored by Saks Fifth Avenue and features such national stores as Ann Taylor, Banana Republic, Brooks Brothers, Coach, Sharper Image, Pottery Barn, William-Sonoma, L'Occitane, Harry & David, and Tiffany. Other national stores include J. Jill, Aveda, and the Tommy Bahama clothing/home decor/dining establishment. If the desert has a "yuppie shopping hangout," this is it.

On the street itself you can buy any upscale service or trinket imaginable, from cashmere blankets to diamond bracelets, cosmetic surgery, designer furniture, hand-engraved stationery, sequined baby booties, couture gowns, and custom-tailored suits. National designers with signature shops here include Escada, St. John, Mondi, and Polo Ralph Lauren.

In the **Desert Crossing** shopping area just off Highway 111, big-box retailers abound. There are Target, TJ Maxx, Circuit City, Payless Shoes, and about a dozen more. Just across the street you'll find Pier I Imports, Best Buy, Cost Plus, and other recognizable chains.

Once you leave Palm Desert and head east, the shopping options decline dramatically, though Indian Wells is attracting more specialty boutiques and local ventures. **The Village** shopping center in this city is better than the average strip mall, with a Ralphs grocery store, Postal Connection, hair salon, cleaners, deli, and several small, high-quality stores selling kitchen items, gifts, and clothing.

Several years ago most of these shops would close their doors for the summer, celebrating a "grand reopening" in September. Some still do take off for a few months, but the majority are open year-round. By the same token, many shops that closed on Sundays a few years ago are now open every day in season. Always call ahead to check on hours, and remember that the retail world in this resort is almost as fickle as the restaurant world, so some shops may have moved, closed, or changed the type of merchandise they offer.

In the following listings, all stores are in Palm Springs, unless otherwise noted.

ANTIQUES AND CONSIGNMENT STORES

Antique Collective
798 and 844 North Palm Canyon Drive
(760) 323-9994
Just as the name suggests, this is a collective endeavor of dozens of individual antiques dealers, offering everything from Bakelite bracelets to beautifully preserved furniture from a variety of eras. The two buildings that house the collections are exceptionally well kept, with the look and feel of glossy retail stores. The staff have all been in the business for years and are knowledgeable about all the goods. If

you're looking for unusual, high-quality gifts or a piece to round out a collection, the collective might be a good place to start.

Bram's
461 North Palm Canyon Drive
(760) 416-2667
This is a real specialty store, featuring antique furniture, art, and accessories from the Arts and Crafts period, roughly 1890 through 1930. There is also a good collection of handmade Mexican sterling silver jewelry of the hefty, rough-hewn variety found decades ago.

Brasfield & Cochran Estate Gallery
222 Via Sol
(760) 318-2522
Because this gallery focuses on buying from the estates of wealthy individuals in California and the Southwest, the selection is always eclectic, with furniture, accessories, collectibles, and art from a wide variety of periods and styles. They also take consignments of quality pieces, primarily from desert residents.

Estate Sale Company
4185 East Palm Canyon Drive
(760) 321-7628
This is the store that brought high-end, professional consignment retail to the desert about 15 years ago. A family-owned business, it's expanded twice and is known as the best place for locals to sell furniture, quality accessories, furs, jewelry, and art quickly. The inventory changes rapidly, and the prices are reasonable for a wide selection that ranges from apartment-grade couches to unusual pieces that were custom-designed and have lost their appeal to the original owners. For some locals a stop at the Estate Sale Company to check out the new stuff is a regular Saturday stop.

Heather James Art & Antiquities
73080 El Paseo Drive, Palm Desert
(760) 346-8926
www.heatherjames.com

This gallery specializes in fine cultural and ethnographic art from all over the world, with emphasis on African, Asian, pre-Columbian, tribal, and classical pieces. At any time, you might find a fine 500 B.C. Attic ware vase, a pair of ancient pottery tomb figures from Jalisco, 19th-century Tantric Buddhist art, or a mask worn by shamans from Borneo in healing ceremonies. The gallery also offers art buying and consultation and has access to sources for fine art from the masters—Van Gogh, Matisse, Monet, Renoir, Degas, Hassam, and many others. You can count on finding museum-quality pieces here, as well as top service.

Lakeridge & Croft Collection
673 North Palm Canyon Drive
(760) 318-9999

You never know what you'll find here in the changing jumble of treasures. Antiques and contemporary consignment furniture, art, glassware, and various collectibles fill the space. Like many of the less well-established antiques shops, the quality is hit-or-miss.

La Maison Jolie
77682 Country Club Drive, Palm Desert
(760) 772-9890

This is one of the most chichi of the desert's many antiques/home decor shops, with absolutely everything that can dress up a wall, tabletop, or special room. The look is predominantly European—Italian pottery, elaborate silk flower arrangements, antique and modern prints, graceful furniture, and lots of little accessories.

Las Palmas Antiques
865 North Palm Canyon Drive
(760) 320-2411

Las Palmas specializes in "home-grown" items from the desert's past, from elaborate custom furniture that once graced a millionaire's home to fixtures, accessories, and interesting home doodads of local origin. The items here tend to be highly decorated and embellished—more High Hollywood Boudoir than midcentury Modern.

Maison Felice
73296 El Paseo Drive, Palm Desert
(760) 862-0021

Here's where you'll find the big statement pieces, from fine European antique furniture to massive architectural elements to elaborate garden accessories and exquisite estate silver. The shop itself is worth a short visit, if only to admire the tasteful merchandising and elegant interior.

Robert Kaplan Antiques
469 North Palm Canyon Drive
(760) 323-7144, (888) 277-8960

A Sotheby's associate, this shop specializes in small items such as clocks, watches, music boxes, fine jewelry, silver, china, and glassware, as well as Tiffany pieces, old paintings, and art objects. There is also a selection of extremely fine furniture and old Russian items. The layout and display are clean, attractive, and easy to navigate. Don't even go in the door unless you're prepared to fall in love with a lovely Art Nouveau brooch, a perfect Russian icon, or an exquisite little writing desk.

Stewart Galleries
191 South Indian Canyon Drive
(760) 325-0878
www.stewartgalleries.com

Stewart's has a huge inventory of paintings by well-known artists in the California Impressionist and Plein Air schools, featuring original oil paintings by artists from the past as well as up-and-coming new talent. Their buyers are also well respected in the art world and often are first on the scene to acquire notable estate paintings from the Modern and Surrealist movements, theory schools, and much more. The antiques side of the business is one of the most popular in the desert, with a changing inventory that includes crystal chandeliers, oriental figures, classic marble statues, fine antique furniture, and decorative accessories. There is always a large selection of bronze sculptures as well.

Two Spirit Gallery
895 North Palm Canyon Drive
(760) 416-3991
There's always something unexpected and beautiful here, from Roseville Potter, Hummels, and Victorian porcelain to ethnic and Native American items. In the little back room is an astounding collection of buttons, beads, and costume jewelry—enough to lose yourself in play for several hours. The wonderful staff will join you in browsing and even put together a necklace, earrings, or a bracelet from the antique and modern beads and findings. The prices are quite reasonable as well.

MIDCENTURY FURNISHINGS AND ACCESSORIES

Although you will find an occasional piece of midcentury furniture or decor at another shop in the valley, this era is almost exclusively represented in Palm Springs. The following shops all feature collections of furniture, home accessories, and memorabilia from the 1940s through the 1970s. The quality and specific items vary greatly from time to time, but they are all quite competitively priced. Most of the goods are on consignment, so you may be able to pick up a piece that has some valley history. Also, the specific area of Palm Canyon Drive where these shops are located has gotten the reputation throughout Southern California as being *the* place to find interesting, unusual, and high-quality midcentury pieces, as well as

those that are simply kitschy and fun. If this is the era that interests you, take a few hours browsing the shops before you make your selection—the comparison may help you find you a better price on a particular piece or an example that's in better condition. To help you in your walking expedition, we've arranged the stores by location, starting with the ones that are closest to downtown Palm Springs and moving north.

Vintage Oasis
373 South Palm Canyon Drive Studio A
(760) 778-6224

Palm Springs Consignment
497 North Indian Canyon Drive
(760) 416-0704

Retrospect
666 North Palm Canyon Drive
(760) 416-1766
Features restored furniture from the period.

Galaxy 500
1007 North Palm Canyon Drive
(760) 320-7776

Dazzles
1035 North Palm Canyon Drive
(760) 327-1446
Also features an extensive selection of Bakelite jewelry.

Okie Dokie
1416 North Palm Canyon Drive
(760) 323-9878

20 First
1490 North Palm Canyon Drive, Suite A
(760) 327-5400

Studio One 11
2675 North Palm Canyon Drive
(760) 323-5104
High-end and rare midcentury furnishings and accessories from the 1930s through the 1970s.

Jonathan Adler is the 21st century's answer to an updated midcentury style. A noted ceramicist, he recently turned his considerable design talents to the decor of the Parker Meridien hotel in Palm Springs, creating a variety of vases, tabletop items, and furniture. Get a catalog from the hotel's concierge or order from www.jonathanadler.com.

Modern Way
2755 North Palm Canyon Drive
(760) 320-5455

BOOKSTORES

Celebritybooks.com
182 North Palm Canyon Drive
(760) 320-6575, (800) 320-6575
www.celebritybooks.com
Well, of course you'd find a store like this
in the desert—chock-full of new, used, rare
and autographed books about, by, and for
celebrities of all kinds. There are books
dealing with Hollywood, movie stars,
sports figures, and royals. The selection
isn't limited to celeb writings and includes
a finely edited collection of local-interest
works, general fiction, mysteries, true-
crime books, gay interest, and science fiction. When an author is in town, you can
bet this store will have the first book
signing. All in all, it's a lovely and interesting little independent bookstore of the
quality you would expect in a much larger
city.

Peppertree Bookstore & Café
622 North Palm Canyon Drive
(760) 325-5311

Peppertree Bookstore
155 South Palm Canyon Drive
(760) 325-4821
www.peppertreebookstore.com
New stores modeled in the tradition of
independent booksellers who know their
merchandise, these are the places that
round out the desert's selection of book-
stores. The owners pride themselves on
selecting books on their merit rather than
because they are on the best-seller lists,
though you will find most of the block-
busters here as well. Author events are
planned to take advantage of the intimate
setting, often making it possible to actually talk to the writers themselves. The
coffee is good, and the ambience is warm
and welcoming.

BOUTIQUES/GIFT SHOPS/SPECIALTY SHOPS

Aristokatz
121 South Palm Canyon Drive
(760) 322-8666
Here kitty-kitty! Cat lovers (or those
owned by cats) will find a lot of love and
humor on the shelves here. Cards, toys,
ceramics, books, calendars, all sorts of gift
items, and even a series of "video catnip"
tapes and DVDs are pretty tempting treats
for those who are fans of all things feline.

Camera Exchange Ltd.
875 North Palm Canyon Drive
(760) 320-6847
For years the only professional camera
store in the desert, this is still the spot
where the pros and knowledgeable ama-
teurs come for advice and materials. They
handle processing for many different types
of film, stock hard-to-find paper and film,
and offer repair, sales, and trade-ins. There
is just no way to find excellent service like
this in one of the big-box camera places.

Clockworks, A Clock Gallery
160 East Tahquitz Canyon Way
(760) 327-2475
New and streamlined, old and elegant—
this shop has them all, along with some
very nice watches and a reliable repair
service for heirloom pieces.

Cohiba Cigar Lounge and Boutique
At The River, Rancho Mirage
(760) 346-4748
Not only can you buy a fistful of premium
cigars, but you can settle down and
smoke them here as well. Smoking accessories and handmade cigars from
Nicaragua, Honduras, and the Dominican
Republic are the highlights.

Cold Nose Warm Heart
187 South Palm Canyon Drive
(760) 327-7747
This is the doggie version of Aristokatz,
featuring everything imaginable for dogs
and the people they own. Handmade dog

bowls, organic dog treats, fine leather collars, high-quality beds, goofy little sweaters, cards, and gift items are all dog-gone charming.

Fame Tobacconist
155 South Palm Canyon Drive
(760) 320-2752, (877) 332-4427

This shop has what they bill as the largest cigar humidor in Southern California, stocked with all manner of exotic cigars from all over the world. Of course they have a wide selection of other smoking goods, including pipes, lighters, cigar and cigarette cases, and—oddly enough—a fine grouping of murderous-looking knives from internationally known knife makers.

Home 101 LLC
392 North Palm Canyon Drive
(760) 318-9886

A fun little catchall gift shop with high-end bath and body products, interesting but not expensive jewelry, cards, books, lighting, and some home furnishings. If you're looking for a tasteful but trendy gift for your host or a last-minute birthday party, this shop will offer a lot of excellent and interesting choices.

Indian Motorcycles
301 North Palm Canyon Drive
(760) 778-6856

Though there are only a few of the famed Indian motorcycles here and this isn't really a "bike shop," you'll find lots of riding-related gear and clothing, as well as some jewelry and tough-guy accessories that are just the thing to give your lazy vacation days a fun edge.

Kitchen Fancy
73930 El Paseo Drive, Palm Desert
(760) 346-4114

Located on El Paseo Drive for 30 years, Kitchen Fancy features a wide selection of unique home accessories, gifts, table linens, greeting cards, candles, barware, and paper goods. They will also gift wrap and ship. This is great place for hostess gifts and hard-to-find items for serious cooks.

Mosaic
155 South Palm Canyon Drive
(760) 322-3485

The sinuous mosaic bench in front of the shop is a signal for the type of gift you'll find inside—witty books and postcards, gorgeous candles and soaps, fun jewelry, a few hard-to-find bits of clothing like Custo T-shirts and Nick and Nora pajamas, room scents, embroidered pillows, picture frames, and lots more. It's all tasteful, a little outrageous, and always changing. Take a few more minutes and check out its next-door sister La Mariposa, for colorful women's clothing and jewelry from Mexico, Morocco, and points south.

Musicians' Outlet
44850 San Pablo Drive, Palm Desert
(760) 341-3171

For professional and serious amateur musicians, this store stocks a wide selection of different instruments—specializing in guitars, keyboards, and drums—as well as a good amount of amplifiers, PA systems, karaoke, tapes, and sheet music. There are a lot of musicians in the valley but, oddly enough, very few stores that cater to their needs. This is the one place outside of Los Angeles that can be counted on to have the guitar strings, drum sets, and knowledgeable staff needed to keep a music group up and running.

Spectacular Shades
73910 El Paseo Drive, Palm Desert
(760) 568-4500

If there's one person in the desert who knows fabulous sunglasses, it's owner Sonia Campbell, who's been stocking the largest selection of upscale shades for many years. Brand names include Oliver People's, Carrera, Dior, Armani, Persol, Fendi, Diva, Kieselstein-Cord, Picasso, Nicole Miller, Calvin Klein, and a lot more. If you're looking for great advice on the most flattering pair for your face, you'll find it here.

Tabletop Elegance
73470 El Paseo Drive, Palm Desert
(760) 674-9234
For the detail-oriented hostess, this shop features a large selection of china, glassware, flatware, and accessories for creating fashionable tabletop settings. The gamut runs from silly paper goods for eating by the pool to supremely elegant collections for formal dinners.

The Treasure House
278 North Palm Canyon Drive
(760) 325-7725
Specializing in inspirational gifts, The Treasure House has been family owned and operated in Palm Springs for over 40 years. They stock work by inspirational artists such as Sandra Magsamen, Millie Keith, Jacqueline Kent, and Jim Shore, as well as handbags by Vera Bradley, painted glass by Joan Baker, and other gift items.

Ulta
At The River, Rancho Mirage
(760) 836-3381
This is a national store, but worth mentioning because of its huge inventory and single-minded focus. As many a hairdresser will say, "It's all about the product." The product here includes every hair potion around, dozens of perfumes, bath and body products, nail polishes, and what seems like an acre of mascara, eyeliner, blush, foundation, lipstick, and gloss. They also have a walk-in beauty bar where you can get a manicure, quickie facial, or bang trim and be out the door for dinner in less than half an hour.

CHILDREN'S CLOTHING AND TOYS/HOBBIES

Dollsville Dolls & Bearsville Bears
292 North Palm Canyon Drive
(760) 325-2241
From highly collectible and fragile dolls to those that are meant for a long, happy life of being dragged from playground to bed, this little shop has them all. There is also a wide selection of stuffed animals, including many collectible lines and future cuddly friends.

Mr. G's for Kids
180 North Palm Canyon Drive
(760) 320-9293
This shop is crammed full of toys for all ages, model kits, books, unusual gifts, and even the classics like yo-yos and paddleballs. They have a small selection of collectibles, plus coloring books, games, and cards. The latest, hottest electronics and large toys aren't here, but it is a charming place with lots of little treasures.

Oilily
The Gardens on El Paseo Drive
Palm Desert
(760) 837-9356
This shop is an explosion of color and features its own signature line of bright, graphic flower prints done up in girl's dresses, tops, shorts, pants, and hand-knit sweaters. There is even a small section for women. The colors are gorgeous, and the workmanship is excellent. The styling is faintly Icelandic, but the vivid pinks, oranges, blues, and greens are anything but staid.

Uncle Don's Hobbies & Supplies
Corner of Town Center Way and Fred Waring Drive, Palm Desert
(760) 346-8856
Uncle Don's was a mainstay in downtown Palm Springs for years and just recently moved to larger, more updated quarters in one of Palm Desert's strip malls. Action figures and models, card and board games, materials for model making, crafts, and collecting are the focus here. This is geared to the older child and adults, not to toddlers or infants.

Wishes Toy Store
78010 Main Street, La Quinta
(760) 564-5246
This shop concentrates on high-quality toys, such as games and mobiles for infant development, fun pool toys, and

card and board games for adults. There's a big selection of intricate balsa-wood models of Ferris wheels and buildings, suitable for children eight and older. The small selection of dolls and books is also top-notch.

COLLECTIBLES

Crystal Fantasy
264 North Palm Canyon Drive
(760) 322-7799
Owners Joy and Scott Meredith are known in town for both their community spirit and their unfailing eye for the best fantasy collectibles and art—representing Harmony Kingdom, faeries, mermaids, dragons, and other magical creatures. There is always a new treasure—incense, candles, gems, jewelry, herbs, oils, stained glass, books, and music.

Legends Celebrity Memorabilia
73260 El Paseo Drive, Palm Desert
(760) 203-1136
This shop offers all types of paper memorabilia, from magazine covers to personal letters and photographs, accompanied by the celebrity's signature and nicely framed for a gift presentation or ready to take home and hang on the wall. Certificates of authentication accompany all the pieces.

River's Ridge
At The River, Rancho Mirage
(760) 674-2111
For mineral enthusiasts, this is a real find. The rock and crystal specimens are truly spectacular, both in size and in quality. There is also a fine collection of Asian art

and jade carvings. The owners have good sources all over the world, so if you don't see what you want, they may be able to find it for you.

Unique Coins
750 North Palm Canyon Drive
(760) 320-3140
This well-respected local shop sells rare coins and currency, as well as fine silver, china, and a small selection of estate jewelry and collectibles. The staff is quite knowledgeable and can find sources for specific coins and rare pieces of jewelry. Many visitors have come to rely on the shop to build their collections over the years.

GARDEN SHOPS

Gubler Orchids
2200 Belfield Boulevard, Landers
(760) 364-2282, (800) 482-5377
One of the country's largest orchid growers, Gubler's set up shop in the high desert in 1975. With temperatures that are 10 to 15 degrees cooler than on the desert floor, year-round sunshine, and the controlled climate of a massive greenhouse, this spot is ideal for these exotic beauties. Gubler's propagates their own orchids and gives tours of the growing areas where they nurture more than 5,000 different orchid hybrids. The selection is huge, and they will ship just about anywhere—even Alaska. Prices are excellent, and the plants are top quality. Gubler's also stocks special potting soil, fertilizer, pots, and baskets, as well as cards, T-shirts, and small gift items.

The Living Desert's Palo Verde Garden Center
47900 Portola Avenue, Palm Desert
(760) 346-5694
www.livingdesert.org
As befits a nursery inside one of the country's most extensive wildlife displays, this garden center features hundreds of rare and hard-to-find desert plants from all

The best sales of the year are in late May and early June, when storeowners know the slow days of summer are just ahead. Few shops advertise, so call your favorite to find out when the big markdowns are scheduled.

over the Southwest and Mexico. In addition, you'll find seeds, books on desert landscaping, and a good selection of attractive pottery.

Moorten Botanical Garden
1701 South Palm Canyon Drive
(760) 327-6555

A Palm Springs Historical Landmark, Moorten Botanical Garden has been in the same spot since 1938, cultivating an astounding variety of cacti, succulents, and other desert plants. There are more than 3,000 varieties here, and something is always in bloom. This is truly a taste of old Palm Springs. Clark Moorten—son of the garden's founders, "Cactus Slim" and Patricia Moorten—is there every day. Just like his parents, he has a true love for the desert and an encyclopedic knowledge of its plants. Take a stroll through the grounds, where specimen plants tower hundreds of feet high and the sounds of doves and other desert birds fill the air. Pick up an exotic plant as a great hostess gift or have it shipped back home. Clark has done the consulting for the desert's most stunning landscapes, and he'll give expert advice on what will work in your climate.

JEWELRY STORES

B. Alsohn's Jewelers
73585 El Paseo Drive, Palm Desert
(760) 430-4211

With a master jeweler and GIA-trained gemologist on staff, this shop features designer jewelry in silver, gold, and platinum; individual gems ready for setting or collecting; and fine watches.

Cousins Estate Jewelers
73350 El Paseo Drive, Palm Desert
(760) 674-8006

From Victorian cameos to heavy gold pieces from the 1980s, the estate jewelry selection offers an ever-changing choice and a look at styles from years past. This shop often gets first crack at estates and

picks the very best items. If you have a longing for something specific, the owners can often find excellent examples for your selection.

DeLuca Jewelers
73655 El Paseo Drive, Palm Desert
(760) 773-1763

Joe DeLuca has owned this business for decades and is one of the desert's most respected jewelry designers. Featured items include original gold pieces, fine diamonds, designer sterling silver, and estate pieces.

Denis Roberge
73995 El Paseo Drive, Palm Desert
(760) 340-5045

All designs are created and manufactured in this elegant space, which is an extension of the Roberge art gallery and Augusta restaurant. The distinctive designs recall classical pieces from Greece or Rome, using 22k gold and large cabochon, colored stones.

Diamonds of Splendor
73400 El Paseo Drive, Palm Desert
(760) 568-6641

Two GIA graduate gemologists own this cozy little space and will create just about any design you have in mind. Originality and quality are watchwords here. They specialize in unusual cuts and faceting, as well as designs that are more traditional and European in style.

El Paseo Jewelry Exchange
73375 El Paseo Drive, Palm Desert
(760) 773-1040

This is a trendy jewelry boutique featuring diamond and gemstone pieces at bargain prices. Designer knockoffs and basics in the latest styles are the specialty.

Emrick Jewels
73896 El Paseo Drive, Palm Desert
(760) 568-4522

Emrick offers a selection of antique and contemporary jewelry that includes Victorian, Art Deco, Art Nouveau, and retro

Moorten Botanical Garden

As every desert old-timer knows, Palm Springs just wouldn't be Palm Springs without Moorten Botanical Garden, a labor of love created by Chester "Cactus Slim" Moorten and his wife, biologist Patricia Moorten.

Nicknamed "Slim" for his tall, lanky form and work as a contortionist, Chester was one of the original Keystone Cops, worked as the stand-in for Howard Hughes, and played parts in many other movies over the years. Poor health led him to the desert in the 1930s with his young wife Patricia, a biologist with a special interest in botany. Together they explored this desolate landscape and worked the Rainbow's End Gold Mine in the high desert. They began collecting desert plants, historic artifacts, and minerals early on and sold them at their shop, located near the site of today's Spa Resort Casino.

As the city attracted socialites, Hollywood royalty, and tycoons in the 1940s, Slim and Patricia created elegant desert gardens and became known for engineering naturalistic waterfalls and pools. They designed and installed landscapes for Frank Sinatra and set up the spare, meticulously "wild" desertscapes at Walt Disney's nearby Smoke Tree Ranch. Disney consulted them in the design of the western-themed Frontierland for the brand-new Disneyland.

The Moortens were also well traveled and packed up their only son Clark for trips down Baja California and into Mexico, collecting plants as far south as Guatemala. These adventures were extensive, and they became familiar not only with the plants but also with the indigenous people and local wildlife. Many rare plants in the Moorten Botanical Garden were collected on these trips.

The Moortens' Mediterranean-style home, "Cactus Castle," sits in the middle of the Botanical Garden, which the Moortens began building in 1938. The setting for many movie scenes and countless weddings and garden parties, the home is

'50s along with a finely edited group of sleek modern works. They also offer appraisals and repair.

Estate Jewelry Collection
73111 El Paseo Drive, Palm Desert
(760) 779-1856
The prices are low enough to keep the pieces moving, and you're likely to find outstanding values from Cartier, Bulgari, David Webb, Tiffany, Van Cleef & Arpels, and other famous designers.

Fort Knoxx Jewelers
156 North Palm Canyon Drive
(760) 325-0505
This is jewelry headquarters for the "fabulous fakes"—moissanite and cubic zirconia set in gold, silver, and vermeil and made to duplicate the real thing. Custom designs, wearable art, and interesting jeweled home accessories are also available.

Moorten Botanical Garden is a Palm Springs landmark, with thousands of varieties of cacti, succulents, and other desert plants. PHOTO BY TOM BREWSTER, COURTESY OF THE PALM SPRINGS DESERT RESORTS CONVENTION AND VISITORS AUTHORITY

a sprawling affair built for the weather, with concrete walls 2 feet thick to keep out the desert heat. For years, the Palm Springs Chamber of Commerce has held its last mixer of the season here, a much-anticipated event that marks the unofficial end of "season" and beginning of summer.

Patricia still lives in the Moorten home, and Clark is now the curator of this botanical wonderland. He is an authority in his own right and among the most knowledgeable experts on succulent plants in America. He tends the garden and propagates many of its plants for sale and is there to greet visitors almost every day. Clark also consults on desert landscaping for clients all over the world.

Frasca Jewelers
73560 El Paseo Drive, Palm Desert
(760) 568-5848
One of the valley's oldest jewelry sellers, Frasca has been on El Paseo Drive for almost 20 years. A full-service store offering high-end gold pieces and platinum, they also offer watch and jewelry repair, pearl restringing, and engraving.

Gail Jewelers
73525 El Paseo Drive, Palm Desert
(760) 776-7150
www.gailjewelers.com
Gail specializes in diamonds and platinum, with a sophisticated selection of designer goods, watches, and gifts. Repair, estate purchases, and appraisals are also available. One of the desert's most respected jewelers, Gail always stocks high-end plat-

inum and high-carat gold in classic as well as contemporary styles.

Hephaestus Jewelers
132 La Plaza
(760) 325-5395

Named for the Greek god of blacksmiths and jewelers, this shop focuses on designer jewelry and also does custom orders and designs. It has a good reputation for quality work and imaginative design using the client's own gems or supplying them from reputable sources.

Leeds & Son
73151 El Paseo Drive, Palm Desert
(760) 568-5266

A family-owned business that's been adorning desert residents since 1947, Leeds spotlights classic designs from such masters as Harry Winston. Custom work features fine diamonds and colored gems, and the timepieces include beauties from Rolex, Damiani, Patek Philippe, Panerai, and more.

Robann's Jewelers
At The River, Rancho Mirage
(760) 341-8142

Robann's is another longtime desert jeweler, family owned and operated for more than 30 years. They specialize in custom pieces and one-of-a-kind original items. They pride themselves on doing all the work on the premises. A certified gemologist appraiser is also on staff.

MEN'S AND WOMEN'S CLOTHING/SHOES/ ACCESSORIES

Belita
73425 El Paseo Drive, Palm Desert
(760) 674-4726

High-fashion clothing that starts at size 14W offers a wonderful option for the plus-size woman who's tired of wearing black and dumpy outfits. This is a fun place with a great selection.

Blonde
At The River, Rancho Mirage
(760) 836-3366

Blonde is the sister to Z Boutique in Palm Springs and offers a bit dressier selection of trendy, California-girl wear. Still, there are racks and racks of great T-shirts and gorgeous jeans. The presentation is a bit jumbled, but it's worth a little bit of extra time to hunt out that new outfit.

Cactus Flower Shoes/Hagar Shoes for Men
73640 El Paseo Drive, Palm Desert
(760) 346-6223

This shop has a good selection of dressy men's and women's shoes, with the emphasis on casual, resort styles. The women's side always has fun, embellished sandals, heels, and mules, as well as nifty belts, purses, and other accessories.

Compliments
74907 Highway 111, Indian Wells
(760) 836-1570

Stop in here for what may be the desert's best and most reasonably priced selection of "Palm Springs babe" jeweled and crystal-encrusted sandals, belts, T-shirts, handbags, jewelry, and resort clothes. You'll always find a good sales rack and a very pleasant staff.

Dot
73573 El Paseo Drive, Palm Desert
(760) 346-5825

Of all the clothing stores in the desert, Dot is the one most resembling a high-end, low-key shop in Los Angeles. It features a beautifully edited collection of men's and women's casual clothes in quality fabrics and subdued colors—rather unusual in Palm Springs. You'll find brands such as Isda, Puma, Three Dots, Big Star, Donald J. Pliner, Isabella Fiore, Magaschoni, and new stars in the design world. Very sophisticated.

Draper's & Damon's
73930 El Paseo Drive, Palm Desert
(760) 346-0559

42396 Bob Hope Drive, Rancho Mirage
(760) 568-1165
When it opened in Palm Springs in 1927, this was the desert's first department store, carrying a dizzying amount of both men's and women's clothes, from tuxedos to walking shorts and everything in between. Times haven't changed much— it's still stuffed full of clothing that's a bit on the fuddy-duddy side, and the service is still excellent.

Edith Morre Inc.
73670 El Paseo Drive, Palm Desert
(760) 346-0561
Often referred to as the "grande dame" of El Paseo Drive women's fashion stores, Edith Morre caters to a mature clientele that adores her tasteful suits, elegant loungewear, and classic jewelry and accessories. The end-of-season sales here are legendary, as the shop closes up for the summer and opens in the fall with all new merchandise.

4 Seasons Swimwear
73400 El Paseo Drive, #4, Palm Desert
(760) 340-2490

The Lodge at Rancho Mirage
64900 Frank Sinatra Drive, Rancho Mirage
(760) 770-6864
This shop specializes in lots of different swimsuits for lots of different ages and body types, from long torsos to those who need a different size for tops and bottoms. Sizes run from 4 to 46, and there are mastectomy suits and designer bikinis, as well as cover-ups, sandals, and accessories.

Joy! A Maternity Boutique
73170 El Paseo Drive, Palm Desert
(760) 773-5450
This shop is new to the desert, a sign that the crowd is growing a bit younger and more family oriented. You'll find well-made

Didn't bring your swimsuit? Brought your old faded one because it's winter and the stores back home are only showing sweaters and coats? You can find a great selection of swimwear, shorts, and warm-weather clothes year-round in the major department stores and most of the trendy boutiques.

casual fashions, lingerie, and sleepwear, as well as good-looking diaper bags, gifts, and baby footwear.

La Mariposa
155 South Palm Canyon Drive
(760) 322-9654
Next door to its sister shop, Mosaic, this colorful place is the spot to go when you need a breezy Mexican cotton skirt and a sexy little top for dinner by the pool. It's full of the kind of bright, free-flowing, casual dresses, skirts, and tops that make vacation really feel different from the norm. Hats, jewelry, wraps, and sandals are part of the mix.

MacMillan's Resort Wear
899 North Palm Canyon Drive
(760) 323-2979
This shop specializes in colorful, cotton and rayon resort clothing for women— bright sundresses, skirts, tops, and shorts by Jams, Reyn Spooner, and Tommy Bahama. If you want the hot "island" style at good prices, this is the spot.

Nomads of the Desert
73191 El Paseo Drive, Palm Desert
(760) 341-8922
Nomads specializes in gorgeous fabrics and embellishments, cut in free-flowing, kind-to-all-figures styles. The handpainted silks, floaty rayons, and cushy velvets come in rich colors and are often heavily embellished. It's a fabulous spot to find ornate, almost-tribal jewelry as well as art-oriented gift items.

Rangoni of Florence Shoes
73151 El Paseo Drive, Palm Desert
(760) 346-6646
Women's high-end brands include Rangoni Firenze, Amalfi, Cole Haan, Donald J. Pliner, Anne Klein, and more, with a specialty in narrow sizes. Men' footwear includes Rangoni, Morescho, and Cole Haan.

Richard Barry Shoes
73750 El Paseo Drive, Palm Desert
(760) 346-2316
Stop here when you're tired of the classics and want a colorful lizard stiletto or a bejeweled little mule in a dozen different colors. There's an excellent selection of unusual women's styles, along with handbags and accessories.

Robert's Fine Shoes
73725 El Paseo Drive, Palm Desert
(760) 340-2929
Offerings here are at the upper end of quality and price. Men's shoes include styles by Bruno Magli, Lorenzo Banfi, and Cole Haan. For women, there's a wide array of shoes, handbags, and accessories from Salvatore Ferragamo, Bruno Magli, Stuart Weitzman, Cole Haan, Icon, and Judith Leiber.

St. John Boutique
73061 El Paseo Drive, Palm Desert
(760) 568-5900
This is a St. John "flagship" store, meaning that the selection is more complete than just about anywhere else in the country. You will find some St. John items in Saks Fifth Avenue down the street, and a nice grouping of off-season pieces at the outlet store in the Desert Hills Premium Outlets, but this is the place for the real deal. Shoes, jewelry, sportswear, evening wear, suits, perfume—it's all here.

Sam Bork Shoes
120 North Palm Canyon Drive
(760) 325-5042
A Palm Springs institution for decades, this shoe emporium offers an unusual selection of both men's and women's shoes. On the men's side, there's a sober group of conservative work and dress shoes, while the women's section is a colorful hodgepodge of color, glitter, and fun.

Sarit
73130 El Paseo Drive, Palm Desert
(760) 341-0664
Every garment here falls into the category of "wearable art," with some more suited for hanging on a wall than draping a female form, but beautiful nonetheless. There are more than 50 international artists represented, as well as contemporary European designers such as Zanella, Dismero Casuals, and Annikki Karvinen.

Subtle Tones
73575 El Paseo Drive, Palm Desert
(760) 346-9651
Everything in the shop is in a muted, pastel shade—whites, blues, soft greens, pinks, and lavenders—with a shot of black thrown in for good measure. Women's casual dresses, tops, pants, shorts, lingerie, and sleepwear are primarily in cotton, linen, washed rayon, and other "pure" fabrics. The high-quality merchandise also includes bedding, bath and beauty products, children's clothing, and furniture.

Trina Turk Boutique
891 North Palm Canyon Drive
(760) 416-2856
Trina Turk is a well-known sportswear designer whose retro-chic designs turn up in Saks Fifth Avenue and other high-end national stores. Trina's second home is in Palm Springs, and she's opened this cool little shop to keep herself entertained while she's in town. Pieces here represent the complete line and are strong on women's outfits that would be perfect by the pool or out for cocktails on a warm spring evening. A bonus—you'll find a few choice vintage pieces and a selection of menswear designed exclusively for the Palm Springs shop.

Troy
73255 El Paseo Drive, Palm Desert
(760) 776-1101
Troy is one of the El Paseo Drive merchants that helped cement the street's reputation as a high-end fashion destination. This lovely shop highlights women's clothing by Oscar de la Renta, Bill Blass, Basier, David Josef, Bob Mackie, and other designers known to offer ornamentation and feminine fit. Troy also has its own private label, a favorite with local ladies who lunch.

The Wardrobe
108 South Indian Canyon Drive
(760) 325-4330
A desert institution, this is a favorite stop for women who want a glamorous black tie look without the El Paseo prices. There's also a good selection of jewelry, lingerie and fun handbags and excellent end-of-season sales.

Z Boutique
155 North Palm Canyon Drive
(760) 325-3050
This tiny space is absolutely stuffed with the trendiest Southern California women's clothes. They were the first to stock Juicy Couture and are always the first in line to show the newest designers in casual, unique, fun clothing. Their second store, Blonde, in The River, is equally full of great finds but somehow doesn't have the folksy, warm vibe that the original does.

GIFT SHOPS IN ATTRACTIONS

These all offer items specific to their nature—often things that can be found nowhere else in the desert. Be sure to check the shops out when you visit.

Children's Discovery Museum
71-701 Gerald Ford Drive, Rancho Mirage
(760) 321-0602
www.cdmod.org
Educational toys and games, museum logo merchandise, and a lot of very fun, very unusual featured items—such as chicken socks, stunt magnets, goofy puzzles and motorized bubble lights—are available here.

Living Desert Zoo and Gardens
47-900 Portola Avenue, Palm Desert
(760) 346-5694
www.livingdesert.org
The shops here offer goods from Africa, including pots, baskets, jewelry and gift items; books, cards, and trinkets with animal and plant themes; and native desert plants, as well as pots, bird feeders, and wind chimes.

Palm Canyon Trading Post
The Indian Canyons
(No street address)
(760) 416-7044
This little shop specializes in Native American crafts and arts from tribes across the country. Merchandise includes paintings, pots, jewelry, leather, sculpture, a variety of crafts, and a good selection of books and cards. To get to this store, follow South Palm Canyon Drive in Palm Springs until it dead-ends, just a few minutes from downtown.

Palm Desert Visitor Center
72990 Highway 111, Palm Desert
(760) 568-1441, (800) 873-2428
vcenter@ci.palm-desert.ca.us
The selection of Palm Desert logo apparel for adults and kids is good quality—comparable to the clothing you'll find in local golf shops—and the prices are much lower.

Palm Springs Aerial Tramway
One Tramway Road
(760) 325-1391, (888) 515-8726
www.pstramway.com
This is the only place to find a replica of the Tram, Tram logo gifts, and maps and posters of the mountain areas around the Tram itself.

Palm Springs Air Museum
745 North Gene Autry Trail
(760) 778-6262
www.palmspringsairmuseum.org
Everything to do with World War II airplanes and pilots is the specialty, with models, maps, books, stickers, posters, and more. There are also some pieces that relate to air warfare since World War II.

Palm Springs Art Museum
One Museum Way
(760) 325-7186
www.psmuseum.org
The small gift shop here offers art jewelry as well as gifts, books, and posters that focus on the latest exhibits, a good children's section, stationery, and some very high-end original pieces such as Dale Chihuly glass.

Palm Springs Official Visitors Center
2901 North Palm Canyon Drive
(760) 778-8418, (800) 347-7746

Palm Springs Uptown Visitors Center
777 North Palm Canyon Drive, Suite 101
(760) 327-2828
www.palm-springs.org
These visitor centers have a wide selection of books on architecture and the city's history, plus good-quality logo merchandise and souvenir items. If you're trying to find an out-of-print or rare book on the city's past, this might be the place to shop.

SPECIALTY FOOD STORES

Bouchee Fine Foods
42410 Bob Hope Drive, Rancho Mirage
(760) 340-5311
This is perhaps the very best little take-out place in the desert—if you long for fresh, gourmet dinners that you can just pop in the oven or microwave. Pick up an entree and several side dishes and totally impress your dinner guests.

Chocolateria/Candy Bouquets
390 North Palm Canyon Drive
(760) 318-1565
A wonderful source for gifts to give while you're in town or to send to friends back home. The selection is mouth-watering, with lots of domestic and international chocolate and candy makers represented. Giftware, ceramics, and the famous "candy bouquets" make this a favorite place to get impressive last-minute presents.

Jensen's Finest Foods
73601 Highway 111, Palm Desert
(760) 346-9393

102 South Sunrise Way
(760) 325-8282

78525 Highway 111, La Quinta
(760) 777-8181
Like many other popular stores in the desert, Jensen's got its start in Palm Springs and expanded to the rest of the area, even adding a store in the mountain community of Idyllwild. This is a combination of supermarket, butcher shop, bakery, wine store, and gourmet foods emporium. You probably want to buy your laundry soap and dog food elsewhere just to save some money, but the food here is absolutely the best, freshest, and tastiest.

Pastry Swan Bakery
68444 Perez Road, Cathedral City
(760) 340-3040
This bakery offers exquisite cakes and cookies, pies, and angelic-looking pastries, plus fresh breads, rolls, and all things yeasty and sugary—the desert's favorite for birthdays, brunches, and special treats. The specialty cakes are elegant and glamorous and can be made up with very little notice for special occasions. Stop by early in the morning for the hot, crusty French bread or a croissant and steaming coffee.

Tulip Hill Winery
At The River, Rancho Mirage
(760) 568-2322
This lovely little shop features a tasting

bar for Tulip Hill wines, a small boutique winery in Northern California. The limited-release wines have won numerous awards and are highly regarded in culinary circles. There's also an olive oil–tasting bar, specialty gourmet foods, chocolates, gifts, wine glasses and accessories, and all kinds of gift items for entertaining.

Van Valkenburg Haus of Chocolates
73655 El Paseo Drive, Palm Desert
(760) 341-8558
The chocolates here are made in the best European tradition—using the finest chocolate, hand-dipped and finished with distinctive shapes and flavors. A gift box of these chocolates will surely earn you major points, no matter who receives it.

SPORTING GOODS

Golf Alley
74040 El Paseo Drive, Palm Desert
(760) 776-4646
In a valley where there are more than 100 golf courses, you can bet that there's a lot of golfers looking for the newest and latest in clubs and gear. When they buy the new, they go to Golf Alley to consign the old. You'll find very good deals on top-brand clubs, as well as a full-service repair shop, custom club fitting, and classic collectors' clubs.

Lady Golf
42412 Bob Hope Drive, Rancho Mirage
(760) 773-4949
Lady Golf has a good selection of pretty shirts, shorts, hats, gloves, and shoes from well-known designers such as Escada and Lauren. The prices are often discounted at the end of the season, which is the best time to shop for all types of golf wear and equipment. Golf shoes and girly golf bags are big here as well. One big feature is the wide selection of sizes, from 2 all the way through 3X.

For the very best deals on golf clothes and accessories, find a friend who belongs to the Vintage Club, Indian Ridge, or another upscale golf/country club. Most of the pro shops in these places offer steeply discounted prices to their members, and the merchandise is top of the line. End-of-season sales slash another 50 percent off.

Lumpy's Discount Golf
67625 East Palm Canyon Drive
Cathedral City
(760) 321-2437

78267 Highway 111, La Quinta
(760) 346-8768
Lumpy's is perhaps the most reliable of the golf superstores in terms of discount prices, with lots of high-tech gear and apparel. They also offer repair service, professional club fitting, and trade-ins.

Pete Carlson's Golf & Tennis
73714 Highway 111, Palm Desert
(760) 568-3263
With 25 years in the desert, Pete Carlson's is the oldest of the big three golf stores and adds tennis apparel and equipment to its extensive selection of pro-line, name-brand goods. The store is huge, and the service is above average.

Roger Dunn Discount Golf
Highway 111 at Date Palm Drive
Cathedral City
(760) 324-1160, (888) 289-9799
Lumpy's, Pete Carlson's, and Roger Dunn are always in hot competition for the title of "largest, best, most" in terms of golf equipment, clothing, and assorted merchandise. Like the others, Dunn offers a very good selection of name brands, often at discount prices.

THRIFT SHOPS AND RESALE CLOTHING

American Cancer Society Discovery Shop
42446 Bob Hope Drive, Rancho Mirage
(760) 568-5967

Run by volunteers from the American Cancer Society, this is a pretty ordinary secondhand shop, though you might get lucky and find a nice piece of jewelry, designer clothing, or items from an estate.

Angel View Prestige Boutiques
886 North Palm Canyon Drive
(760) 327-0644

Angel View Thrift Mart
454 North Indian Canyon Drive
(760) 322-2440

These two shops benefit the Angel View Crippled Children's Foundation, a charitable organization that has been around the valley for many years. The Thrift Mart is insanely cluttered and busy, with people dropping off garage sale rejects at all hours. It takes a lot of stamina to go through this place. The Prestige Boutique, however, is the showcase for the best-quality goods that have been donated—men's and women's clothing and accessories in good condition.

Celebrity Seconds
333 North Palm Canyon Drive
(760) 416-2072

This is a tiny place crammed full of outrageously over-the-top women's clothing and accessories, along with a few choice pieces from the estate of Ginger Rogers. This shop has been featured several times on national television, and it's certainly

worth a look. The Ginger Rogers items move very slowly, probably because of their elevated price tags.

City of Hope
35688 Cathedral Canyon Drive
Cathedral City
(760) 321-2266

The City of Hope is a national cancer research institute in Southern California, and this shop is one of many that sell items to benefit the organization. There's always something here—antiques, books, jewelry, household items, and clothing. The atmosphere says "thrift store," so you'll have to hunt a bit, and the selection varies from day to day.

Eisenhower Medical Center Auxiliary Collectors Corner
71280 Highway 111, Rancho Mirage
(760) 346-1012

This well-run shop often gets high-end items of furniture and accessories. They also have a small selection of men's and women's clothing, housewares, and odds and ends. Overall, the presentation and quality are good, though the prices are a bit steep for used merchandise. Be sure to call ahead, as their hours are somewhat erratic and they do close for a period in the summer.

Jade
787 North Palm Canyon Drive
(760) 324-8825

This shop offers women's clothing on consignment and specializes in what they call the "Hollywood" side of fashion—splashy, sparkly, and not for the timid. The clothes are great for a costume party or a fun night out clubbing, and the prices are so low that you can wear a piece once and then donate it to one of the desert's charity thrift shops without a bit of guilt.

Patsy's Clothes Closet
4109 East Palm Canyon Drive
(760) 324-8825

Next door to the Estate Sale Company, Patsy's is a good place to find the

The Desert Hills Premium Outlets have many stores that offer 10 percent off for shoppers 50 years and older who make their purchases on a Tuesday. You can also download coupons at their Web site, www.premiumoutlets.com.

sequined dress from the '80s, furs with Beverly Hills origins, and the odd designer outfit, plus a lot of more-ordinary women's clothing, shoes, and accessories. Prices are fair, and the owners are a hoot—they'll dress you up in a feather boa and have you batting your eyes in a nanosecond.

Revivals
611 South Palm Canyon Drive
(760) 318-6430

68929 Perez Road, Unit K
Cathedral City
(760) 328-1330
All of the proceeds from the two Revivals stores go to the Desert AIDS Project, one of Southern California's most progressive and active organizations helping individuals living with HIV/AIDS. Donations come from all over, and you can find just about anything here—cowboy boots, dinner glasses, furniture, art, you name it. The prices are very good. The volunteers also accept and handle donations earmarked for the benefit of the local Shelter from the Storm, a shelter for abused women and their children.

OUTLET SHOPPING

Desert Hills Premium Outlets
West of Palm Springs on I-10, Fields Road exit
(909) 849-6641
On I-10 to the west of Palm Springs, the Desert Hills Premium Outlets are an attraction unto themselves, and if you're planning a trip, better make it early on a weekday before the busloads of tourists and day-trippers start swarming. There are more than 200 shops here, running the gamut from home furnishings to electronics, jewelry, clothing, china, silver, luggage, lingerie, and diamonds. The quality of the stores is high, with international names such as Gucci, Furla, Hugo Boss, St. John, Bose, Calvin Klein, and more. If you've shopped outlets before, you should know to ask the sales staff a few pointed questions about the merchandise. You will

Want the best deals at factory outlets? Shop late in the day before a major holiday such as Thanksgiving. Merchandise will already be marked down in anticipation of the sale after the holiday, and you'll be able to beat the hordes.

want to find out if the items in the store are from stock that would sell in a full-price store, or if they have been manufactured specifically for the outlets. Many companies will make "down-market" versions of their goods for the outlets, skimping a little here and changing a little there. There's nothing wrong with that, but you should be aware of what you are buying and how good a deal it really is.

OUTDOOR MARKETS

College of the Desert Street Fair
43500 Monterey Avenue
College of the Desert Campus,
Palm Desert
(760) 773-2567
www.codstreetfair.com
This event is run by the College of the Desert Alumni Association to benefit the community college, and it's been a profitable venture since its beginning. Hundreds of vendors set up for this weekly event on the COD campus just north of Highway 111 in central Palm Desert. The parking lots are clogged with shoppers by 8:00 A.M., so it's a good idea to get there early. The competition for vendor space is fierce, and the rules are strict. It's a very well-run event. Wear your walking shoes and bring cash for small purchases such as produce and food. Most vendors accept credit cards, but do you really want to use your Visa for that tie-dye souvenir T-shirt? The street fair runs both Saturday and Sunday year-round, starting at 7:00 A.M. both days. It closes at noon from June through September and at 2:00 P.M. October through May.

The height of the date harvest is in February, and this is the optimum time to get fresh-from-the-palm dates. Check out vendors at the Thursday-night VillageFest in Palm Springs and the Saturday-morning College of the Desert Street Fair in Palm Desert.

Palm Springs VillageFest
North Palm Canyon Drive between
Amado and Baristo Roads
(760) 320-3781
www.palm-springs.org

Up through the 1980s, Palm Springs was a place that rolled up the streets after 6:00 P.M. Stores closed, restaurants opened late only on the weekends, and there wasn't a darn thing to do at night. That left both visitors and locals feeling like farmers or kids with a curfew—early to bed and early to rise.

That changed when the city started VillageFest in 1991 as an attempt to bring life to the streets and encourage weekenders to come on Thursday rather than Friday. Today this weekly street fair attracts from 4,000 to 5,000 people on the quietest, hottest summer night. During high season, attendance is often as high as 12,000. It took several years for local merchants to get on board, but now virtually all the shops on the central part of Palm Canyon Drive stay open past 6:00 P.M., new restaurants have bloomed with outdoor seating, and the event has become an integral part of the city's personality. In 2005 VillageFest received a series of upgrades, including a certified organic farmers' market, elimination of the kiddie rides, better live entertainment, and strategies to make it more accessible for wheelchairs. Organizers have also decided to strictly enforce rules that all crafts must be handmade and that the artists themselves must work the booths. This is one event that's a must, with music spilling from the nightclubs, shoppers walking their dogs and picking up art, street entertainers, an extensive farmers' market, and the added bonus of being able to wander in and out of all the shops on the street.

ATTRACTIONS

Like any other resort destination, the Palm Springs area has its fair share of attractions and diversions for visitors looking for a change from the endless round of sun and play. But don't expect a string of amusement parks or cookie-cutter playgrounds. With one or two exceptions, the attractions here are truly representative of the forces that have defined the desert and shaped its character: its Native American and western heritage, its natural resources, its weather, and its highly individual pioneers.

If you're on a limited schedule or visiting for the first time, there are three "must-see" attractions that are suitable for all ages and will give you a deep appreciation of this area's personality.

If you've ever thought to yourself, "Oh, Palm Springs is just swimming pools and golf courses," you'll think very differently after a visit to the Indian Canyons, the Palm Springs Aerial Tramway, or the Living Desert. Each of these spots offers a highly individual look at the interaction between man and nature. Each place is absolutely unique to the desert, and, above all, each one is great fun. You can use your visit as an opportunity for education and wonder or just have a good time petting Nubian goats, hiking to waterfalls, and enjoying a view that stretches all the way to Mexico. Put these three on the top of your list and make room for a few more each time you visit.

Opening and closing hours can vary, so be sure to call ahead or check the Web sites for last-minute information.

Although most of these attractions can be seen and visited perfectly well on your own, several tour companies provide guides and programs that are outstanding. Taking at least one trip with one of these outfits is worth the price many times over in the knowledge and appreciation of the desert that you'll gain. Because the prices and hours of the tours can change dramatically depending on the operator and time of year, we suggest you always call ahead to make sure you won't be disappointed.

Unless otherwise noted, all establishments accept major credit cards. All the attractions listed are in Palm Springs, unless otherwise noted.

PRICE CODE

Prices are given only as a range and are per person, using the following code. If there is no price code next to an attraction's listing, that attraction is free.

$	$2 to $10
$$	$11 to $20
$$$	$21 to $50
$$$$	more than $50

ATTRACTIONS

Agua Caliente Cultural Museum
Village Green Heritage Center
219 South Palm Canyon Drive
(760) 323-0151
www.accmuseum.org
This small and beautifully arranged space is the center of the tribe's growing efforts to preserve the Cahuilla history and culture. Permanent and changing exhibits display just some of the museum's Southern California basketry collection of more than 400 pieces, as well as contemporary arts and artifacts from the Tahquitz Canyon Archaeological Collection, one of the most extensive excavation projects in California.

The Palm Springs Aerial Tramway offers a summer pass, good for unlimited rides May through August. If you're planning to ride up more than three times over a summer stay, this is the best value.

With some of the world's best examples of the work of Cahuilla basket weavers and their neighboring tribes, the full collections are available to researchers and students on request. More baskets, artifacts, and archival photographs are displayed in the lobby of the tribe's Spa Resort Casino at 100 North Indian Canyon Drive in Palm Springs. The museum is open Wednesday through Saturday from 10:00 A.M. to 5:00 P.M. and Sunday from noon to 4:00 P.M.

Cabazon Cultural Museum   Free
(No street address)
(760) 827-2946
www.cabazonindians-nsn.gov
Currently not much more than a few dozen artifacts housed in the tribal offices adjacent to the Cabazon's Fantasy Springs Resort Casino, the Cabazon Cultural Museum has long-standing plans for a new building, but no firm dates for construction have been set. It's worth a look if you're going to the casino to gamble or attend a concert, but right now it doesn't merit a separate trip.

The Cabazon Cultural Museum is located near Indio, 22 miles east of Palm Springs. Take I-10 and exit at Golf Center Parkway. Go north to Indio Springs Parkway, turn east, and follow the signs. The hours of operation vary, so it's best to call for details.

Cabot's Old Indian   Free
Pueblo Museum $$ (guided tours)
67616 East Desert View Avenue
Desert Hot Springs
(760) 329-7610
www.cabotsmuseum.org
A California state historic site, this is one of the oddest attractions in the area, verging on the creepy. Built in the style of a Hopi pueblo, the building is the work of Cabot Yerxa, the man who "discovered" hot mineral water in Desert Hot Springs.

A wanderer and explorer who grew up in a family of Indian traders, Yerxa headed for the Klondike in 1899 when he was just 16, following other prospectors searching

for gold. He became fascinated with the Inuit culture, collecting curios and artifacts and learning the language. When his father bought land in Cuba, he joined him and later set up a cigar factory in Key West. The family moved on to Riverside and invested in orange groves, and Cabot established a homestead on 160 acres on the present site of Desert Hot Springs. His search for reliable water led to his discovery of the first hot mineral springs in the area.

He later enlisted in the army and finally returned to the desert in 1937. Two years later he started building his life's work, a reflection of his personal interpretation of Indian belief.

Cabot believed that symmetry retains evil spirits, so the doorways and floors slant, the walls are uneven, and the windows form puzzles of multishaped glass. He learned how to make adobe bricks and scavenged most of the building materials from abandoned homesteads. The result is a four-story, 35-room maze with 150 windows, 5,000 square feet, and innumerable narrow staircases and winding halls.

Touring Cabot's Old Indian Pueblo is not for those who are claustrophobic, but it's a fascinating look at one man's obsession. It's open Friday and Saturday from 10:00 A.M. to 3:00 P.M. and is closed July through September.

Children's Discovery Museum
of the Desert $
71-701 Gerald Ford Drive, Rancho Mirage
(760) 321-0602
www.cdmod.org
Kids will be in their glory at this hands-on heaven. Trunks full of vintage clothes and costume props encourage the imagination, a scaled-down grocery store lets little ones play more make-believe, and there's always some wonderfully untamed activity, such as sloshing paint on an old VW, that makes this a brilliant place for small children and their parents.

Parents must always stay with their children and are encouraged to join in the activities. Check the Web site for such events as free family fun nights, toddler parties, and holiday activities. Classes and special programs for ages one through four are planned throughout the week.

If you're looking for a safe, relatively inexpensive place to spend some quality time with the family, this is one of the desert's gems. The museum is open Monday through Saturday from 10:00 A.M. to 5:00 P.M. and on Sunday from noon to 5:00 P.M. It is closed on Monday from May through December. For more information, check the listing in the Kidstuff chapter.

General George S. Patton Memorial Museum   Free
(No street address)
(760) 227-3483

In early 1942 Major General George S. Patton Jr. was tapped to set up the Desert Training Center and start an emergency mission to train men and machines to stop Germany's advance into North Africa. He selected a site of almost 18,000 square miles, making it the largest military installation and maneuver area in the world. Joseph Chiriaco, one of the first area residents Patton met when he came to the desert, donated the site where the museum now stands.

The Desert Training Center became operational in early April 1942. Four days later, General Patton and the troops took their first desert march. Within 15 days, all units at the center had been on a desert march. Within 23 days, he had conducted 13 tactical exercises, including some with two nights in the desert. As Patton explained to his men, "If you can work successfully here, in this country, it will be no difficulty at all to kill the assorted sons of bitches you meet in any other country."

Patton was at the Desert Training Center for less than four months before he was sent overseas to start planning the North African campaign. More than a million troops eventually trained for desert warfare here. Along with a facility housing an eclectic assortment of memorabilia, the museum has some of the original tanks used in training operations. If you look closely, you can still see some of the tracks

these relentless machines made in the desert sand more than 60 years ago.

The museum is open daily from 9:30 A.M. to 4:30 P.M. It's located on Chiriaco Summit, 30 miles east of Indio. Take I-10 and take the Chiriaco Summit exit.

Most nature tours include stops to do a little bit of exploring and walking, so wear closed-toe shoes and comfortable clothes. The same guideline applies if you're visiting the Indian Canyons or Living Desert on your own. Leave the flip-flops back at the pool.

The Indian Canyons $
38-500 South Palm Canyon Drive
(760) 325-3400, (800) 790-3398
www.indian-canyons.com

Tahquitz Canyon $$
500 West Mesquite Avenue
(760) 416-7044

Located on Agua Caliente tribal land, just a few minutes' drive from downtown, Andreas, Murray, and Palm Canyons are true, natural palm oases, with waterfalls, streams, and cool canopies of towering palm trees. To reach the canyons, follow South Palm Canyon Drive in Palm Springs until it dead-ends, just a few minutes from downtown. Palm Canyon and Andreas Canyon also have the world's largest stand of naturally occurring palm trees. This is one of the desert's three "must-see" attractions, along with the Living Desert and the Palm Springs Aerial Tramway.

Listed on the National Register of Historic Places, the canyons are the ancestral home of the Agua Caliente Band of Cahuilla Indians and are owned and operated by the tribe. Andreas Canyon was the largest gathering place, the center of social life during the hot summer months. Here you can spot faint petroglyphs and an impressive stone outcropping where the women of the tribe used to grind grain. Picnic tables and a parking lot are as far as most visitors go, but make the effort and take a short hike to nearby Murray Canyon. This small palm oasis is the access point to the area's famous "Seven Sisters" hiking spot, where waterfalls tumble down from the mountains, going through seven immense natural stone bowls before settling into a peaceful stream.

Palm Canyon is the largest of the three canyon-oasis areas. It stretches through palm-lined canyons and streams for 15 miles, and at the top it intersects Highway 74 on its way to Idyllwild. You can drive right up to the trading post and take a stroll to a lovely waterfall, or you can put on your hiking boots and venture out for a full day of wandering and dreaming. This truly is one of the most beautiful spots in the entire desert and an absolute must for those who want to get close to the true heart of Palm Springs. Be warned, though: It's easy to lose your bearings, and the rocks can be slippery and treacherous. Always let people know where you're going, take a map and cell phone, and wear the right shoes and clothes.

If you're staying around the trading post, be sure to check out the maps, books, and fine-quality Native American arts and crafts from tribes around the country. Have a cold drink and strike up a conversation with the people behind the counter—they're a wonderful resource for tales and inside information about the canyons.

Tahquitz Canyon, just a few blocks from downtown Palm Springs, is also on the National Register of Historic Places. For years the area was scarred by graffiti and littered with trash. Then, with income provided from the Indian Canyons and the new Spa Resort Casino, the tribe fenced the canyon land, cleaned it up, and built the Tahquitz Interpretive Center, where visitors can learn about the area's history. This is the place to sign up for a guided hike that leads directly to Tahquitz Falls, a breathtaking spot with a huge waterfall that runs year-round.

The Indian Canyons and Tahquitz Canyon are open daily from 8:00 A.M. to 5:00 P.M. August through June; in July they're open from 8:00 A.M. to 5:00 P.M. Friday through Sunday. Tahquitz Canyon may close in the summer; beginning in June, be sure to phone to get up-to-date information. A two-hour, moderate-to-difficult hike is the only way visitors can view Tahquitz Canyon, and reservations are required.

Joshua Tree National Park $-$$
Joshua Tree National Park Visitors Center
74485 National Park Drive
Twentynine Palms
(760) 367-5522
www.joshua.tree.national-park.com
Joshua Tree National Park is a beautiful desert wilderness area covering 794,000 square miles just south of the town of Twentynine Palms. Rock climbers are drawn to the park's enormous boulder formations. Photographers and visitors come from all over the world to enjoy the beauty of the "high desert." In the spring the park can be carpeted overnight with dozens of species of wildflowers. There are also numerous examples of cacti and Joshua trees. There are 35 miles of trails for hikers and nine primitive campsites with fire grates and picnic tables for campers. Permits are required for backcountry camping. Pets must be on a leash and attended at all times. They are not allowed on nature trails.

The park is open year-round. A seven-day pass costs $10 per vehicle. A $125 individual annual pass is available if you are planning on multiple visits. The visitor centers are open daily from 8:00 A.M. to 5:00 P.M. The Oasis Visitor Center is located at the Twentynine Palms entrance. The Cottonwood Visitor Center is at the south entrance. The Black Rock Canyon Visitor Center is at the campground southeast of Yucca Valley. For more information, check the listing in the Kidstuff chapter.

Knott's Soak City U.S.A. & Rocky Point $$$
1500 Gene Autry Trail
(760) 327-0499
www.soakcityusa.com

A full-fledged water park with 18 slides and rides, Knott's is an exceptionally clean, well-run facility that caters to all ages. The 800,000-gallon wave pool is as close to the beach as you can get in Palm Springs, and the waves are actually big enough to get in a little boogie board action.

Toddlers are well served here as well, with the gentle Gremmie Lagoon and Kahuna's Beach House, a family water playhouse. Tubes and life vests are provided at no charge. There are extra fees for locker rentals and parking. Leave your chairs, barbecues, food, and drink behind, because they aren't allowed inside. Likewise, come in appropriate swimwear—long pants and denim aren't allowed in the pool or activity areas.

This is a fine place to spend an afternoon, particularly if the kids are chafing under orders to keep the noise down at the hotel pool. Knott's is open March through September. For more information, check the listing in the Kidstuff chapter.

Living Desert Zoo and Gardens $ (summer)–$$
47-900 Portola Avenue, Palm Desert
(760) 346-5694
www.livingdesert.org

One of the three "must-see" attractions (along with the Indian Canyons and Palm Springs Aerial Tramway), the Living Desert is a unique combination of zoo, botanical garden, and wildlife education/breeding center. There are so many different activities and events going on that it's a good idea to call before you visit or check the daily schedule on the excellent Web site for updated events, programs, special tours, demonstrations, or lectures.

The Living Desert is dedicated to showcasing the animals and plants of the world's different deserts. Many of the animals here are critically endangered, largely because modern hunting equipment—

Despite its harsh appearance, the desert is an extremely fragile environment. Taking just "a few" souvenirs such as rocks or flowers can cause damage that takes years to repair. Stay on marked trails, enjoy the beauty, and take lots of photos to remember your visit.

jeeps, helicopters, telescopic sights, and automatic weapons—has given man an immense advantage over animals in the desert. The Living Desert has been successful in increasing the world's population of slender-horned gazelles, sand cats, addax, and Arabian oryx, and this is one of the few places in the world where these beautiful creatures can be seen up close.

The animals live in exacting re-creations of their natural habitat, with room to roam. Along with the African wildlife, the park showcases North American animals and birds of prey. The After Sundown exhibit features locals such as bats, scorpions, owls, mice, and snakes that are active only after dark. Coyotes, wolves, mountain lions, badgers, and bobcats are all part of the crowd, as they live wild in the mountains surrounding Palm Springs.

Village WaTuTu is an authentic replica of a North African village, with grass-thatched huts around the Elder's Grove, where storytellers weave tales from African and Native American folklore. There are a Petting Kraal, African domestic livestock, and leopards, hyenas, camels, birds, and plants from the region.

Featured in *Sunset Magazine,* the Wortz Demonstration Garden gives homeowners and landscape architects ideas for using drought-resistant plants in their own homes or projects. The Palo Verde Garden Center offers a variety of cacti, succulents, flowering ornamentals, wildlife food, desert plants, and arrangements, as well as landscaping and horticultural books, videos, and garden ornaments.

You should plan on at least three to four hours to see everything. This place has thought of everything to make a visit pleasant, including lots of shade trees and misted rest spots, two excellent gift shops, restaurants, first aid stations, baby-changing stations, and ATMs.

One of the "star" attractions at the Living Desert is the periodic Starry Safari Overnight Adventure. This features a wildlife presentation, nighttime walk around the park, dinner, and tales around the campfire. Participants bring their own sleeping bags and tuck into the park's four-person tents for the night. The program is tailored to adults and children older than eight. Singles and couples without children are welcome. Reservations are required.

The Living Desert is open daily from 9:00 A.M. to 5:00 P.M. September 1 through June 15, with the last admission at 4:00 P.M.; it is closed on December 25. It's open daily from 8:00 A.M. to 1:30 P.M. June 16 through August 31, with the last admission at 1:00 P.M. Regular, non-narrated shuttle service is available throughout the park for an extra charge. Parking is free.

Moorten Botanical Garden $
1701 South Palm Canyon Drive
(760) 327-6555

A living museum with nature trails that weave around 3,000 varieties of giant cacti, trees, succulents, flowers, birds, and turtles, Moorten Botanical Garden has been a Palm Springs landmark since 1938. The one-acre site is packed with rare and exotic plants, grouped according to the desert region where they naturally grow, including Arizona, California, Texas, Colorado, Mexico, South America, and Africa.

Perhaps the most striking feature of this quirky, slightly Wild West site is the age of its plants and their density on this relatively small site. Specimens here reach monumental proportions and bloom in abundance just as they do in the wild. Monstrous agaves, crested *Cereus*, towering cardon and exotic boojum trees, a two-story *Pachypodium*, and more than a dozen different aloes from southern Africa and Madagascar are a few of the standouts. Turtledoves, hummingbirds, lizards, and other small wild creatures are at home

in the gardens and add to the feeling of being enclosed in a magical dreamscape.

The Cactarium, a greenhouse that protects some of the most rare and unusual species from the brutal summer sun and cold nights, is a treasure house of world-class specimens found virtually nowhere else outside of private collections or their native habitat.

Many unusual botanical specimens are for sale, along with other souvenirs. No matter the day, one member of the Moorten family is always on hand to talk about the plants, the garden, and old Palm Springs. This is the most authentic, down-to-earth of all the man-made attractions in the desert. In fact, as Clark Moorten will tell you, it's not really man-made, just "man-maintained."

The botanical garden is open from 9:00 A.M. to 4:30 P.M. Monday through Saturday and from 10:00 A.M. to 4:00 P.M. on Sunday; it is closed on Wednesday.

The Mysterious Integratron $
2477 Belfield Boulevard, Landers
(760) 364-3126
www.integratron.com

A sun-bleached dome about 20 miles from Joshua Tree National Park, the Mysterious Integratron is a legendary site in UFO circles. It's just down the road from Giant Rock, a freestanding boulder that's seven stories high, covers 5,800 square feet, and has a place in Native American lore as a site where elders received teachings from spirits.

The Integratron began to take shape in 1947 when George Van Tassel, a Lockheed engineer and former test pilot for Howard Hughes, left his job, leased four square miles around Giant Rock, and moved his family to a campsite by the boulder. He claimed that his weekly meditations led to an encounter with aliens from the planet Venus who invited him onto their ship and gave him tips on rejuvenating living cells with sound.

Combining these tips with theories involving the earth's magnetic field and the locations of both the Great Pyramid in

Egypt and Giant Rock, Van Tassel started building his "rejuvenation chamber" in 1954.

For the next 18 years, UFO conventions and donations from thousands of believers kept the family afloat, but when Van Tassel died in 1978, the Integratron was not fully finished and the work was abandoned.

The Integratron still stands, a pristine white dome looking as if it was painted yesterday. The 38-foot-high, 50-foot-diameter structure was built without nails, screws, or any metal framing to enhance its magnetic properties. The upper level is engineered to amplify sounds, with a central spot on the wooden floor that creates an almost living vibration. Here, two sisters who bought the property a few years ago give sound baths using Tibetan crystal bowls and explain the workings of "the Dome."

Although the Integratron has been featured on many TV shows, including one on the Discovery Channel, very few locals even know of its existence. This is truly an "Insider Place" and well worth the visit. Be sure to call or visit the Web site for driving directions, as the street address will be of little help.

Self-guided tours, private group tours, sound baths, retreats, and workshops are held throughout the year. Because of ongoing restoration and times when the facility is rented to large groups, opening times vary. Check the Web site for updates.

Oasis Date Gardens   Free
59-111 Highway 111, Thermal
(760) 399-5665, (800) 827-8017
www.oasisdategardens.com
A working date garden since 1912, Oasis is the oldest date grower in the valley. And it boasts the oldest date palm in the valley—planted in 1919, this giant towers 80 feet above the Oasis Ranch Store. In addition to hundreds of date palms in various stages of maturity, the 175-acre garden has a palm arboretum for propagation, a packing house, the ranch store, and a garden cafe. If you're taking one of the tours that goes to the eastern end of the valley, chances are good that it includes a stop

---

Bring a sweater or light jacket if you're taking the Tram ride. It's always 30 to 40 degrees cooler at the top than it is on the desert floor.

---

at Oasis for free date samples, a rest break, and an opportunity for shopping.

Oasis ships its many varieties of fresh dates all over the world. Pick up a couple of packages for yourself and send some home to your friends. There's no souvenir that says "Palm Springs" more than a box of sweet golden-brown dates. The facility also gives daily tours at no charge. In season, Oasis is the home base for Camel Safari rides, so if you've harbored a desire to go a few blocks on top of the "ship of the desert," this is the place. Call for dates and prices. Oasis is open from 8:00 A.M. to 5:00 P.M. Monday through Saturday.

Palm Springs Aerial Tramway   **$$$**
One Tramway Road
(760) 325-1391, (888) 515-8726
www.pstramway.com
The third of the desert's "must-see" attractions (including the Indian Canyons and the Living Desert), the Palm Springs Aerial Tramway soars from sea level in rugged Chino Canyon on the north edge of Palm Springs to the 8,516-foot Mountain Station. Temperatures at the top of the Tram are generally about 30 to 40 degrees cooler than they are in the desert, and the pine-scented mountain wilderness is a bracing contrast to the glitz and glamour down below.

The trip up takes about 15 minutes and offers a spectacular view from the world's largest rotating tramcars. The cars hold around 80 people and are very stable, though you'll get a little "lift" when they pass under the cable towers. At the top you can have a delicious cafeteria-style meal inside or outside on balconies that give a view of the entire valley floor. A short film about the Tram's making is good for history buffs and helps to explain why

Want the ultimate summer romantic date? Pick a full-moon night and get the Tram's Ride 'n' Dine special. Have a leisurely dinner while the sun sets, then head for Lookout Point, about a half mile from the Mountain Station. With clear weather you can see the moonlight shining on the Salton Sea and northern Mexico.

the Tram promoters call its building "the eighth wonder of the world."

Twenty years after the Tram opened for its first ride in 1963, it was designated a historical civil engineering landmark. Of five supporting towers, the first is the only one that can be reached by road. The other four and the 35,000-square-foot Mountain Station were all built with men and materials flown in place by helicopters—more than 23,000 flights in all.

In 2000 the original tram cars were replaced, and the entire facility—designed by famed midcentury architect and Palm Springs resident Albert Frey—was given a much-needed interior updating.

The top of the Tram is right in the middle of the Mount San Jacinto State Park and Wilderness and is the hub for 54 miles of hiking trails. The trails are easy to walk and are clearly marked, so you can strike off on your own and pick a pretty spot to have a picnic lunch. The free, guided nature walks are also a wonderful way to learn about the natural environment at the Top of the Tram.

One of the joys of spending a winter vacation in Palm Springs is the choice of sunbathing by the pool or playing in the snow—or even doing both in the same day. Snow at the top of the Tram is virtually guaranteed by Christmas. During the winter months the Winter Adventure Center offers cross-country ski and snowshoeing equipment rental; or you can bring your own. Sleds and cold-weather clothes are also for sale in the Mountain Station gift shop. Really hardy types can even camp out in the snow.

Day permits are available at the Ranger Station in Long Valley, a short walk from the Mountain Station, and are required for any extensive hiking or backpacking beyond Long Valley. Permits are also required for overnight camping at the primitive campsites in four designated campgrounds. Requests for advance permits can be made in person or in writing—no phone or fax requests are accepted. Check the Web site for details.

Tram cars depart at least every half hour, starting at 10:00 A.M., Monday through Friday, and starting at 8:00 A.M. on weekends and during holiday periods. The last car up is at 8:00 P.M., with the last car down being at 9:45 P.M. Ride 'n' Dine specials that give a discount for a ride and a meal are available after 3:00 P.M.

Palm Springs Air Museum $$
745 North Gene Autry Trail
(760) 778-6262
www.palmspringsairmuseum.org

The Palm Springs Air Museum is dedicated to World War II aircraft and has one of the world's largest collections of flying World War II airplanes. Yes, we said flying. These planes are in perfect working condition and are pressed into service for flight demonstrations and hands-on exhibitions throughout the year, particularly on significant military anniversary dates.

The planes, along with rare combat photography, enormous murals, artifacts, and memorabilia, are grouped into the major regions of combat, the European and the Pacific Theaters. Ongoing history and education programs are part of the lure here, along with a remarkable group of docent volunteers, all of whom served in World War II themselves and make up the irreplaceable living history component of the Air Museum.

Large-scale model ships and gorgeous vintage automobiles are also displayed in the museum's air-conditioned hangars. There is also a fine library, computers with flight simulators, and a gift shop stocked with models and flight-related souvenirs. The institution is on a 10-acre site that

Vintage planes and automobiles are on display at the Palm Springs Air Museum. PHOTO BY JACK HOLLINGSWORTH, COURTESY OF THE PALM SPRINGS DESERT RESORTS CONVENTION AND VISITORS AUTHORITY

includes visitor parking, ramp access to the Palm Springs International Airport for visiting display aircraft, exterior displays, and an aircraft ramp for special shows and flight demonstration viewing.

The Air Museum is open daily from 10:00 A.M. to 5:00 P.M.

Palm Springs Art Museum   **$**
101 Museum Drive
(760) 325-7186
www.psmuseum.org
Founded in 1938, the Palm Springs Art Museum is one of the country's finest small fine arts/natural history institutions. Its patrons over the years have been the most affluent and famous of the desert's visitors and residents, from Walter Annenberg to Kirk and Anne Douglas, Steven Chase, and William Holden. All contributed large amounts of money, art, and love to building a world-class facility.

Named the Palm Springs Desert Museum for more than 50 years, the institution changed its name in 2005 to the Palm Springs Art Museum, more accurately reflecting its focus on the fine and performing arts. The museum's permanent art collection features 19th-, 20th-, and 21st-century works focusing on contemporary California art, classic western

---

The Palm Springs Art Museum offers free admission from 4:00 to 8:00 P.M. each Thursday, during the weekly VillageFest. Make an evening of it by touring the museum, having an early dinner, and shopping for fresh produce and crafts, all within a 4- to 5-block radius.

American art, Native American art, pre-Columbian art, Mexican art, European modern art, glass studio art, American mid-20th-century architecture, and American photography.

In addition, the Annenberg Theater keeps an eclectic calendar from ballet to modern dance, opera to jazz, and comedy to drama. The museum offers art classes, special events, lectures, films, two sculpture gardens, a cafe, and a new online museum store filled with unique items you won't find anywhere else.

In the newly re-installed Denney Western American Art Wing, fans of classic western art such as paintings and sculptures by Charles Russell and Frederic Remington can view their works alongside contemporary works such as Alexis Smith's image of a modern-day desperado or Arlo Namingha's sculpture inspired by traditional Hopi kachinas.

In the spacious upstairs galleries, added with the museum's major expansion a few years ago, visitors can view a major survey of 20th-century art, with approximately 100 paintings, works on paper, and sculpture by well-known artists. From early modernists to the contemporary, some of the artists are Alexander Archipenko, Marc Chagall, Amedeo Modigliani, Alberto Giacometti, Henry Moore, Barbara Hepworth, Franz Kline, Sam Francis, Helen Frankenthaler, Frank Stella, Robert Motherwell, Robert Arneson, William Wiley, Dale Chihuly, DeWain Valentine, Peter Voulkos, and Edward Ruscha.

Along with outstanding traveling exhibitions of major artists, the museum is known for its natural history and science wing. Here the changing exhibits appeal to all ages and are always focused on learning through fun. Past exhibits have included the world of dinosaurs, nocturnal desert wildlife, earthquakes, and more.

Special children's and family programs are a recent addition to the museum during the summer months. Check the Web site for current events and activities. For more information on the Annenberg Theater, see the listing in the Arts and Entertainment chapter.

The museum is open from 10:00 A.M. to 5:00 P.M. Tuesday, Wednesday, Friday, and Saturday; from noon to 8:00 P.M. on Thursday; and from noon to 5:00 P.M. on Sunday. It is closed on Monday and major holidays. Docent-guided tours are available at 2:00 P.M. Tuesday through Saturday and are free with admission.

Salton Sea   Free
(No street address)
(760) 393-3059
www.saltonsea.ca.gov

A State Recreation and Wildlife Refuge, the Salton Sea is 35 miles long and 227 feet below sea level. A massive inland sea created when the Colorado River broke free of its dams and flooded the area back in 1905, it is primarily an agricultural drainage basin, taking runoff from irrigation in the fields served by the Colorado River. The runoff is both salty and rich in fertilizer. The high nutrient levels from agricultural runoff cause periodic algae "blooms" that suck up oxygen on the sea's surface and kill thousands of fish, a fact of life that sometimes can be smelled all the way to Palm Springs.

Today the sea is most famous for its role as a winter stopover for migratory birds. As many as 380 of this country's known bird species have been counted here—almost half of all the species in the United States. During December and January millions of birds use the Salton Sea each day, and there's more bird and wildlife diversity here than any other place in California. Because it's such a vital resource for wildlife, many environmental and political groups are searching for ways to nurse the area back to health.

The area has a fascinating history and an uncertain future. One of the best ways to learn about both is to take a nature tour with one of the desert companies that specialize in this area. It will be an unforgettable experience and a rich opportunity for photos of bubbling mud pots, an inland sea, and the remains of Salton City, once touted as the desert's most exciting new recreation area. Salton Sea lies 30 miles south of Indio on Highway 111.

The Village Green Heritage Center $
221 South Palm Canyon Drive
(760) 323-8297

The Village Green Heritage Center sits in a well-groomed little park right in the middle of Palm Canyon Drive and features two 19th-Century pioneer homes. The McCallum Adobe, the oldest remaining building in Palm Springs, was built in 1884 for John McCallum, the first permanent white settler. Although adobe was eminently suited for the desert climate, few people in the area knew how to make the bricks, and this was an oddity at the time.

Palm Springs' first hotel operator, Dr. Welwood Murray, built the second structure, Miss Cornelia's "Little House," in 1893. The house was constructed of railroad ties from the defunct Palmdale Railway and purchased by the sisters Miss Cornelia White and Dr. Florilla White in 1913. In 1961 the Palm Springs Historical Society acquired the home and furnished it with antiques donated by local residents.

Between the two old homes, there's a vast and interesting collection of photographs, paintings, clothing, tools, books, Indian artifacts, and furniture from the earliest pioneer days of the city. Also in the Village Green complex are the Agua Caliente Cultural Museum and Ruddy's 1930s General Store Museum, a re-creation of a turn-of-the-century general store, complete with authentic fixtures and dry goods. The Village Green is all the more interesting for its location, showing an immediate contrast between the city's

modern shops and restaurants and the modest dwellings of the past.

From mid-October through May, the Village Green complex is open from noon to 3:00 P.M. on Wednesday and Sunday and from 10:00 A.M. to 4:00 P.M. Thursday through Saturday.

TOURS
Aerial Rides/Tours

Nostalgic Warbird &
Biplane Rides $$$$
Palm Springs International Airport
(760) 641-7335, (800) 991-2473
www.nostalgicwarbirdrides.com

An FAA-rated pilot with more than 20 years behind the controls of every type of aircraft from gliders to fighters and Boeing 737s, Mike Carpentiero has been flying gliders since 1984 and operating this company since 2003.

The thrilling flights allow passengers to take the controls of a 1941 open cockpit World War II Stearman trainer or sit side by side in a 1928 TravelAir biplane. Rides are tailored to the individual—daredevil or serene—and can include acrobatics. A video

CLOSE-UP

Bruce Poynter, Desert Guide Extraordinaire

Every tour operator and hotel concierge knows Bruce for his endless store of knowledge and unfailing enthusiasm. Even though he's been taking visitors out on desert tours for more than 15 years, he still gets genuinely excited about spotting a red-tailed hawk, reciting a mind-boggling assembly of geologic facts, or capturing a gentle rosy boa so the children and adults in his tour group can see one of the desert's most delicate and harmless snakes up close.

Right out of high school Bruce joined the Air Force and spent most of his enlistment working with the fire rescue crews in Vietnam at the height of the conflict, earning a Commendation Medal as sergeant. The experience sharpened his appetite for firefighting, and he joined the Indio Fire Department as soon as his military service ended.

The next 20 years were spent in emergency medical services as a fire department captain, emergency medical transport specialist, and instructor in first aid, CPR, and desert survival. Named Firefighter of the Year and Emergency Medical Technician of the Year, Captain Poynter was known all over the valley for his humor, daring, and professionalism. He'd probably still be there today if not for an injury he sustained while trying to move an accident victim out of oncoming traffic on a rainy night.

The injury ended his fire department career and opened the door for a new one. As Bruce was recovering, the first tours were beginning in the desert, and the organizers called on his expertise to help design scripts and find trails through the hills. A match made in heaven. Over his more than 30 years in the valley, Bruce has hiked or four-wheeled on every possible path from Joshua Tree to Mexico, exploring on his own, traveling with herpetologists from the University of Califor-

of the adventure is optional. Considering that a one-hour flight can cost as much as $500, that's a souvenir worth having.

Rides are offered October through May, and reservations are required.

Sailplane Enterprises $$$$
Jacqueline Cochran Airport in Thermal
(909) 658-6577
www.sailplaneenterprises.com
The specialty here is motorless flight for two in sailplanes piloted by FAA-certified pilots. The company has a large fleet and can manage as many as 100 flights a day, with a variety of rides and packages on the menu.

Sailplane Enterprises is open October through May. Reservations are required.

Balloon Tours

All three of the desert's hot-air balloon companies offer early-morning rides over the agricultural areas at the eastern end of the valley. Competent pilot/guides, colorful craft, and a champagne reception at

nia to round up rattlesnakes for their venom, and unraveling the history and barren beauty of the desert for his friends.

In his career as tour guide extraordinaire, Bruce has starred in travel programs for the Travel Channel, BBC1, BBC2, and Travel Tokyo. He's been quoted and fawned over in *Sunset* magazine, *Men's Journal, Palm Springs Life,* the *New York Times, Los Angeles Times, Chicago Tribune,* and dozens of other publications.

Today he splits his time between training other guides and leading tours for families and Fortune 500 companies. Although he's often on call for VIP groups, he also consults with Big Wheel Tours and is their lead guide and trainer. It's practically impossible to name a natural desert attraction or sight that Bruce hasn't studied and burned into his brain—the Palm Springs Aerial Tramway, Indian Canyons, Joshua Tree National Park, Salton Sea, Mecca Hills Wilderness, Santa Rosa National Monument, the Living Desert, Idyllwild—and all come alive with insider tips and knowledge that he has

Bruce Poynter has been educating tour groups about the history, geology, and botany of the desert for more than 20 years. PHOTO COURTESY OF BIG WHEEL TOURS

amassed over a lifetime of living here.

You may be fortunate to take a tour with one of the guides who trained under Captain Poynter. If you're really lucky, you'll get the man himself.

the end of your flight are part of the package. This is an expensive way to see the desert, but the experience of floating soundlessly above the date groves and ranch houses of this rich farmland is incomparable.

All of the balloon companies offer virtually the same experience, which includes optional transportation to the launch site and from the landing site, a chase vehicle to make sure your craft has help if you land away from the predetermined site, a pilot to guide the craft in the air, crew to assist the launch and landing, champagne

at the end, and a lovely certificate as a memento of the trip. Because of strict FAA rules, the balloons all travel over the same fields. Be aware that the high winds in the late winter and early spring can cause pilots to cancel flights at the last minute. Because all the flights are early in the morning to avoid the afternoon thermal updrafts, you might even get a 4:00 A.M. call canceling the trip.

A Dream Flight $$$$
(760) 776-5785

Balloon Above the Desert $$$$
83-232 East Avenue 44, Indio
(760) 776-5785, (800) 342-8506
www.balloonabovethedesert.com

Fantasy Balloon Flights $$$$
(760) 568-0997, (800) 462-2683

Bike Tours

Adventure Bike Tours $$-$$$
70-250 Chappel Road, Rancho Mirage
(760) 328-0282
www.adventurebiketours.info
This outfit offers four-hour guided group
bike tours and supplies helmets, refreshments, and chase vehicles throughout the
tours. Riders can also rent the "E-Bike," an
electric bike designed by Lee Iacocca, the
genius behind Chrysler and a desert resident.

Big Horn Bicycle Adventures $$$
302 North Palm Canyon Drive
(760) 325-3367
Big Horn specializes in guided tours
around the city of Palm Springs, including
one that goes to the Indian Canyons and
another that takes riders around the old
Las Palmas neighborhood where the
biggest names in Hollywood used to live.
They also rent and sell electric bikes.

Nature and Sightseeing Tours

Big Wheel Tours $$$-$$$$
P.O. Box 4185, Palm Desert 92270
(760) 779-1837
www.bwbtours.com

*Legitimate tour companies are licensed
by the Public Utilities Commission,
carry extensive insurance, and have
guides who are CPR-certified. If you
have any doubts, ask for these creden-
tials up front.*

Each of its hiking, off-road, and bicycle
tours is meticulously researched, informa-
tive, and entertaining; the guides are first-
rate, and the destinations show imagination
and creativity.

Its new off-road tours, including one
that goes into Joshua Tree National Park,
over the San Andreas Fault, and through
historic gold-mining areas, use Ford Expe-
dition vehicles.

Big Wheel offers popular destinations
such as the Indian Canyons and the Palm
Springs Aerial Tramway as well as more
scenic and remote areas. The Borrego
Springs Time Machine tour includes hikes
to a calcite mine and wildlife spotting.
Another gem is the trip to the Salton Sea,
where over three million birds visit on an
average winter day.

Tours to Idyllwild, the Coachella Valley
Preserve, and other spots can be tailored
for different levels of ability, from expert
hikers to mobility-impaired visitors.

Celebrity Tours of Palm Springs $$
4751 East Palm Canyon Drive, #C
(760) 770-2700, (888) 805-2700
www.celebrity-tours.com
This is the original tour company in the
desert, taking visitors around in air-
conditioned buses to gape at places where
celebrities used to live. Locals often call it
the "dead stars tour," because so many of
the famous names are long gone. Even so,
it's a good way to get your orientation and
see the neighborhoods that made Palm
Springs famous way back when.

Covered Wagon Tours $$$$
P.O. Box 1106, La Quinta 92253
(760) 347-2161, (800) 367-2161
www.coveredwagontours.com
Authentically built covered wagons pulled
by draft mules and driven by guides who
play to the "Wild West" history of the
desert can be a delightful way to learn a
little bit about the desert—a smidgen of
history wrapped in a lot of entertainment.
Barbecue cookouts over a campfire and
country-western serenades as the sun

goes down are part of the fun, and the wagons are equipped with padded seats and rubber wheels for a relatively smooth ride. The tours take place in the Coachella Valley Preserve, a lovely desert spot with a small natural palm oasis. Departure times and offerings vary, so be sure to call for information and directions.

Desert Adventures $$$$
67-555 East Palm Canyon Drive
Suite E-106, Cathedral City
(760) 324-5337, (888) 324-5337
www.red-jeep.com

Desert Adventures is the company that started the entire nature tour business in the desert, back in the early 1990s. At that time, they spent hundreds of hours researching their information and developing tour programs that many of the other companies have copied. Winners of the prestigious Phoenix Award from the Society of American Travel Writers for their environmentally progressive policies and highly trained guides, Desert Adventures was once the only way to see the desert as its original inhabitants did.

Over the years, however, intense competition from newer tour companies and a series of less than stellar business decisions have eroded their place at the top of the heap. Desert Adventures' tours are still some of the best in the desert, but their guides can be a scruffy lot, and their prices are among the highest. The pick of the tours is the Mystery Canyon excursion, which takes participants in a red jeep through the agricultural areas in the eastern desert out to Painted Hills, an area of steep canyons and rock formations that straddles part of the San Andreas Fault.

Elite Land Tours $$$$
555 South Sunrise Way, Suite 200
(760) 318-1200, (800) 514-4866
www.elitelandtours.com

Elite Land Tours specializes in backcountry exploration from the air-conditioned comfort of the massive all-terrain Hummer H2. This is the tour that would be featured on *Lifestyles of the Rich and Famous*—it

Some tour companies include hotel pickup and drop-off in their prices; others do not. Some also provide water and snacks along the way. Find out before you book, as the cost of water, snacks, and special hotel transportation can add up quickly.

includes gourmet lunches and personalized DVDs for bragging opportunities back home. There's only one drawback: Although the Hummer is ideally equipped to go over the gnarliest road, the operators are a little hesitant to take these shiny new vehicles into areas where the terrain might rough up their beautiful new paint. Oh well. The tour guides are always up-to-date on the area's history and current ecological issues, and the tour menu offers good variety, including a Night Discovery Tour with special night vision equipment to spot the desert's elusive wildlife.

Outdoor Adventures
42-335 Washington Street, Suite F-121
Palm Desert
  Aerial Adventures $$$$
  (888) 786-8747

  Joshua Tree National Park
  Scenic Tour $$$
  (760) 285-1608
  www.joshutatreetour.com

  A Taste of Palm Springs $$$$
  (877) 656-2453
  www.palmspringsfuntrips.com

Aerial Adventures offers 30-minute helicopter flights over certain areas of Palm Springs. Because of concerns about disturbing wildlife, particularly the endangered Peninsular Bighorn Sheep, these flights may be eliminated or greatly curtailed in the future.

The Joshua Tree tour goes out every Tuesday and Thursday in air-conditioned buses, traveling to Joshua Tree National Park with expert local guides. With the exception of one hour off the vehicle for photos and

If the winter rains have been kind, the desert will be a carpet of wildflowers as early as February, lasting as late as May in the high desert. The Palm Springs Art Museum staffs a wildflower hotline and also does wildflower tours if the season warrants it. Call the museum at (760) 325-7186 in mid-February.

short walks, plan on spending all your time on the highway and park roads.

A Taste of Palm Springs is a Thursday excursion that includes a celebrity home tour, Ride 'n' Dine on the Palm Springs Aerial Tramway, and a final stop at the VillageFest street fair in Palm Springs. There are better values and more knowledgeable guides with other companies.

PS Windmill Tours $$
(760) 251-1997, (877) 449-9463
www.windmilltours.com
Billed as the only working tour of a wind farm in the world, this is a unique opportunity to get up close to the towering windmills that dot the hills in the San Gorgonio Pass outside of Palm Springs. The wind farms sprouted there in the 1970s when tax breaks for alternative power were plentiful. By the time the tax breaks were phased out, the technology had become efficient enough to allow the operators to generate power at a profitable rate. According to geologists, this is one of the most consistently windy places on earth. The tour is fascinating, full of hard facts and unusual photo opportuni-

ties. Windmill Tours is located north of Palm Springs, near the intersection of I-10 and 20th Avenue. Call for directions.

Sky Watcher $$
73-091 Country Club Drive, Suite A42
Palm Desert
(760) 831-0231
www.sky-watcher.com
This company specializes in tours of the sky, with telescopes and sky binoculars, storytelling, and "space candy" (Mars and Milky Way). Program tours are offered at the La Quinta Resort and Club on Friday and Saturday evenings, beginning at dark and lasting two hours. Call for times, days, and pricing or contact the resort.

Trail Discovery/Desert Safari $$$$
P.O. Box 8394, Palm Springs 92263
(760) 325-4453, (888) 324-4453
www.palmspringshiking.com
Company president and lead guide Scott Scott (yes, that's really his name!) has been hiking in the desert for years and is considered quite the expert. He's a delightful companion as well, adapting each tour to the participants' interests and ability levels.

Scott offers three main tours—to the Indian Canyons, Joshua Tree, and the Palm Springs Aerial Tramway. He also offers five or six "expedition" excursions that are a bit more difficult, more detailed, and just as much fun. If you're in town during a full moon, the Moonlight Expedition is a must. All tours include transportation, loaner hiking packs, water, snacks, and admissions when needed.

PARKS, RECREATION, AND SPORTS

With its near-constant sunny days and exceptionally low humidity, the Palm Springs area delivers the three things outdoor sports enthusiasts want: weather, weather, and weather. Even snow lovers can get their winter fix by taking a trip up the Palm Springs Aerial Tramway for snowshoeing and cross-country skiing or by driving just a few hours for excellent downhill skiing in nearby Big Bear and Arrowhead ski resorts.

There's so much for the golfer here that the sport gets its own chapter—with more than 100 courses throughout the valley, including some excellent public courses, it's the number one outdoor activity and the one that gets the most attention from the press.

Back in the early days of the desert, when movies stars and the wealthy "discovered" Palm Springs, though, golf was nonexistent. In those days tennis was the sport of choice, followed by horseback riding in the hills surrounding the town. Tennis continues to be popular, with the Indian Wells Tennis Gardens hosting major international tennis tournaments and dozens of public courts throughout the valley. Most major hotels have tennis courts, and many offer pro lessons and amateur play matching. Horseback riders, sadly, have lost a lot of the open desert that used to be their roaming grounds, though the Desert Riders group is quite active in maintaining and building new trails in the foothills.

Polo is a major sport in the eastern end of the valley, and even if you've never picked up a mallet, it's a great spectator activity. You may even be tempted to sign up for a lesson or two so you can experience this "sport of kings" firsthand.

It almost goes without saying that if you're a swimmer, you've found your spot. Every hotel in the valley has a pool. For lap swimming and lessons, several of the cities offer Olympic-size pools and expert instruction.

Public parks for picnics, soccer, skateboarding, and just plain romping around are dotted throughout the desert. And for the furry travelers, Palm Springs and Palm Desert both have off-leash dog parks.

To help you find your way around the sports side of the desert, we've grouped our listings by sport, with subcategories for geographic locations where appropriate. Sports activities with no address listed are companies that primarily provide tours and offer pickup and drop-off.

Keep in mind that many of the public parks and public pools have hours that vary by season. Public parks are free. Public facilities for such sports as tennis, fishing, and swimming usually charge a nominal fee. Always call the public spots to make sure you know their hours, available activities, and information about fees.

Well-marked bike trails in Palm Springs include the Heritage Trail and various loops around town and through the country club areas. Maps are available at no charge through the Palm Springs Leisure Center, on Baristo Road between Sunrise Way and Airport Road. Trails that connect among the other cities are still works in progress. The Leisure Center is the best place to find current information and directions. Call (760) 323-8272.

PRICE CODE

Unless otherwise indicated, all credit cards are accepted. Price ranges apply to charges for one person in high season. No price ranges are indicated for public facilities, as many are free, and fees for others change with the season. Always call ahead to make sure the public facilities are open. Many close or curtail hours during the summer months.

$	Up to $10
$$	$11 to $25
$$$	$26 to $50
$$$$	$51 and up

BIKING

Adventure Bike Tours $$-$$$
70-250 Chappel Road
Rancho Mirage
(760) 328-0282
www.adventurebiketours.info
This outfit offers guided group bike tours with bikes, helmets, refreshments, and full-support chase vehicles. Bike rentals are also available.

Bighorn Bicycle Adventures $$$
320 North Palm Canyon Drive
Rancho Mirago
(760) 325-3367
This company specializes in downtown tours of Palm Springs and does hiking tours. Trek bikes are the vehicles of choice, and the company also sells and rents electric bikes.

Big Wheel Bike Tours $$$-$$$$
P.O. Box 4185, Palm Desert 92270
(760) 779-1837
www.bwbtours.com
This group has perhaps the most knowledgeable and personable bike guides in

---

Check the local newspaper, **The Desert Sun,** *for organized bike rides and hikes throughout the week. Most are just a few dollars, and many are free. If your hotel has bikes to rent or loan—and many do—ask the concierge for a bike trail map and do some family exploring for a few hours.*

---

the desert. Choose a wild ride down Highway 74 or a leisurely circle in the mountains and over the San Andreas Fault. Custom tours, rental bikes, and delivery are all available.

BOWLING

Fantasy Lanes Family Bowling Center $
84245 Indio Springs Parkway, Indio
(760) 342-5000
Located in Fantasy Springs Casino, this is a glossy alley with 24 lanes, neon pins, glowing lanes and gutters, laser lights, and fog machines. A snack bar, arcade, pool table, lounge, and proximity to more flashing lights in the casino make this a far cry from the dingy bowling alleys of *Laverne and Shirley* days.

FISHING

Lake Cahuilla $
(No street address)
(760) 564-4712
This is a Riverside County Park that is stocked on a regular basis. Only nonmotorized boats are allowed. Fishing licenses are required. To get to Cahuilla, go east on Highway 111 east from Palm Springs to Jefferson Street in Indio; then take a right and go about 6 miles.

Whitewater Trout Farm $
9160 Whitewater Canyon Road
Whitewater
(760) 325-5570
www.campingfriend.com/whitewater
troutfarm/
This trout hatchery is set up for family fun. Whitewater supplies the license, tackle, and bait for a low fee, charges by the pound for fish caught, and will even clean and cook your catch if you want. Picnic tables and grills are available. To reach Whitewater from Palm Springs, go north on Indian Canyon Drive to I-10, west to the Whitewater exit, and then 5 miles to the hatchery.

HIKING

There are hundreds of miles of hiking trails all over the foothills around the desert cities. Most were originally created by the Cahuilla Indians for travel among bands, for hunting, and as trade routes. The Desert Riders, a dedicated band of horse riders that's been around since the early days, are responsible for the excellent maintenance of the trail system and for creating new trails on a regular basis. Trail maps are available from the various hiking companies for a small fee. It's advisable to check with these companies for seasonal trail closures—many of the most popular trails recently have been closed to hikers during the winter months. Winter is lambing season for the endangered Bighorn Sheep.

Big Wheel Tours   **$$$**
P.O. Box 4185, Palm Desert 92270
(760) 779-1837
www.bwbtours.com
Big Wheel's hiking tours are the same high quality as their bike tours, with guides who are both entertaining and highly seasoned. They'll put together a custom tour, or you can choose from hikes into Joshua Tree National Park, the Indian Canyons, and other areas, including the top of the Tram.

Joshua Tree Hike & Fitness   **$$**
(760) 366-7985
This company only does hikes and specializes in the beautiful natural areas in Joshua Tree National Park. Half-day or full-day hikes are available for all fitness levels. Guides will either meet you at the site or pick you up at your hotel.

Palm Springs Art Museum   **$**
101 Museum Way
(760) 325-7186
www.psmuseum.org
Twice a week from November through April, a naturalist conducts these museum-sponsored hikes. Routes vary according to the season, and most are suitable for all fitness levels.

With so many trails right on the edge of the cities, you can spend a morning hiking and be down in plenty of time for lunch, a quick shower, shopping, and pool time.

Trail Discovery/Desert Safari   **$$$**
P.O. Box 8394, Palm Springs 92263
(760) 325-4453, (888) 324-4453
www.palmspringshiking.com
The owner of this little company is most likely the guide for your tour—Scott Scott probably knows more about the hiking trails in and around Palm Springs than any other human in the valley, and the experience of hiking with him will be a delight. Scott will meet you at the site or pick you up at your hotel.

HORSEBACK RIDING/POLO

Coyote Ridge Stable   **$$$$**
Morongo Valley
(760) 363-3380
www.coyoteridgestable.com
In the high desert about 20 minutes from Palm Springs, this stable takes guests on wrangler-guided rides through the mountains overlooking the valley. Rides are gentle and suitable for beginners.

Eldorado Polo Club   **$-$$$$**
50950 Madison Street, Indio
(760) 342-2223
The desert's original polo club, this sprawling facility offers lessons as well as regular international competitions and celebrity tournaments. Bring a picnic and enjoy the game up close from the grassy lawn next to the field. Admission to tournaments is usually just a few dollars. Polo lessons can cost upward of $100.

Empire Polo Club   **$-$$$$**
81-800 Avenue 51, Indio
(760) 342-2762
Empire began life as the little kid on the

The late Sonny Bono and Frank Bogert, both former mayors of Palm Springs, riding through the Indian Canyons. PHOTO COURTESY OF PALM SPRINGS HISTORICAL SOCIETY

polo block in Indio and is now best known for its special events, as well as many important international tournaments. The grounds are huge—even more extensive than Eldorado—and often host balloon festivals, concerts, rodeos, art shows, and other open-air activities in the winter. The restaurant is excellent. Lessons are also available for all skill levels. As is the case with Eldorado Polo Club, tournament admission is just a few dollars, and polo lessons can cost $100 and more.

Ivey Ranch Equestrian Center $$$$
73605 30th Avenue, Thousand Palms
(760) 343-4251
Primarily a boarding facility for local horse owners, this equestrian center also offers special events and occasional trail rides. Ivey has been operating its facility for more than 25 years and has only recently opened to the public. Now it's becoming popular as a site for private parties and themed events for the many business and convention groups meeting in the desert throughout the year. Call for information on planned trail rides—just a few each year—that are open to the public.

Los Compadres Stable $$$$
1849 South El Cielo Road
(760) 320-3209
The place where all of the Desert Riders stable their mounts, this is one of the valley's oldest sports facilities. It's also home to the once-popular "Mink and Manure Club" where stars and the wealthy would saddle up for social trail rides and cocktails. Private and semiprivate lessons and boarding are available.

Smoke Tree Stables $$$$
2500 Toledo Avenue
(760) 327-1372
This was once "out in the country," and now the stables are surrounded by pricey homes and condos and bordered by an excellent golf course. Smoke Tree is adjacent to Smoke Tree Ranch and has always been a part of it, stabling horses for the homeowners there and offering rides and

lessons to the public. The crusty wranglers know their business, and it's not chatting up visitors, so just relax in the saddle and enjoy the ride through the wash and up into the Indian Canyons.

Vandenburg Equestrian Center $$$$
69380 Converse Road, Cathedral City
(760) 328-4560
This is a far cry from the Wild West, down-to-earth atmosphere of Smoke Tree. A professionally run facility with lessons in English- and western-style riding, Vandenburg caters to the experienced horseback rider or the rider who wants expert instruction and one-on-one attention. If you have ever wondered if there's a horse in your future, take a lesson here for a good introduction to equestrian etiquette and expectations.

Willowbrook Riding Club $$$$
20555 Mountain View Drive, Desert Hot Springs
(760) 329-7676
This is a good place to ride when it gets too hot on the desert floor. Desert Hot Springs is usually a good 10 degrees cooler. There's a fine cross-country course, and you can take lessons in English flat and hunter's techniques.

ROCK CLIMBING

Joshua Tree National Park $
(No street address)
(760) 367-5500
Rock and boulder climbers from all over the world consider the park to be one of the best spots for challenging and beauti-

---

If you make your home in Palm Desert for more than half the year and have the utility bills and other ID to prove it, you can get a resident card, which entitles you to amazing discounts on public golf and other recreational activities in Palm Desert.

---

ful scrambling. The park has no facilities, but there are always a few outfitters and guides available at small shops near the entrance. To reach the park, take Highway 62 north of Palm Springs to Joshua Tree.

Uprising Outdoor Adventure Center $$$
1500 North Gene Autry Trail
(760) 320-6630
Next to Knott's Soak City U.S.A., this is one of the country's largest outdoor man-made climbing facilities. It's misted and shaded and offers a variety of walls and skill levels, and the instruction is top level.

ROLLER HOCKEY/SKATING

Big League Dreams Sports Park $$
33700 Date Palm Drive, Cathedral City
(760) 324-5600
A covered in-line hockey facility is one of the many sports features in this family park, which also offers softball, basketball, and video sports.

Palm Desert Skate Park
Palm Desert Civic Center Park
73510 Fred Waring Drive, Palm Desert
(760) 346-0611
Open from sunrise to 10:00 P.M. and lighted in the evenings, this is a first-class facility for skateboarders and in-line skaters.

Palm Springs Skate Park
401 South Pavilion Way
(760) 323-8272
The desert's newest skate park has all the goodies for skateboarders and in-line skaters—boxes, spines, rails, hips, wedges, and 9-foot bowls.

The Palm Springs Olympic-size pool at the Pavilion near downtown is the best spot in the valley for lap swimming and costs just a few dollars. Go early in the morning and pack a picnic lunch to enjoy later in the adjacent Sunrise Park.

SOCCER

Palm Desert Soccer Park
74735 Hovely Lane, Palm Desert
(760) 568-9697
This offers five full-sized, lighted fields with picnic pavilions, tot and toddler lots with perimeter seating, three horseshoe courts, three shuffleboard courts, and a basketball court, as well as paths for walking, jogging, biking, or in-line skating. The park is closed annually from April 1 to June 31 for renovation.

SWIMMING
La Quinta

YMCA of La Quinta
Fritz Burns Park
78060 Frances Hack Lane
(Corner of Avenidas Bermudas and Avenue 52)
(760) 341-9622
One of the desert's few public swimming pools, this one offers open swim, lap swim, and lessons for all ages, from tiny tots to seniors, who want a gentle water workout.

Palm Springs

Palm Springs Swim Center
Sunrise Park, corner of Sunrise Way and Ramon Roads
(760) 323-8278
This is a first-rate public facility, open year-round. The temperature is maintained at an even 80-84 degrees—no small feat for a 50-meter Olympic-size pool. The center offers lessons and classes for all ages, spacious lawns and picnic tables, a sundeck, and a children's section.

Indio/Coachella/Mecca

Pawley Pool Family Aquatic Complex
46-350 South Jackson, Indio

Public Tennis Courts

COACHELLA

Bagdouma Park
84620 Bagdad Street
(760) 347-3484
Four courts.

INDIO

Indio High School
81750 Avenue 46
(760) 775-3550
Six courts.

LA QUINTA

Fritz Burns Park
78060 Frances Hack Lane
(760) 777-7090
Six courts.

La Quinta High School
79255 Westward Ho
(760) 772-4150
Six courts.

PALM DESERT

Cahuilla Hills Park
45825 Edgehill Drive
(760) 568-9697
Two courts.

Community Center Park
73510 Fred Waring Drive
(760) 773-2326
Six lighted courts.

Palm Desert High School
43570 Phyllis Jackson Lane
(760) 862-4300
Six courts.

PALM SPRINGS

DeMuth Park
4365 Mesquite Avenue
(760) 323-8272
Four courts, lighted from 6:00 to 10:00
P.M.

The Plaza Racquet Club
1300 Baristo Road
(760) 323-8997
Nine lighted courts. A privately owned
facility open to the public, this club
charges by the hour and offers equipment rentals as well as lessons.

Ruth Hardy Park
700 Tamarisk Avenue
(760) 323-8272
Eight courts, lighted from 6:00 to 10:00
P.M.

RANCHO MIRAGE

Whitewater Park
71-560 San Jacinto Drive
(760) 324-4511
Four lighted courts.

Bagdouma Community Pool
84-626 Bagdad Avenue, Coachella

Mecca Community Pool
65-250 Coahuilla Street, Mecca
www.indio.org

The swimming pools are outdoors and are
closed in the winter months. When the days
heat up, the pools normally open around
the end of March and stay open through
the summer. The exact days and times vary
according to the season, and according to

The desert wilderness is fragile and carefully protected. If you long to go off-roading, you'll have to do it as a paying guest with one of the local tour companies.

available city funding, so always check the Web site before planning to swim.

Pool rentals are available at all locations on weekend evenings. Reservations must be made in person and paid in full at the time of reservation.

TENNIS

Tennis has always been a big sport in the desert, which has consistently sunny and dry weather even in the dead of winter. The story has it that Charley Farrell and Ralph Bellamy founded the Palm Springs Racquet Club after they were kicked off the courts at El Mirador Hotel. The Racquet Club's main attraction, besides the cocktails and pretty girls around the pool, was its top-notch courts.

Today the Indian Wells Tennis Garden is the site of major tennis tournaments and has hosted virtually every major tennis star in the country. Tournaments for seniors, juniors, and all skill levels abound during the season, and most large hotels offer courts for their guests. Public courts are plentiful in the desert, and though they may not be as luxurious as the ones at the Racquet Club or Tennis Gardens, they are well maintained and very popular. Court time is first-come, first-served, and players are asked to limit their court time to a few games when there are other players in line.

 Many of the desert's public parks make ideal places for reunion picnics, barbecues, and large get-togethers. Just make sure to check with the city's recreation department to get up to speed on rules and regulations.

PUBLIC PARKS

Cathedral City
(760) 770-0340 (City Hall)
www.cathedralcity.gov
Cathedral City has four parks with playground equipment and picnic and barbecue areas. The best of these is Panorama Park, located at the intersection of Tachevah Way and Avenida Maravilla. Panorama Park has tennis and basketball courts, as do the others, but they are of a higher quality here. All of the city's parks are very heavily used, particularly for family gatherings and parties, year-round. Unfortunately, the city has no parks and recreation department and does not treat the parks as a high priority. Any ballplaying is strictly on an ad hoc, pickup game basis, and regular organized recreation does not exist. The parks are open during daylight hours each day.

Indio
www.indio.org
Indio has eight public parks with a variety of amenities, including softball fields, basketball courts, barbecue areas, tennis, and playground equipment. As one of the most family-oriented cities in the desert, Indio has always put parks and public recreation near the top of their quality-of-life priority lists. The parks are well maintained and offer good equipment, spacious grounds, and a friendly environment for picnics, children's play, and basketball or tennis games. Two of the best are North Jackson Park just south of I-10 on Jackson Street, and South Jackson Park at the intersection of Jackson and Date Streets. Both parks have softball fields, barbecue areas, and playground equipment. North Jackson Park also has tennis courts. Call the Planning Department at (760) 342-6541 for park hours and to schedule events.

La Quinta
www.la-quinta.org
La Quinta Community Center (77-865 Avenida Montezuma; 760-564-9921) is a

Palm Desert's Family Parks

Without a doubt, Palm Desert has the valley's best-planned and most extensive public parks and recreation programs. The city began with a plan and has adhered to a long-range vision as a balanced community that provides lots of amenities for its residents as well as super-high-end shopping and dining for visitors. Its serendipitous location right in the middle of the valley cities has made it a magnet for retail, which in turn has churned out sales tax revenue to help fund the parks and keep them in top shape.

The showplace of the city's parks is the Civic Center Park. With an extensive rose garden and sculpture walk, it is also a sprawling, green landscape with a meandering stream, picnic spots, lots of room to run and throw Frisbees, and walking paths that are lighted and well patrolled for a safe, fun outing. The park's huge amphitheater is filled with hundreds of families on hot summer nights, here to enjoy a picnic supper and watch the free movies and concerts. Lighted tennis courts, sand volleyball courts, two skate parks, baseball fields, and two dog parks are part of the complex, which always seems to be expanding and improving.

Palm Desert is part of the Coachella Valley Recreation and Park District (CVRPD), which also covers Indio. The California Association of Recreation and Park Districts has given the CVRPD its award for Outstanding Large District five times, most recently in 2005. It would have been easy and less costly, in the short term, to just let the CVRPD cover the parks part of the city plan. The Palm Desert city council, though, has taken its "balanced city" mission seriously, and the investment in the parks system has paid off by making the city a desirable residence with strong property values.

By using city money to fund the Civic Center Park and several other installations, and relying on the district to take care of the community center, Palm Desert has created a public recreation umbrella that offers something substantial for every age. The community center has a full-size gym with weight rooms, aerobic equipment, racquetball courts, showers, and locker rooms.

Licensed after-school programs, toddler classes to help kids make the transition from home to kindergarten, and camps for times when school is out of session are all available here. Throughout the year, there are youth and adult basketball leagues, adult coed softball games, cross-country track meets, and girls' volleyball. The list goes on. And anyone can enjoy the parks and recreation programs, resident or not. Of course, fees are a bit higher for nonresidents, but they're still a bargain.

newly renovated park that features a lighted baseball field with covered stadium seating, an amphitheater, new lighted basketball courts, a playground, a barbecue area and tables, and a 6,000- square-foot community center, which offers a variety of classes, sports programs, and child care facilities. The only other park in La Quinta is Coral Mountain Regional Park near Avenue 58 and Lake

Although the weather truly is suitable for year-round sports, plan your activity for early in the day if you're here in the summer months. By 10:00 A.M. the temperature is approaching the day's high.

Cahuilla. Coral Mountain has no facilities or recreational equipment.

Palm Desert
Parks and Recreation Department
73-510 Fred Waring Drive
(760) 346-0611
city Web site: www.cityofpalmdesert.org
Palm Desert currently has 12 parks for humans and two for dogs. Combined, the various human parks offer facilities for just about every activity a family could wish for: baseball, softball, and soccer fields; basketball, tennis, shuffleboard, and horseshoe courts; a skate park; picnic areas; tot and toddler lots; playground equipment; and a huge amphitheater for public concerts and movies. One of the most-used parks is Palm Desert Civic Center Park (43-900 San Pablo Avenue; 760-568-9697). Facilities here include softball fields, basketball courts, soccer fields, barbecue areas, playground equipment, tennis and racquetball courts, and walking paths. Palm Desert State Park is located within this park. The Palm Desert Soccer Park (74-735 Hovley Lane) has five lighted soccer fields for different skill levels; basketball, horseshoe, and shuffleboard courts; and playgrounds for little children.

Check the city Web site for new additions, hours, and activities throughout the year.

Palm Springs
Parks and Recreation Department
401 South Pavilion Way
(760) 323-8272
Palm Springs operates eight parks with a wide variety of amenities, including softball fields, batting cages, picnic shelters and barbecue areas, playground equipment, a skate park, a swimming pool, and tennis courts. The best of these are Sunrise Park (adjacent to the Parks and Recreation Department at 401 South Pavilion Way) and DeMuth Park (4365 Mesquite Avenue). Sunrise Park features the Palm Springs Swim Center and expansive park grounds with playground equipment and picnic areas. This park is also adjacent to the city's library and baseball stadium. DeMuth Park is in constant use, with several softball fields, tennis courts, picnic and barbecue areas, and playground equipment.

The city's Web site (www.palmsprings.org) doesn't offer much specific information on park hours or events, but it does have a good annual recreation schedule for downloading.

Rancho Mirage
www.ci.rancho-mirage.ca.us
Whitewater Park (71-560 San Jacinto Drive; 760-324-4511) features four lighted tennis courts, two basketball courts, two racquetball/handball courts, an informal play area, picnic facilities, a children's playground, a life-size fire engine, a water feature, and walking paths.

Rancho Mirage's park system is a true baby compared to those of any of the other valley cities, with minimal acreage and equipment. (Three other smaller parks have no recreational amenities.) On the other hand, Rancho Mirage probably has a smaller percentage of families than the other cities, so the parks do not get a lot of use. Even on the busiest weekends, the tennis and racquetball courts are usually the only areas with waiting lines.

GOLF

The Palm Springs area wasn't always famous as a golf destination. In fact, when the movie stars first made this their preferred playing field, the only sport was tennis or perhaps a leisurely lap around the pool. However, once the first course was built—O'Donnell Golf Club in Palm Springs—the die was cast. The desert's weather makes this the perfect spot for year-round golf, with a few summertime adjustments like teeing off at the crack of dawn. There are now between 100 and 110 courses in the valley, depending on who's counting, Some of the largest estates here have their own minicourses, and even the airport has a putting green.

Major golfing events such as the Bob Hope Chrysler Classic, the Nabisco Championship (formerly the Dinah Shore), and the Skins Game are played and televised here each year. The valley's golf course designers include such top names as Pete Dye, Arnold Palmer, Gary Player, and Ted Robinson—and they have done some of their finest work here in the Coachella Valley.

Dedicated golfers will find a huge selection of course styles, from easy, flat vistas of green to challenging courses filled with hills, desert landscaping, water hazards and tricky transitions. Water reserves from deep natural underground aquifers keep the courses green, and almost all are safeguarding that color with measures that conserve and recycle the water.

In addition to the stunning natural beauty all around, it's the grass, the weather, and the sunshine that make playing golf in the desert a very different and challenging experience.

A lot of golfers come to the valley with experience playing on soft, uniform bent grass, mowed to a cut-velvet consistency. But the desert's scorching summer temperatures make it necessary to have a "double-planting" on each course—a Bermuda base for the summer and an overseeding of bent grass when the days cool off.

Putting on this combo turf can be challenging, as Bermuda seems to have a mind and strong personality of its own. Golf writer Kathy Bissell had these tips for the readers of the *Desert Golf Guide* recently:

- Unless it's cut for the U.S. Open stimpmeter readings, play less break than you would for bent. In fact, if the break looks subtle, sometimes it's best just to hit it straight. Bermuda has grain, which mainly means it sort of bends with the sun. So if you're out first thing in the morning and playing for something bigger than a nickel a hole, look carefully at the grass blades to see if the blades are pointed away from the rising sun. It's like nap on corduroy.
- If you're putting against the direction of the grass blades, your ball is going to come to a stop in a hurry, almost as if it had brakes. And if you're putting with the grass blades, the ball will roll faster and farther, so you don't have to hit it so hard.

A few other tips will make your desert golf experience pleasantly memorable, such as respecting the weather and taking advantage of booking services for tee times at coveted courses.

The ultra-low humidity really does make the temperature feel cooler, and many a golfer has gotten dizzy and sunburned before learning to use sunscreen and drink water throughout the play. Take a cue from the pros—wear a hat or visor and sip water at each tee. Go easy on the alcohol or just save it for the 19th hole, when you can celebrate your score at leisure.

When you take a look at the fees, dues,

and memberships for the courses listed here, you may be tempted to give up and start looking for the nearest miniature golf course, complete with windmills and smiley bear hazards. True, there are clubs that cost $300,000 to join and charge $250 for a single round. But there are also dozens of courses open to the public at very reasonable rates, and many of these are top courses, no matter what they charge. Desert Willow's Firecliff and Mountain View courses in Palm Desert and Landmark Golf Club in Indio—all public-access courses—would likely be exclusive members-only country clubs if they were located anywhere else in the country.

If you're a guest at the Westin Mission Hills in Rancho Mirage, Marriott Desert Springs in Palm Desert, Rancho Las Palmas in Rancho Mirage, or La Quinta Resort & Club in La Quinta, you'll have playing privileges at these world-class facilities.

Most private and semiprivate clubs offer guest privileges to their members, and many have reciprocal agreements with clubs across the country. All in all, there are a lot of options for any golfer who likes variety.

The listings for golf courses are organized first by geography, breaking the valley down into three areas. West Valley includes Sky Valley, Desert Hot Springs, Palm Springs, and Cathedral City. Central Valley covers Rancho Mirage, Palm Desert, Indian Wells, and Thousand Palms. East Valley includes Bermuda Dunes, La Quinta, and Indio. Within these three areas, the courses are grouped according to whether

they are private, private/reciprocal, semiprivate, or public.

When two yardages are given for a course, they are for the men's and women's tees respectively.

PRICE CODE

Unless otherwise indicated, all credit cards are accepted. Price ranges apply to one round of golf for one person in high season. Although no price ranges are given for those golf courses that are private, private/reciprocal, or semiprivate, we have included the latest information on annual membership fees and monthly dues.

$	Up to $25
$$	$26 to $75
$$$	$76 to $150
$$$$	$151 and up

WEST VALLEY

Private Courses

Caliente Springs Golf Course
70200 Dillon Road, Sky Valley
(760) 329-2979
Built in 1998, this is a short 9-hole, par-3 course that is open to members and their guests only. It's built along a hillside and is mostly up and down with no flat lies. A basic clubhouse offers club rental and food and beverages, and there is a driving range. Tee times are first-come, first-served.
Par: 27; **Yardage:** 785/624
Membership fees/dues: $211 annually for individuals; $345 annually for couples

O'Donnell Golf Club
301 North Belardo Road
(760) 325-2259
The desert's original golf course, this is the perfect spot for a mellow game. Set right up against the foothills next to the Palm Springs Art Museum and behind the Hyatt Regency Suites, it's a lovely, peaceful layout with two par 5s and a 207-yard par 3.

Par: 35; **Yardage:** 2655
Membership fees/dues: $6,000 initiation;
$275 monthly

Outdoor Resorts/RV Resort
69-411 Ramon Road, Cathedral City
(760) 324-8638
This is a par-3 course with Bermuda
greens and many of the same features
you would find on a regulation course, at
a reduced size.
Par: 27; **Yardage:** 1801/1771/560
Membership fees/dues: included in residential fees

Private/Reciprocal Courses

Canyon Country Club
1100 Murray Canyon Drive
(760) 327-1321
This 18-hole course was designed by
architect Billy Bell Sr. in 1961 and is a classic, mature course with beautiful groom-
ing. One of the first golf courses in Palm
Springs, it's surrounded by million-dollar
homes and has a breathtaking view of the
hills that shelter the Indian Canyons.
Par: 72; **Yardage:** 6904/6496/6005/5796
Membership fees/dues: $15,000 annually;
$600 monthly

Seven Lakes Country Club
4100 Seven Lakes Drive
(760) 328-9774
This short executive course is kept in top
condition. The par 3s are generally less
than 125 yards, with water on eight of the
holes.
Par: 58; **Yardage:** 2712/2608
Membership fees/dues: $2,000 annually

Semiprivate Courses

Cathedral Canyon Country Club
68-311 El Paseo Real, Cathedral City
(760) 328-6571
The scenic, tree-lined courses are fairly

light and require a variety of shot-making
skills. Water comes into play on almost
every hole.
Par: 72; **Yardage:** 650/6172/5433
Membership fees/dues: $3,500 initiation;
$345 monthly

Date Palm Country Club
36-200 Date Palm Drive, Cathedral City
(760) 328-1315
A Ted Robinson course established in 1971,
this is a mature course dotted with seven
lakes and lined with lovely old trees. No. 8
is the highlight—a 175-yard hole that
needs an accurate tee shot over one of
the lakes.
Par: 58; **Yardage:** 3083
Membership fees/dues: $1,950 annually
for residents

Desert Crest Country Club
16-900 Crest Avenue
(760) 329-8711
Built in 1966 by an unknown architect, this
is a well-maintained, level course with four
lakes, lots of trees, and a consistent 100-
yard average on all the holes.
Par: 72; **Yardage:** 6876/6614/6205/5359
Membership fees/dues: none; greens fees
apply

Desert Princess Country Club
28-555 Landau Boulevard, Cathedral
City
(760) 322-2280
www.desertprincesscc.com
The three courses are mostly flat and well
kept-up, with water coming into play on 17
holes. The Cielo course is located in a wash
and features six holes with a Scottish-links
style.
Par: 72; **Yardage:** 6706/6269/5835/5326
Membership fees/dues: $5,415 annually
for residents; $6,770 annually for nonresi-
dents

Mesquite Golf & Country Club
2700 East Mesquite Avenue
(760) 323-9377
Built in 1985 amidst the condos and apartments of Mesquite Country Club, the

course plays over and along a streambed and is quite a bit more challenging when the stream is running hard after a rainfall. It's flat and well bunkered and has eight small lakes and lots of palm trees.

Par: 72; **Yardage:** 6328/5944/5281

Membership fees/dues: $2,000 initiation; $2,500 annually

Mission Lakes Country Club
8484 Clubhouse Boulevard, Desert Hot Springs
(760) 329-8061

A 1970 Ted Robinson course, this is often windy where three of the holes are located into the mountains. The long par 3s are also a challenge—five of them measure 200 yards or more.

Par: 71; **Yardage:** 6742/6404/5862/ 6401/5862/5505

Membership fees/dues: $209 monthly for residents only

Public Courses

Cimarrón Golf Resort $$$
67-603 30th Avenue, Cathedral City
(760) 770-6060
www.cimarrongolf.com

This is a 36-hole links-type course designed by John Fought in 1999. It has gorgeous views from all angles and large greens with subtle breaks. It's a challenging layout that will have even seasoned golfers fighting for par. Walking is allowed, and tee times can be booked 60 days in advance with a credit card.

Par: 71; **Yardage:** 6858/6474/5879/5127 (long course)

Par: 56; **Yardage:** 3156 (short course)

For the very best deals on clothes and gear, check the pro shops at the country clubs. If you're the guest of a member, you can get amazing prices that beat those of the best discount place.

Desert Dunes $$-$$$ winter
Golf Course $$ summer
18-550 Palm Drive, Desert Hot Springs
(760) 251-5368
www.desertdunesgolfclub.net

Robert Trent Jones Jr. designed this course in 1989, giving it a unique Scottish-links style with natural sand dunes. The par-3 fifth hole needs a long tee shot over desert landscaping to a sharply undulating green.

Par: 72; **Yardage:** 6876/6614/6205/5359

Hidden Springs Country Club
15-500 Bubbling Wells Road
Desert Hot Springs
(760) 329-8816

This is a fairly long, well-kept executive course with three ponds and Bermuda greens.

Par: 29; **Yardage:** 1506/1410

Membership fees/dues: $800 single/ $1,050 couple for residents; $900 single/ $1150 couple for nonresidents

Indian Canyons $$-$$$ winter
Golf Course $$ summer
1097 Murray Canyon Drive
(760) 327-6550

Formerly known as Canyon South, this is one of the most scenic and windless courses in the valley. It's right up against the Indian Canyons on the southern edge of Palm Springs, and the views are magnificent. There are some tough par 3s to test your skills.

Par: 71; **Yardage:** 6328/5944/5281

Palm Springs $-$$ winter
Country Club $ summer
2500 Whitewater Club Drive
(760) 323-2626

Built in 1957, this is a mature course with tree-lined fairways and greens that are both well conditioned and well protected.

Par: 72; **Yardage:** 6201/5869/5129

Sands RV Country Club
16-400 Bubbling Wells Road,
Desert Hot Springs
(760) 251-1173
This short, wide, 9-hole course is a beginner's dream, with few trees and no bunkers.
Par: 32; **Yardage:** 2127/1832
Membership fees/dues: $600 annually

Tahquitz Creek $$-$$$ winter
Golf Resort $-$$ summer
1885 Golf Club Drive
(760) 328-1005
Billy Bell Sr. built one of the courses in 1957, and Ted Robinson added his touch to the other in 1995. The Legend is a well-maintained, tree-lined course with lots of shade in the summer. The Resort course has water in play on seven holes, with No. 7 featuring an island fairway.
Par: 72; **Yardage:** 6649/6249/5828/5206

Tommy Jacobs $$ winter
Bel Air Greens $ summer
1001 South El Cielo
(760) 322-6062
www.tommyjacobsbelairgreens.com
A 9-hole executive course owned by former PGA player Tommy Jacobs, this features Bermuda greens and short holes, with water on five of the holes and strategically placed traps.
Par: 32; **Yardage:** 1768/1570/1397

CENTRAL VALLEY
Private Courses

Avondale Golf Club
75-800 Avondale Drive, Palm Desert
(760) 345-3712
This 18-hole desert course has tree-lined fairways and two big lakes surrounded by undisturbed mountain views.
Par: 72; **Yardage:** 6782/6400/5781/5501
Membership fees/dues: $12,500 initiation; $485 monthly

Bighorn Golf Club
255 Palowet Drive, Palm Desert
(760) 341-4653
Bighorn, one of the top courses in the valley, was built in 1991 and 1998 by Arthur Hills and Tom Fazio. Carved into the Santa Rosa Mountains off Highway 74, it's a dramatic and challenging course with ups and down that can be as much as 400 feet. The views of the mountains and desert below are gorgeous.
Par: 72; **Yardage:** 7049/6648/6235/5764/5012
Membership fees/dues: $350,000 initiation; $20,000 annually

Chaparral Country Club
100 Chaparral Drive, Palm Desert
(760) 340-1501
A Ted Robinson–designed 18-hole executive course with lots of bunkers and water on 13 holes, this is known as the "little monster."
Par: 60; **Yardage:** 3916/3664/3269/3103
Membership fees/dues: $7,500 initiation; $1,450 annually

The Club at Morningside
39-033 Morningside Drive
(760) 321-1555
A Jack Nicklaus 18-hole links-style course, this is a test of skill all the way through, with contoured fairways, water hazards, and deep bunkers.
Par: 72; **Yardage:** 6773/6404/6200/5618/5448
Membership fees/dues: $100,000 initiation for equity members; $45,000 for nonequity members; $13,000 monthly

Desert Horizons Country Club
44-900 Desert Horizons Drive, Indian Wells
(760) 340-4651
A challenging championship 18 holes, this course is known for the ninth hole, a skill test that requires a 180-yard shot over water to a three-tiered, hourglass-shaped green.

A favorite pastime is playing golf on one of the more than 100 courses in the Palm Springs area. PHOTO BY JACK HOLLINGSWORTH, COURTESY OF THE PALM SPRINGS DESERT RESORTS CONVENTION AND VISITORS AUTHORITY

Par: 72; **Yardage:** 6609/6163/5792/5458 **Membership fees/dues:** $50,000 initiation; $975 annually

Desert Island Golf & Country Club
71-777 Frank Sinatra Drive, Rancho Mirage
(760) 328-0841
This 18-hole course wraps around a huge lake that surrounds an island housing the Desert Island condos. Narrow fairways and lots of bunkers surrounding the greens make it a challenge.
Par: 72; **Yardage:** 6686/6310/5705/5604

Membership fees/dues: initiation varies; $567 monthly

Eldorado Country Club
46000 Fairway Drive, Indian Wells
(760) 345–4770, ext. 3331
One of the desert's oldest courses, Eldorado is mature and well maintained. It's mostly level with out-of-bounds on every hole.
Par: 72; **Yardage:** 6808/6346/5856/5330 **Membership fees/dues:** $130,000 initiation; $14,000 annually

Indian Ridge Country Club
76-375 Country Club Drive, Palm Desert
(760) 772-7222
Arnold Palmer designed these 36 holes with strategically placed bunkers and good use of water. Successful play demands a bit of planning. The greens are large and curvy, with wide contoured fairways.
Par: 72; **Yardage:** 6915/6671/6289/5914
Membership fees/dues: $95,000 initiation; $840 monthly

Ironwood Country Club
49-200 Mariposa, Palm Desert
(760) 346-7811
The scenic South course is rated among the desert's toughest, winding through the desert with many challenging holes from the back tees. The easier North course has great views as well, with water hazards and fairways lines with condos and homes.
Par: 72; **Yardage:** 7265/6902/6489/5608 (South course)
Par: 70; **Yardage:** 6065/5696/5248 (North course)
Membership fees/dues: initiation amount on request; $710 monthly

The Lakes Country Club
161 Old Ranch Road, Palm Desert
(760) 568-4321, ext. 134
With water on 23 of the 27 holes, this beautiful course also features rolling terrain and lots of bunkers, making it a good challenge for an average golfer.
Par: 72; **Yardage:** 6700/6283/5703/5378 (North/East nines)
Par: 72; **Yardage:** 6630/6220/5688/4996 (East/South nines)
Membership fees/dues: no initiation fee; $4,500 annually for homeowners only

Monterey Country Club
41-500 Monterey Avenue, Palm Desert
(760) 346-1115
Another Ted Robinson 27-holer, this is a tight target course with narrow fairways lined with condos on both sides, and lots of bunkers and water.

Par: 71; **Yardage:** 6108/5790/5264 (East/West nines)
Par: 72; **Yardage:** 6185/5898/5417 (West/South nines)
Par: 71; **Yardage:** 6005/5720/5698/5231 (East/South nines)
Membership fees/dues: $7,000 initiation; $436 monthly for individuals; $467 monthly for couples

Palm Desert Greens Golf
73-750 Country Club Drive, Palm Desert
(760) 346-2941
Only in the desert would you find a lovely executive 18-hole course in the middle of a mobile home park. Bermuda greens are large and beautifully maintained.
Par: 63; **Yardage:** 4079/3681
Membership fees/dues: included in residential fees

Portola Country Club
42-500 Portola Avenue, Palm Desert
(760) 568-1592
Another mobile home park and another 18-hole golf course. This one is located on 27 acres with many lakes and water hazards.
Par: 54; **Yardage:** 2124/1913
Membership fees/dues: included in residential fees

The Reserve
74-001 Reserve Drive, Indian Wells
(760) 837-4840
Built up against the mountains in one of the desert's most exclusive country clubs, this 18-hole course can be tricky. The subtle elevations fool most newcomers, who soon find that they need to step up the club work.
Par: 72; **Yardage:** 7034/6556/5946/5380

Summer rates for play are dramatically lower than those for high season. Just be sure to book the earliest possible tee times. By 10:00 A.M. the thermometer is well on its way to 100, and the afternoons from 1:00 until after sundown are the hottest parts of the day.

Membership fees/dues: $250,000 initiation; $19,000 annually

Shadow Mountain Resort
45-700 San Luis Rey, Palm Desert
(760) 346-8242
The facility includes a clubhouse, driving range, putting green, gear rental, and snack bar. The 18-hole course has lots of palm trees, a bit of water, and lots of bunkers.
Par: 70; **Yardage:** 5393/5154
Membership fees/dues: $1,500 initiation; $298 monthly

The Springs Club
1 Duke Drive, Rancho Mirage
(760) 328-0590
Water is a factor on 11 of the 18 holes, and the undulating greens have lots of bunkers. Fairways are well kept and lined with mature trees.
Par: 72; **Yardage:** 6637/6279/5889/5614
Membership fees/dues: $25,000 initiation; $770 monthly

Tamarisk Country Club
70-240 Frank Sinatra Drive
Rancho Mirage
(760) 328-2141
Established by Billy Bell Sr. in 1952 and remodeled by Ron Fream in 1987, this is a mature course with lots of trees. It's mostly flat, but the putting greens have breaks that will be a challenge. New tees were built in 2004.
Par: 72; **Yardage:** 7003/6623/6303/5996/5652
Membership fees/dues: $80,000 initiation; $10,920 annually

Thunderbird Country Club
70-612 Highway 111, Rancho Mirage
(760) 770-6199
This is one of the desert's first clubs and is still one of the most exclusive. This was Frank Sinatra's desert headquarters when he was alive. It's a flat, narrow course with water, bunkers, and palm trees to create a few challenges.

Par: 71 (men's), 72 (women's); **Yardage:** 6460/6179/5854
Membership fees/dues: $100,000 initiation; $12,500 annually

Toscana
43-199 Via Lucca, Indian Wells
(760) 404-1444
Built in 2004, this is the first Palm Springs–area golf course designed by Jack Nicklaus in more than 15 years. Two courses, each designed to play at more than 7,300 yards from the "golden bear" tees, have separate tees to give variety.
Par: 72; **Yardage:** 7349/7048/6863/6562/6336/6043/5990
Membership fees/dues: $120,000 initiation; $1,000 monthly

Tri-Palms Estates Country Club
32-700 Desert Moon, Thousand Palms
(760) 343-3669
This is a fairly average 18-hole course, with water on most of the holes and wide fairways.
Par: 70 (men's), 72 (women's); **Yardage:** 5465/5346
Membership fees/dues: included in residential fees

The Vintage Club
75-001 Vintage Drive West, Indian Wells
(760) 862-2076
A Tom and George Fazio design, this is one of the most sought-after courses. The Desert course is short and tight with compact little greens that demand precise shots. The Mountain course is just the opposite—a wide-open layout for easy drives.
Par: 72; **Yardage:** 6301/5892/5664/4770 (Desert course)
Par: 72; **Yardage:** 6830/6422/6045/5663/5166 (Mountain course)
Membership fees/dues: $300,000 initiation; $21,000 annually

Private/Reciprocal Courses

Indian Wells Country Club
46-000 Club Drive, Indian Wells
(760) 345-2561

Harry Rainville designed the first 27 holes in 1956, and Ted Robinson came along to build the next nine in 2001. The Cove is a rolling course with wide-open fairways, large greens, a few doglegs, and water on three holes. The Classic features lots of mature trees, a few elevated greens, and a good amount of water and bunkers.
Par: 72; **Yardage:** 6478/6095/5665 (Classic course)
Par: 72; **Yardage:** 6558/6229/5658 (Cove course)
Membership fees/dues: $48,500 initiation; $580 monthly

Marrakesh Country Club
47-000 Marrakesh Drive, Rancho Mirage
(760) 568-2660

A Ted Robinson course established in 1967, this is much harder than it looks. There are lots of bunkers, hilly terrain, four lakes, and strategically placed trees. The longest par 4 is 304 yards.
Par: 60; **Yardage:** 3614/3497/3220
Membership fees/dues: $12,500 initiation; $2,100 annually

Mission Hills Country Club
34-600 Mission Hills Drive
Rancho Mirage
(760) 324-7336

With 54 holes and a variety of architects, including Pete Dye, Desmond Muirhead, Ed Seay, and Arnold Palmer, Mission Hills offers a great variety of different skill levels. The Arnold Palmer course features a flat link-style layout with Tiff Dwarf greens and lots of bunkers. Pete Dye's Challenge course is a stadium setup with rolling hills and very deep bunkers. Undulating greens, mature trees, and gently rolling terrain are the signatures on the Dinah Shore course.

Par: 72; **Yardage:** 7221/6906/6286/5684
Membership fees/dues: $50,000 initiation; $624 monthly

Palm Valley Country Club
76-200 Country Club Drive, Palm Desert
(760) 345-2742

Ted Robinson designed the Championship course with sharply undulating greens and spectacular views. The Challenge course is a tough, short challenge with water hazards on 15 holes.
Par: 63; **Yardage:** 4232/3909/3433 (Challenge course)
Par: 72; **Yardage:** 6545/6191/5724/5295 (Championship course)
Membership fees/dues: $30,000 initiation; $555 monthly

Santa Rosa Country Club
38-105 Portola Avenue, Palm Desert
(760) 568-5717

A desert course with 18 holes on 80 acres, this is a challenging layout, with two large lakes and tree-lined fairways.
Par: 70; **Yardage:** 5568/5271/4750
Membership fees/dues: $1,500 initiation; $290 monthly

Sunrise Country Club
71-601 Country Club Drive, Palm Desert
(760) 328-1139

A mature 18-hole executive course, this will have you reaching for every different club to deal with the water and sand.
Par: 64; **Yardage:** 3837
Membership fees/dues: $5,000 initiation for equity members; $156 monthly

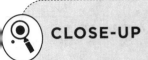

Bob Hope Chrysler Classic

The Palm Springs Golf Classic—now the Bob Hope Chrysler Classic—was played for the first time in 1960, and its first winner was golf legend Arnold Palmer, who set a tournament record of 22 under par that remained unbroken for almost 20 years. That year, Arnie went on to chalk up eight more victories, dominating the field in his best year as a pro. Five months after winning the Classic, he shot a final round 65 to make one of the most dramatic comebacks in the history of the U.S. Open. That game made him a legend and elevated golf into the national consciousness as a top sport. Palmer won the Classic again in 1962 and 1968 and was a runner-up in 1965 and 1966.

The Classic's early years determined the format and traditions, which remain to this day. Bob Rosburg is credited with creating the tournament's unique five-day format played over four different courses. The founding courses played were Thunderbird, Tamarisk, Bermuda Dunes, and Indian Wells Country Clubs. The tradition of the Classic Girls began in the event's early years, with the earliest tournaments having a Classic Queen. Debbie Reynolds, Jane Powell, and Jill St. John were early titleholders.

From the very first year, the Classic attracted Hollywood's hottest stars to compete in the tournament's pro-am competition: Bing Crosby, Burt Lancaster, Kirk Douglas, Phil Harris, Desi Arnaz, Ray Bolger and Hoagy Carmichael. Dwight Eisenhower was the first former president to play in the tournament. Bob Hope, the biggest star of all, played in the early years, added his name to the tournament (the Bob Hope Desert Classic) in 1965, and later became the Classic's chairman of the board. The Classic had another huge draw—a $50,000 prize offered for a hole in one. For the first three years of the tournament, the Classic purchased an insurance policy from Lloyd's of London for a hole-in-one payoff—and the $50,000 was won in each of these years.

The combination of Arnie's victories and the hole-in-one bonanza were strokes of marketing genius and luck, and the Classic, which was televised for the first time in 1961, was a prime factor in making the sport popular. The annual tournament also brought images of the desert into homes all across the country, promoting the desert's sun and lifestyle in the winter when the rest of the nation was locked deep in ice and snow.

Frank Sinatra made his Classic debut in 1972. Other stars of the era who played often were Jack Benny, Andy Williams, Lawrence Welk, Sammy Davis Jr., Jackie Gleason, and Dean Martin. Gerald Ford joined the field in 1977, making him the second former president to play in the tournament. Willie Mays, Joe Louis, Johnny Bench, Merlin Olsen, John McKay, Maury Wills, and Bear Bryant were among the sports-world stars who teed it up in the Classic during the 1970s. Barbara Eden was the first Classic Queen of the '70s, reigning over a court that wore outfits with "Bob," "Hope," and "Classic" emblazoned across the front. Other queens during the decade were Gloria Loring, Brucence Smith, Linda Carter, Lexie Brockway, and Terry Ann Browning. The last four also held the title of Miss World USA. Beginning in 1975 the Bob Hope Classic Girls became the ambassadors of the Classic, as there was no longer a queen. By this time, Bermuda Dunes, Indian Wells, and La Quinta served as the host courses on a rotating basis. Eldorado and Tamarisk rotated as the fourth course in the lineup each year.

In the 1980s Chrysler, which had been a major sponsor for several years, added its name as title sponsor, increasing the total purse by 228 percent. A new course, PGA West, joined the course rotation in 1987, and the game became even more competitive, with 10 different winners in 10 years.

The biggest single news event at the Classic during the 1990s didn't even involve the world's top professionals. In 1995, the team of President Bill Clinton, President George H. W. Bush, President Gerald R. Ford, tournament host Bob Hope, and defending champion Scott Hoch teed it up for the tournament's opening round. This was the first time a sitting president had played during a PGA Tour event and perhaps the first time three presidents had played together—ever.

In 1990 the tournament began with a $1 million purse, increasing to $3 million in 1999. Today, for the first time in its history, the Classic has its own permanent course, a development that will allow more money to go to charity. The Classic Club, as it is known, has 40 acres of landscape, with 30 acres of lake and water features, 14 bridges, 150 acres of turf, and almost 5,000 specimen pine trees. It is joined by Bermuda Dunes Country Club, La Quinta Country Club, and PGA West for the five days of play. It is a semi-private, daily-fee golf course, so members of the public can hit balls on the same greens as the giants of the game.

Over the years the Classic has donated more than $42 million to desert charities, helping support and sustain every good cause, from Guide Dogs of the Desert to Eisenhower Medical Center. The Classic Ball is still the most prestigious charity event around, with tickets selling for $500 a person and every heavy hitter in town showing up for a glimpse of the winners and the stars who will entertain them. Since its very first year, this star-filled sports event has been a vital player in the valley's life, bringing in thousands of visitors, millions of dollars, and priceless publicity from all over the world.

Semiprivate Courses

Desert Falls Country Club
1111 Desert Falls Parkway, Palm Desert
(760) 340-4653
www.desert-falls.com
One of the few courses in the area with a Scottish links-style design, this is a long 18-hole course with very large greens.
Par: 72; **Yardage:** 7084/6702/6230/5792/5298
Membership fees/dues: $17,000 initiation; $4,740 annually

Ivey Ranch Country Club
74-580 Varner Road, Thousand Palms
(760) 343-2013
A regulation 9-hole course, this has doglegs and out-of-bounds on several holes. The greens are bent grass, and the fairways are narrow.
Par: 70; **Yardage:** 2633/2473/2322
Membership fees/dues: $2,500 initiation; $2,300 annually

Rancho Las Palmas Country Club
42-000 Bob Hope Drive, Rancho Mirage
(760) 862-4551
There are three separate Ted Robinson courses: the North is hilly and long; the South winds through condos and is quite narrow; and the West is a short play with the most water and best scenery.
Par: 71; **Yardage:** 6113/5677/5290 (West/North nines)
Par: 71; **Yardage:** 6025/5662/5300 (North/South nines)
Par: 70; **Yardage:** 6128/5725/5256 (West/South nines)
Membership fees/dues: no initiation; $4,150 single/$5,100 family annually

Mountain Vista Golf Club at Sun City Palm Desert
38-256 Del Webb Boulevard
Palm Desert
(760) 200-2200
Most of the 36 holes are bordered by homes on this flat, roomy course with large greens and little elevation change. There are water hazards on 11 holes.

Par: 72; **Yardage:** 6720/6162/5305 (Santa Rosa course)
Par: 72; **Yardage:** 6669/6202/5635/5053 (San Gorgonio course)
Membership fees/dues: no initiation; $4,385 annually for 150 rounds

Oasis Country Club
42-300 Casbah Way, Palm Desert
(760) 345-2715
With 22 lakes and excellent greens, this is one of the most fun courses in the area. There are six par 4s and 12 par 3s.
Par: 60; **Yardage:** 3489/3118/2728
Membership fees/dues: $2,200 initiation; $2,700 annually

Palm Desert Country Club
77-200 California Drive, Palm Desert
(760) 345-2525
Billy Bell Sr. designed these 27 holes in 1958, and they've matured nicely. The wide fairways are challenging and lined with trees. Maintenance is very good, with recently added trees, flower beds, and bunkers.
Par: 72; **Yardage:** 6643/6370/5843 (Regulation course)
Par: 60; **Yardage:** 1635/1539
Membership fees/dues: $2,200 initiation; $3,900 annually

Palm Desert Resort Country Club
77-333 Country Club Drive, Palm Desert
(760) 345-2781
These 18 holes are in top condition, with many bunkers, nine lakes, bent-grass greens, and wide fairways.
Par: 72; **Yardage:** 6616/6343/5978/5462
Membership fees/dues: $3,500 initiation; $5,000 annually

Rancho Mirage Country Club
38-500 Bob Hope Drive, Rancho Mirage
(760) 324-4711
A gentle, rolling 18 holes with tight fairways and small greens, this offers a good challenge for skilled golfers.
Par: 70 (men's), 72 (women's); **Yardage:** 6111/5823/5309

Membership fees/dues: $7,500 initiation; $3,600 annually

Suncrest Country Club
73-450 Country Club Drive, Palm Desert
(760) 340-2467
A longer-than-average 9-hole executive course, Suncrest has bunkered greens and two holes with water.
Par: 66; **Yardage:** 2473/2250
Membership fees/dues: $1,505 annually for residents

Woodhaven Country Club
41-555 Woodhaven Drive East, Palm Desert
(760) 345-7513
A tough course set in the midst of condos, these 18 holes feature narrow fairways, small greens, and lots of trees, bunkers, and water.
Par: 70; **Yardage:** 5794/5254
Membership fees/dues: $5,000 initiation; $3,000 annually for residents; $4,000 annually for nonresidents.

Public Courses

Desert Springs
JW Marriott   **$$$ winter**
Resort and Spa   **$$ summer**
74855 Country Club Drive, Palm Desert
(760) 341-1756
Both courses have wide fairways surrounded by bunkers, lakes, and palm trees. They are mostly level, are beautifully kept up, and allow for lots of wiggle room off the tee.
Par: 72; **Yardage:** 6761/6381/6143/5492 (Palms course)
Par: 72; **Yardage:** 6627/6323/6023/5262 (Valley course)

Desert Willow   **$$$$ winter**
Golf Resort   **$$–$$$ summer**
38-995 Desert Willow Drive
Palm Desert
(760) 346-7060
www.desertwillow.com

Every golfer needs a guru, and a great place to find one is the Faldo Golf Institute at Marriott's Shadow Ridge. Short-game and full-swing sessions include a coupon for a round of golf and a video analysis comparing your swing with Masters champion Nick Faldo. Call (760) 674-2700.

This 36-hole course offers five sets of tees for golfers at all skill levels and is one of the most beautiful in the desert, combining true desert landscaping with more traditional "greenscapes." Do your best to stay in the fairways or you'll be deep into sand at every turn.
Par: 72; **Yardage:** 7056/6676/6173/5642/5079 (Firecliff course)
Par: 72; **Yardage:** 6913/6470/6097/5573/5040 (Mountain View course)

Emerald Desert   **$$ winter**
Country Club   **$ summer**
76-000 Frank Sinatra, Palm Desert
(760) 345-4770, ext. 3331
This 9-hole course has six lakes, bentgrass greens surrounded by sand traps, and narrow fairways.
Par: 28; **Yardage:** 1325/1246

The Golf Center at Palm Desert   **$**
74-945 Sheryl Drive, Palm Desert
(760) 779-1877
This 9-hole course, with driving ranges and eager-to-help instructors, is a good place for beginners to learn.
Par: 27; **Yardage:** 1056/875

The Golf Resort   **$$$ winter**
at Indian Wells   **$$ summer**
44-500 Indian Wells Lane, Indian Wells
(760) 346-4653
www.golfresortatindianwells.com
Ted Robinson designed this 36-hole layout in 1986, and each 18-hole course has three tee positions. The greens are beautiful, with excellent views from the shorter West course. The East course features lots

of water hazards and rolling, parallel fairways.
Par: 72; **Yardage:** 6500/6157/5408

Marriott's Shadow   **$$$ winter**
Ridge Resort   **$$ summer**
9002 Shadow Ridge Road, Palm Desert
(760) 674-2700
www.golfshadowridge.com
This 18-hole desert course, designed by
Nick Faldo in 2000, is a challenge, with
large greens and bunkers, elevation
changes, and waste areas.
Par: 71; **Yardage:** 7006/6621/6204/5158

Mission Hills   **$$$ winter**
North   **$$ summer**
70-705 Ramon Road, Rancho Mirage
(760) 770-9496
www.troongolf.com
This is a heavily landscaped Gary Player
course with rolling fairways, bunkers, and
lakes dotted over the 18 holes.
Par: 72; **Yardage:** 7062/6643/6044/4907

Pete Dye at Westin   **$$$ winter**
Mission Hills Resort   **$$ summer**
71-501 Dinah Shore Drive
Rancho Mirage
(760) 328-3198
www.troongolf.com
A links-style layout with large, curving
greens and rolling fairways, this 18-holer
features lots of pot bunkers and railroad
ties.
Par: 70; **Yardage:** 6706/6158/5587/4841

EAST VALLEY

Private Courses

Bermuda Dunes Country Club
42-360 Adams Street, Bermuda Dunes
(760) 345-2771
A 1959 Billy Bell Sr. course, this features
hilly terrain with trees lining the fairways
and a few water hazards.
Par: 72; **Yardage:** 6927/6542/6081/5484
(One and Two nines)
Par: 72; **Yardage:** 6716/6360/5857/5484

(Three and One nines)
Par: 72; **Yardage:** 6749/6434/6016/5410
(Two and Three nines)
Membership fees/dues: $25,000 initiation;
$590 monthly

The Club at PGA West
55-955 PGA Boulevard, La Quinta
(760) 564-3980
www.pgawest.com
PGA West is one the desert's most coveted plays, and the three different courses
offer a lot of variety. The Nicklaus course
is beautifully landscaped with flowers,
desert grasses, and water off the fairways.
The Weiskopf is long and challenging, and
the Palmer is one of the most challenging,
long-play courses in the valley.
Par: 72; **Yardage:** 6951/6365/5658/4822
(Jack Nicklaus)
Par: 72; **Yardage:** 6950/6462/5995/5226
(Arnold Palmer)
Par: 72; **Yardage:** 7165/6654/6129/5536
(Tom Weiskopf)
Membership fees/dues: $110,000 initiation; $674 monthly

The Hideaway
52-500 Village Club Drive, La Quinta
(760) 777-7400
www.hideawaygolfclub.com
A 2001 Pete Dye 36, this has water on
every hole but one. Fairways are long and
rolling, greens are large, and there are lots
of bunkers and doglegs.
Par: 72; **Yardage:** 7337/6752/6206/5574/
5160 (Pete's course)
Par: 72; **Yardage:** 6963/6462/5921/5503/
5201 (Clive's course)
Membership fees/dues: $150,000 initiation; $750 monthly

La Quinta Country Club
77-750 50th Avenue, La Quinta
(760) 564-4151
www.laquintaresort.com
Driving accuracy is the demand on this
mature course with lakes, bunkers, undulating greens, and fairways lined with trees.
Par: 72; **Yardage:** 7060/6554/6175/
5786/5338

Membership fees/dues: $60,000 initiation; $708 monthly

La Quinta Resort & Club: Citrus Course
50-503 Jefferson Street, La Quinta
(760) 564-7620
www.laquintaresort.com
Pete Dye put some moxie into this design, offering an abundance of sand and water, bent-grass greens, and stunning views.
Par: 72; **Yardage:** 7151/6811/6396/5641/5326
Membership fees/dues: $92,500 initiation; $609 monthly

Mountain View Country Club
80-375 Pomelo, La Quinta
(760) 771-4311
A 2003 Arnold Palmer stunner, this 18-holer is becoming very popular, offering a strategic challenge for the skilled player and some satisfaction for the midlevel golfer.
Par: 72; **Yardage:** 7386/6845/6319/5697/5340
Membership fees/dues: $82,000 initiation; $7,500 monthly

Outdoor Resorts/Indio Motorcoach Resort
80-394 Avenue 48, Indio
(760) 775-7255
www.outdoor-resorts-indio.com
This is an extremely short, par-3, 18-hole course with small, well-protected greens.
Par: 64; **Yardage:** 1456
Membership fees/dues: included in residential fees

The Palms Golf Club
57-000 Palm Drive, La Quinta
(760) 771-2606
www.thepalmsgc.org
This 18-holer is a park-style course cut out of the middle of a date drove. A stream comes into play on a few holes, and there are some sharp doglegs.
Par: 70 (men's), 71 (women's); **Yardage:** 7029/6642/6244/5557
Membership fees/dues: $40,000 initiation; $428 monthly

The Plantation
50-664 Monroe Street, Indio
(760) 775-3688
A Brian Curley–Fred Couples design on the desert floor, this 18-holer still offers a good test, with its good use of mounds and bunkers.
Par: 72; **Yardage:** 7049/6591/6181
Membership fees/dues: $50,000 initiation; $6,000 annually

The Quarry at La Quinta
1 Quarry Lane, La Quinta
(760) 777-1100
An absolutely stunning Tom Fazio design, this 18-holer winds through 375 acres and an abandoned rock quarry. The entire course is sodded, and a spectacular 70-foot waterfall is the background for the 10th and 17th holes.
Par: 72; **Yardage:** 7083/6634/6248/5882/5226
Membership fees/dues: $150,000 initiation; $1,250 monthly

Rancho Casa Blanco Country Club
84-136 Avenue 44, Indio
(760) 775-7116
Bermuda greens, water, and bunkers dot this short, pretty course.
Par: 54; **Yardage:** 1302
Membership fees/dues: included in residential fees

Rancho La Quinta Country Club
48-500 Washington Street, La Quinta
(760) 777-7799
In 1993 Robert Trent Jones Jr. designed a traditional course with large greens and a beautiful, tranquil setting. Jerry Pate came along in 2000 with a dramatically oversize companion, all spacious greens, large

Winter days are perfect for golfers—dry, sunny, and warm. Just remember that the sun goes down as early as 4:00 P.M. and the temperature drops dramatically at the same time.

lakes, and lots of desert landscaping.
Par: 72; **Yardage:** 7063/6452/5986/5311
(Jones course)
Par: 72; **Yardage:** 6972/6474/5941/5224
(Pate course)
Membership fees/dues: $105,000 initiation; $675 monthly

The Tradition
78-505 Old Avenue 52, La Quinta
(760) 564-1067
A traditional Arnold Palmer 18, this goes out of the box with five par 5s and five par 3s. The 17th hole is a short par 4 raised 150 feet above the green.
Par: 72; **Yardage:** 6541/6163/6085/5540
Membership fees/dues: $150,000 initiation; $14,400 annually

Semiprivate Courses

Heritage Palms Golf Club
80-055 Fred Waring Drive, Indio
(760) 772-7334
A well-maintained 18 holes with excellent mountain views, this has a signature fourth hole, a par 4 with a lake running down one side.
Par: 72; **Yardage:** 6727/6293/5577/4885
Membership fees/dues: $2,950 annually for residents only

Indian Palms Country Club
48-630 Monroe Street, Indio
(760) 347-2326
A real old-timer, this still has the original nines built in 1948. The other two nines were built around 1980. One of those, the Royal, has water hazards on eight holes.
Par: 71; **Yardage:** 6709/6439/5859
(Indian/Mountain course)
Par: 71; **Yardage:** 6713/6254/5622 (Mountain/Royal course)
Par: 71; **Yardage:** 6700/6227/5547
(Indian/Royal course)
Membership fees/dues: $3,475 annually

Indian Springs Country Club
79-940 Westward Ho, La Quinta
(760) 200-8988
www.indianspringsgc.com
Originally built by John Gurley Sr. in 1962, the 18 holes were rebuilt by Dave Ginkel in 2000, featuring several bunkers and lakes with contoured freeways.
Par: 72; **Yardage:** 6741/6104/5297
Membership fees/dues: $4,000 annually for homeowners; $4,500 for others

La Quinta Resort & Club: Mountain and Dunes Courses
50-200 Avenue Vista Bonita, La Quinta
(760) 564-7610
www.laquintaresort.com
Both courses have the traditional Pete Dye railroad ties used in the many bunkers. Greens are large and undulating. The Dunes course has plentiful water hazards, and the Mountain course features a natural setting up against the Santa Rosa Mountains.
Par: 72; **Yardage:** 6747/6230/5735/5222
(Dunes course)
Par: 72; **Yardage:** 6756/6230/5481/5219/4894 (Mountain course)
Membership fees/dues: included with Citrus course

Norman Course PGA West
50-664 Monroe Street, Indio
(760) 775-3688
www.pgawest.com
Greg Norman's 2000 design uses desert landscaping in a links-style course with some contouring and lots of penalties for the golfer who strays from the fairway.
Par: 72; **Yardage:** 7049/6591/6181
Membership fees/dues: $50,000 initiation; $6,000 annually

PGA West Resort Courses
56-150 PGA Boulevard, La Quinta
(760) 564-7170
www.pgawest.com
Pete Dye designed the Stadium course in 1986, and he stuffed it full of deep pot bunkers, sand, water, and sidehill lies. Jack Nicklaus's companion course, designed in 1987, is a quieter brother, with elevated

tees, huge tiered greens, and forced shots over water.
Par: 72; **Yardage:** 7266/6739/6166/5700/5092 (TPC Stadium course)
Par: 72; **Yardage:** 7204/6522/6061/5627/5023 (Nicklaus Tournament)
Membership fees/dues: $110,000 initiation; $645 monthly

Shadow Hills
80875 Avenue 40, Indio
(760) 200-3375
Established in 2004 with a second nine opening this year, this course is a test for skilled players, while still giving some slack to those who are out for the fun of it.
Par: 35; **Yardage:** 3235/2385 (9 holes); 6730/5043 (18 holes)
Membership fees/dues: included with residence

Public Courses

Indio Golf Course $
83-040 Avenue 42, Indio
(760) 347-9156
This is one of the longest par-3 courses in the entire country, with holes that range from 120 to 240 yards. A 1964 Larry Hughes 18-holer, it gets lots of play year-round.
Par: 54; **Yardage:** 3004/2662

Landmark $$$ winter
Golf Club $$ summer
84-000 Landmark Parkway, Indio
(760) 775-2000
www.landmarkgc.com
These two courses are both a challenge and a delight to play, with the natural setting and variety of terrain. Three lakes, rolling sand dunes, desert plantings, lots of slopes, and different soil types keep it interesting.
Par: 72; **Yardage:** 7123/6510/5856/5015 (North course)
Par: 72; **Yardage:** 7044/6500/5905/5094 (South course)

Palm Royale $$ winter
Country Club $ summer
78-259 Indigo Drive, La Quinta
(760) 345-9701
An 18-hole, 1985 Ted Robinson design, this has a short par 3 and lots of hazards—water on nine holes, palms lining the greens, and lots of bunkers and grass humps.
Par: 54; **Yardage:** 1984/1689

SilverRock $$$ winter
Resort $$ summer
79-179 Ahmanson Lane, La Quinta
(888) 600-7272
www.silverrock.org
This is Arnold Palmer's newest course—opened in 2005—and it was chosen as a host course for the 2006 Bob Hope Chrysler Classic. The first course is a tough 7,570 yards, with water features throughout.
Par: 72; **Yardage:** 7553/7101/6639/5974/5306/4885

Trilogy Golf Club $$$
60-151 Trilogy Parkway, La Quinta
(760) 771-0707
www.trilogygolfclub.com
Gary Pinks designed this well-bunkered 18 holes in 2002 and this course has hosted the PGA Tour's 2003, 2004, 2005, and 2006 LG Skins Game.
Par: 72; **Yardage:** 7200/6883/6455/6044/5542/4998

CLINICS AND SCHOOLS

Cimarrón Golf Academy
Cimarrón Golf Resort, Cathedral City
(760) 770-6060
Jim Wilkinson, PGA. Individual/group lessons, specialty schools, corporate outings, junior clinics. Personalized instruction. Open year-round.

College Golf Center of Palm Desert
College of the Desert, Palm Desert
(760) 341-0994
Full-service golf center and pro shop. PGA

For great last-minute tee times and price savings, check into the local companies that have good connections with the courses. This may be the only way to secure a round at one of the most exclusive clubs.

and LPGA instruction. Night-lighted and misted practice range.

Desert Princess Country Club & Resort School of Golf
Cathedral City
(760) 322-1655
www.desertprincess.com
PGA instructors dedicated to improving your game while you have fun learning. All levels.

The Faldo Golf Institute
Marriott's Shadow Ridge, Palm Desert
(760) 674-2700
State-of-the-art equipment and video analysis of every part of the game.

Indian Wells Golf School
Golf Resort at Indian Wells
(760) 346-4653
Golf package with video analysis, small classes, on-course lessons, course time, and practice facilities.

Jim McLean Golf School
PGA West, La Quinta
(760) 564-7144
Video private lessons, corporate clinics, golf schools, junior academies, taught in Superstations by master instructors trained by Jim McLean.

Tahquitz Creek Golf Academy
(760) 328-1005
Full- and half-day schools, clinics, and private and group lessons. Free junior and adult clinics daily January through May. Complete practice center. Customized programs.

Troon Golf Institute
Westin Mission Hills Resort, Rancho Mirage
(760) 328-4303
PGA and LPGA golf professionals providing golf schools and private instruction.

BOOKING SERVICES

Advance Golf
(760) 324-3560
Customized individual or group bookings. Play exclusive private clubs or premier resorts. Also tennis services.

Desert Connection
(760) 324-3668
Specializing in golf tours and travel services for the Japanese tourist. One-day, three-day, or one-week golf school for Japanese players.

Golf à la Carte
(760) 320-8713
www.palmspringsgolf.com
Advance bookings for individuals and groups. The desert's original tee-time booker.

Next Day Golf
(760) 345-8463
Discount tee times. Call between 5:00 and 10:00 P.M. for golf the next day. Booking individuals and groups.

Palm Springs Golf Vacations
(760) 346-3331, (800) 774-6531
Customized golf packages; corporate, group, or individual golf outings; tee-time specialists. Japanese-speaking guides.

Par-Tee Golf
(800) 727-8331
Advance reservations; corporate, individuals, and package golf outings.

Stand By Golf
(760) 321-2665
Deep-discount tee times for following-day play on all of the desert's top courses.

ANNUAL FESTIVALS AND EVENTS

Special events in the Palm Springs area follow the weather patterns—when it's hot, the pace slows to a crawl, but when the temperatures cool off, it's impossible to fit everything in. Literally dozens of fund-raising galas, golf tournaments, film festivals, art shows, and sporting events fill the calendar from late September all the way through April, tapering off dramatically in May.

There are lots of high-priced dinners and dances, to be sure, but most of the events in this section are geared to be affordable to the typical vacationing family. There are also ample opportunities for free entertainment, from concerts in the park to street fairs and art festivals to car shows and bike rides.

Despite its close historical ties to Hollywood stars, the Palm Springs area was never associated with "the industry" until Sonny Bono started the Palm Springs International Film Festival in 1990. Since then the slate of film festivals has grown enormously, and there seems to be a new specialty festival appearing every season. Many of these little festivals screen films that are virtually impossible to find outside of big-city art houses. And most of the festivals are held at the refurbished Camelot Theatre, close to downtown Palm Springs. A fixture in Palm Springs since its star-studded opening in 1967, the Camelot eventually closed and remained vacant for seven years until it was bought in 1999. Ric and Rozene Supple made upgrades and launched the Camelot as the desert's home for foreign and art films.

Golf tournaments are also popular in Palm Springs. The desert has more than 100 golf courses, and it seems as though there is no end to the hunger for more, bigger, and fancier. Many of the top pros on the PGA circuit either have homes here or have laid out a fabulous course or two. Combine the abundance of golf with the desert's many charities, and you have a lot of opportunities to raise funds, particularly if a tournament benefits a popular charity or can boast celebrity players.

Each year there are tournaments that aren't successful enough to be repeated, and others that change names or lose sponsors. Because of this, our listings cover only those tournaments that have been played for at least three consecutive years and have secured courses or sponsors for another year to come. Also, because several of the tournaments rely solely on volunteers rather than paid staff, prices and exact schedules may not be available until a few months before the event.

In this chapter we've highlighted the most prominent and long-lived annual events, knowing that more will pop up by the time this book is in your hands. The events are organized by month, with ongoing fairs and events grouped together at the beginning of the chapter. Some of the events may change months, duration, and location, and prices are sure to change. The prices given were current at the time of publication and are printed here for reference only. Use this chapter to help you plan your visit, but be sure to confirm the details with the listed phone numbers and Web sites.

All the events listed take place in Palm Springs, unless otherwise noted.

ONGOING FAIRS AND EVENTS

Throughout the Year

College of the Desert Street Fair
43500 Monterey Avenue, Palm Desert
(760) 773-2567
www.codstreetfair.com
Every Saturday and Sunday from 7:00 A.M. to 2:00 P.M. (7:00 A.M. to noon June through September), locals and visitors crowd into this sprawling fair, which features more than 300 vendors selling everything from tacos to fine art and cheap sunglasses. The College of the Desert Alumni Association, an organization that carefully vets the vendors for quality and honesty, runs the fair. The farmers' market is a highlight—come early to get the freshest produce. The fair takes place in a large open area in the middle of the campus of College of the Desert. Enter the parking lot from Monterey Avenue, just south of Fred Waring Drive. Wear comfortable shoes and bring cash for food and small items. Free admission and street parking. For more details, see the listing in the Shopping chapter.

First Friday
North Palm Canyon Drive between Amado Road and Tachevah Drive
(760) 778-8415, (760) 325-8979
On the first Friday of every month, the shops, restaurants, and galleries on North Palm Canyon's Heritage District stay open until 9:00 P.M., offering music, refreshments, and a festive atmosphere conducive to wandering and shopping. This area is full of consignment and antiques shops, boutiques specializing in real and faux retro items, and art galleries. Free admission and street parking.

Indio Open-Air Market
Riverside County Fairgrounds
46350 Arabia Street, Indio
(800) 222-7467
Every Wednesday and Saturday night from 4:00 to 10:00 P.M., this flea market/street fair caters mostly to the Mexican-American population, with authentic food, Spanish-language music and videos, and new and used brand-name merchandise. The market takes places on the grounds of the Riverside County Fair and National Date Festival. Free admission and street parking.

Palm Springs VillageFest
North Palm Canyon Drive between Amado and Baristo Roads
(760) 320-3781
www.palm-springs.org
Held from 6:00 to 10:00 P.M. each Thursday, VillageFest is the granddaddy of all the other street fairs and regular art strolls. The brainchild of City Councilman Tuck Broich back in 1991, it's been growing and attracting more shoppers every year. A good portion of downtown Palm Canyon Drive closes to street traffic on this night. Shops and restaurants all along the 4-block VillageFest strip stay open late, and the area becomes an absolute magnet for locals and visitors. Children and dogs are welcome, and there's lots of live music, interesting food, and good-quality arts and crafts, as well as a farmers' market. Free admission and street parking. For more details, see the listing in the Shopping chapter.

May through September

Summer of Fun Concerts & Movies in the Park
Palm Desert Civic Center Amphitheater
73510 Fred Waring Drive, Palm Desert
(760) 346-0611
www.palm-desert.org
From the last Thursday in May through the first Thursday in September, the City of Palm Desert hosts free movies and concerts in the park. Concerts begin at 7:30 P.M. Movie preshow festivities with cartoons and prize giveaways start at 7:00 P.M. The movie starts at sunset.

This has become a huge community gathering, so get there well before the start times to get a good spot. You're welcome to bring all types of picnicking gear, such as food, soft drinks, low lawn chairs, and blankets, but alcohol is not allowed.

October through April

Art Walk at the Art Place
41-801 Corporate Way, Palm Desert
(760) 776-2268
From 6:00 to 9:00 P.M. on the first Friday of the month, October through April, the many art galleries and design-supported businesses in the business park area of Palm Desert open their doors to welcome the public. It's similar in concept to the El Paseo Art Walk, but the atmosphere is less high-toned, and the art—much of it from artists who are showing in their own studios—can be a very good value. Free admission and street parking.

October through May

El Paseo Art Walk
El Paseo Drive, Palm Desert
(760) 346-8885
www.elpaseo.com
From 5:00 to 9:00 P.M. on the first Thursday of each month from October through May, the dozens of art galleries and boutiques along El Paseo Drive stay open late for artist exhibitions, receptions, entertainment, and refreshments. This event offers even the most inexperienced art lover a good chance to view world-class art in a casual, friendly, no-pressure atmosphere. It's also a good opportunity to check out the menus and make a decision on where to eat later, as El Paseo is home to a great many restaurants, from white-tablecloth fancy to good family pizza places. Free admission and street parking.

World Affairs Council of the Desert Speaker Program
Renaissance Esmeralda Resort
44-400 Indian Wells Lane, Indian Wells
(760) 322-7711
www.worldaffairsdesert.org
A nonpartisan and nonprofit group, the World Affairs Council focuses on noted international professors, political figures, and reporters discussing issues that have significance to U.S. foreign policy.

Tickets for the evening are $45 for members, $55 for nonmembers. Held monthly on Sunday evenings from October through May, the programs begin with a reception at 5:00 P.M., dinner at 6:00 P.M., and a speaker's presentation.

November through May

Desert Arts Festival
400 North Palm Canyon Drive
(760) 323-7973
Held on the last weekend of the month during daylight hours, this regular art event features fine art in all media, plus jewelry and other crafts by artists from throughout Southern California. The fair is on the grounds of the city's first park—Frances Stevens Park—and right in the middle of the action on Palm Canyon Drive. Park, explore the art, and have lunch or dinner downtown for an enjoyable, inexpensive day that's entertaining for most ages. Free admission and street parking.

JANUARY

Palm Springs International Film Festival
1700 East Tahquitz Canyon Way
Suite #3
(760) 322-2930, (800) 898-7256
www.psfilmfest.org
World and U.S. premieres, parties, lectures, and presentations and more than 100 new films are on the program, which

If you volunteer at one of the film festivals, you'll get free passes for some great movies. Lots of golf tournaments also have good deals for their volunteers.

often isn't finalized until very close to opening night. The black-tie gala awards program and dinner is one of the hottest events in an event-filled season in the desert, with everyone vying for tables close to the stars.

Screenings and other events take place at various movie theaters and hotels in Palm Springs in early January. Individual tickets are $9.00 for films before 5:00 P.M. and $10.00 after 5:00 P.M. Platinum Passes allowing the holder to view every movie are $350. Opening- and closing-night tickets are $50. Tickets to the awards gala are $350. There are also coupon books that offer package discounts.

Palm Desert Golf Cart Parade
El Paseo Drive, Palm Desert
(760) 346-6111
www.golfcartparade.com
The Palm Desert Chamber of Commerce started the Golf Cart Parade in 1964 as a lark for the locals. Today they take it pretty seriously—more than 100 fantastically decorated golf cart "floats" parade down the toney El Paseo shopping district and attract around 25,000 spectators. Marching bands, jugglers, clowns, and other entertainers join the carts.

It's a pretty old-fashioned event in many respects, beginning with a Rotary Club pancake breakfast and ending with a street festival that offers live entertainment and children's activities. Entry proceeds benefit local charities. The event is now held in mid-January after occurring in November for many years.

Bob Hope Chrysler Classic
Call for locations
(760) 346-8184
www.bhcc.com

The Classic has been the desert's top tournament since it began back in 1960. A lot of local tourism promoters give this event credit for creating millions of dollars' worth of publicity for the desert. In mid-January, while the rest of the country is deep in snow and ice, a whole lot of TV sets are tuned to scenes of the sport's best pro and celebrity golfers hitting balls on brilliant green courses drenched in sunshine.

Traditionally, the tournament has been played on four courses, which vary from year to year. In the past most of these courses have been private, with little room for spectators and no provisions for public play. Starting in 2006, the Classic has its own two courses, both of which welcome public play. Each of the new courses also has lots of open space for the TV crews and spectator galleries. The Classic course at NorthStar, a new Palm Desert development, was an outright gift to the tournament. The second course—SilverRock Resort in La Quinta—is one of the most spectacular new courses in the desert. With this change, the Classic has been able to increase its annual charity contributions—$1.5 million in 2005.

Clubhouse badges are $75 for the entire event and allow access to the clubhouse, where there's a good chance of seeing the players up close. Daily tickets are $20 to $25, with an additional $10 for clubhouse access. Parking is limited, so come early. Preferred parking tickets are available at the NorthStar location only and cost $25 for the weekend or $15 for one day. Children under 12 are admitted free when a paying adult accompanies them.

Southwest Arts Festival
Empire Polo Club Forum Area
81-800 Avenue 51, Indio
(760) 347-0676
www.southwestartsfest.com
Held in late January or the first weekend in February from 10:00 A.M. to 4:00 P.M., this judged and juried outdoor art fair features western and southwestern-themed

art and crafts in all media. The 200-plus artists and craftspeople are primarily from the western United States, showing and selling works that range from the traditional to the contemporary. There is always lots of live entertainment, food, wine, and beer. Admission is $6.00 for adults, $5.00 for seniors, and $4.00 for children. Valet parking is available.

FEBRUARY

Steve Chase Humanitarian Awards
Palm Springs Convention Center
277 North Avenida Caballeros
(760) 323-2118
www.desertaidsproject.org
When renowned interior designer Steve Chase left his extensive art collection to the Palm Springs Art Museum, he also created a tradition of continuing support for his chosen charity, the Desert AIDS Project. This social event in early February began as a VIP cocktail party at the museum and has evolved into a glamorous all-out gala, attracting a guest list of the most affluent and influential names in the desert, as well as a lot of heavy hitters from Hollywood. Tickets are $325 per person for the cocktail reception, dinner, silent auction, entertainment, and awards show. Parking is free on-site or nearby on the street.

Tour de Palm Springs Bike Event
Palm Springs Pavilion in Sunrise Park
Sunrise Way between Baristo and
Ramon Roads
(760) 568-2800
www.tourdepalmsprings.com
One of the largest charity bike rides in the country, the Tour attracts as many as 10,000 riders, so it's smart to get there early for sign-ups. Route maps for the different rides are given out on the morning of the event, so everyone starts out with the same level of knowledge. A spaghetti dinner the night before is great for carb-loading for the 5-, 10-, 25-, 50-, and 100-mile rides. Registration for this early

February event is $20. Parking is free on the street.

Palm Springs Modernism Show
Palm Springs Convention Center
277 North Avenida Caballeros
(948) 563-6747
www.palmspringsmodernism.com
This annual show and sale in mid-February features 75 noted national and international dealers exhibiting vintage furniture and decorative arts and crafts from all design movements of the 20th century. The Friday-evening preview party gives collectors first dibs on their favorite items and benefits the Palm Springs Preservation Foundation, the organization that was instrumental in preserving and publicizing many of the city's most important midcentury buildings. Book signings and lectures are also scheduled for the weekend.

Admission is $10 per day for Saturday and Sunday, and $50 per person or $80 per couple for the Friday-evening preview. Parking is free at the Convention Center or on nearby streets.

Riverside County Fair and
National Date Festival
Riverside County Fairgrounds
46350 Arabia Street, Indio
(800) 811-3247
www.datefest.org
This old-time combination of county fair, carnival, and Arabian Nights dress-up celebration has been held for more than 40 years on the fairgrounds in Indio, and it's worth at least one visit during its 10-day run in mid-February. Bring your camera and wear good walking shoes, because there's a lot to see. No outside food or drink is allowed, so make sure to bring extra cash for snacks, trinkets, and rides.

In the past there have been some concerns about safety, with the odd fight and purse snatching. The fair officials have really stepped up security, adopting a no-nonsense approach to trouble or its appearance, so you should be able to enjoy a good family outing without worry.

CLOSE-UP

The Palm Springs International Film Festival and Sonny Bono

The late Sonny Bono created this 10-day event in 1990, midway through his term as mayor of Palm Springs. It began as an upstart festival focusing on emerging filmmakers and top international films not yet in general release. And it began on a shoestring, with seed money from the City of Palm Springs. Bono's name and film industry connections were the key to its initial success, though a lot of the city's longtime residents took a dim view of spending city money to support an unproven event.

At the time, the city had seen several years of retail and visitor exodus to newer shops and hotels in the other end of the valley, and its balance sheets were looking fairly anemic. But Sonny promoted the festival as a way of attracting the Hollywood heavy hitters and young stars who could make the city "hip" again and help reverse its slide into obscurity.

When Sonny went on to become a congressman, he continued his efforts with the festival, often putting his own money and staff to work when times were shaky. When he died in a skiing accident in 1998, his widow Mary won a special election held to fill his vacated congressional seat. She also stepped up to head the film festival, making sure his vision was continued. In 2004 Congresswoman Mary Bono resoundingly won the 45th District congressional election with a 67 percent majority, earning her fourth term in office. Her support of the festival has never wavered, and she has been a key player in keeping sponsorship money flowing.

Seeing hotel rooms and restaurants full of visitors during the festival's run has validated the event as a real economic boon to the city, and Palm Springs has remained its primary sponsor, recently committing funds through 2010. As Mayor Ron Oden said in 2005, "This is our signature event. It gets our name out there to the international community."

As the festival has grown in prestige and name recognition, other sponsors

---

Some of the highlights are the Arabian Nights costume contests, camel and ostrich races, nightly live concerts featuring popular Mexican and country-western groups, and, of course, all the fried fair food you can eat. There are also cooking and art demonstrations, a livestock "nursery," and a petting zoo for the little ones.

A large part of the event is typical county fair stuff, with more than 7,000 exhibits of livestock, agriculture, horticulture, photography, wood carving, and junior achievement displays. Adding to the often-frenzied atmosphere are lots of carnival rides and booths, multiple entertainment stages, off-track betting on horse races, and nightly musical pageants featuring the fair's official Queen Scheherazade and her court. Past fairs have also included Mexican rodeos, mon-

have stepped up, including Tiffany & Co. (which presents the annual awards gala), the Cities of Indian Wells and Palm Desert, *The Desert Sun* newspaper, Mercedes-Benz, the Agua Caliente Band of Cahuilla Indians, and the National Endowment for the Arts.

Savvy programming and support from Hollywood insiders have helped the festival grow into one of the most prestigious and cutting-edge film events in the country, screening more than 200 films from 60 or more countries. Past honorees have included Kirk Douglas, Susan Sarandon, Sophia Loren, Nicole Kidman, Kevin Spacey, Samuel Jackson, and many others. Films premiered here have gone on to win dozens of Oscars and Oscar nominations. The festival has an attractive film sales and distribution record and is seen by American distributors as one of the best Academy Award campaign marketing tools.

Today Sonny Bono's little film festival has become the largest revenue-generating film festival in the country, with a box office of more than $750,000. In 2005 it scored 105,000 admissions, second only to the Seattle Film Festival with 157,000. In contrast, the venerable San Francisco Film Festival had 95,000 admissions, and Robert Redford's Sundance Film Festival

Kevin Spacey was one of the many honorees at the Palm Springs International Film Festival. Congresswoman Mary Bono, whose late husband Sonny Bono founded the festival, is its primary spokesperson. PHOTO COURTESY OF THE PALM SPRINGS INTERNATIONAL FILM FESTIVAL.

racked up just 45,000.

In short, the Palm Springs International Film Festival has brought Hollywood back to Palm Springs, just as Sonny Bono envisioned it would.

---

ster truck demonstrations, and freestyle motorcycle contests.

Parking is plentiful and inexpensive around the fairgrounds. Admission is $7.00 for adults, $6.00 for seniors, $5.00 for children 5–12, and free for children under 5. A daily unlimited-ride pass is $20, and a season pass good for admission every day is $25.

Frank Sinatra Celebrity Invitational
Indian Wells Country Club
46-000 Club Drive, Indian Wells
(760) 674-8447, (800) 377-8277
www.sinatragolf.com
This late-February event is two days of golf and three nights of entertainment, including a black-tie gala, plus the popular Ladies Luncheon and Fashion Show. Non-golf events are held at the Renaissance

Esmeralda Resort and Spa. It's smaller than the Bob Hope Chrysler Classic and doesn't have the professional status of the Skins game, but the Frank Sinatra Invitational is the best golf tournament for star spotting and celebrity photo opportunities. Held to benefit the Barbara Sinatra Children's Center at Eisenhower Medical Center, this tournament boasts an atmosphere that harks back to the golden days of the desert, when seeing a movie star on the golf course was just par for the day.

Tickets are $20 per day. Parking is $5.00. If you want to be right there with the celebrities, you can buy a Platinum Entry for $10,000 or a Gold Entry for $4,000.

Keith McCormick's Palm Springs Exotic Car Show & Auction
Downtown Parking Garage
300 South Indian Canyon Drive
(760) 320-3290
www.classic-carauction.com
This two-day show and auction of rare and vintage automobiles hold in late February is a good excuse to daydream and see the beautiful vehicles up close. Get an ice cream, check out all the cars, and do some window-shopping along Palm Canyon Drive while you're at it. Another identical event is held in downtown Palm Springs in November. Admission for the event is $10 per day or $15 for both days. On-street parking is free nearby.

L'Affaire Chocolat
Miramonte Resort & Spa
45-000 Indian Wells Lane, Indian Wells
(760) 327-3309
A chocolate addict's dream event, this aromatic afternoon features chocolate cooking demonstrations, chocolate tastings, and a chef's chocolate competition, plus live and silent auctions. The sweet women of Les Dames d'Escoffier Palm Springs host this scholarship fund-raiser for young women interested in pursuing education in the culinary arts. Tickets are around $30. The location is tentative, as this event has already outgrown two hotel homes and attracts more and more people each year.

MARCH

Hike for Hope
Indian Canyons
(760) 202-3885
www.hike4hope.com
A family-oriented, noncompetitive hiking event in the beautiful Indian Canyons, this benefits the City of Hope National Medical Center and its research on women's cancer. There are nine different routes for easy, moderate, and strenuous hikes. The event brings as many as 1,000 women and their families together for a fun and exhilarating morning of hiking and companionship in early March.

Early registration is $25 for adults and $20 for children 14 and younger or adults 55 and older. Regular registration is $30 for adults and $25 for youth and older adults. Registration includes Indian Canyons admission, a T-shirt, goodie bags, snacks, and various prizes.

Pacific Life Open
Indian Wells Tennis Garden
78-200 Miles Avenue, Indian Wells
(800) 999-1585
www.pacificlifeopen.com
Begun more than 30 years ago as a small-scale tennis tournament at the stadium at the Hyatt Grand Champions resort, this event has morphed into one of the most prestigious events on the professional tennis circuit. The two-week tournament held in early to mid-March typically starts with a strong field of 96 men and 96 women competing for $5 million in prize money and is televised during the finals. There are eight tennis courts, set up in stadiums ingeniously designed to give every spectator excellent lines of sight, even from the nosebleed seats. Every one of today's top competitors plays here at some point.

The adjoining grounds are set up with food, entertainment, and vendors. Bring a hat, some sunscreen, and money for snacks; and be prepared for an exciting day up close with the best tennis players in the world.

Series passes go from $630 to $6,000, but take heart—individual tickets range from $14 to $66. It's a good idea to buy your tickets online well in advance, because the good seats go fast, particularly those for the last two days. Parking is $7.00, with a shuttle to take you to the stadium. Day play begins at 10:00 A.M. and evening sessions start at 10:00 P.M.

Cabazon Indio Powwow
Fantasy Springs Resort Casino
84-245 Indio Springs Parkway, Indio
(760) 342-5000, (800) 827-2946
www.fantasyspringsresort.com
A three-day festival in March that celebrates Native American dance, music, culture, and food, the powwow attracts hundreds of the best Indian dancers from all over the country, as well as artisans displaying and selling beadwork, paintings, pottery, leather crafts, jewelry, and more. Designed to bridge the Indian and non-Indian cultures, the event encourages visitors and invites everyone to join in the intertribal dancing. Another three-day powwow is held here in November, with much the same format and details. Admission is free. The powwow is held adjacent to the Fantasy Springs Casino, and parking is free in their lots.

Native American Film Festival
Camelot Theatres
2300 East Baristo Road
(760) 778-1079
www.camelottheatres.com
One of the newest of the desert's many film festivals, this four-day event in mid-March includes feature films by Native American filmmakers, filmmaker and celebrity guest panel discussions, a short-film program, and a program of Native American storytelling. Opening- and closing-night screenings and parties give attendees a chance to mingle with the producers and stars of a relatively new movie genre.

Tickets are $8.00 in advance and $10.00 on the day of screening. Opening- and closing-night movies and receptions are $10 in advance and $15 on the day of the event.

La Quinta Arts Festival
La Quinta Civic Center
78150 Calle Tampico, Suite 215
(760) 564-1244
www.lqaf.com
Marking its 25th year in 2007, this open-air festival held in mid-March has become known as one of the most noteworthy juried art events in the country. More than 250 artists, selected from close to 1,000 entrants, sell and display sculpture, paintings, photography, drawings, prints, jewelry, and fine crafts in a nicely designed garden setting with live entertainment and food and beverages.

Multiday passes for the Friday–Sunday show are $15. Regular admission is $10 for adults. Children 12 and younger are admitted free. There's a separate $50 fee for the early-evening preview on Thursday, which also features "A Taste of La Quinta," with food and wine from local chefs. The outdoor show is held on the grounds of the La Quinta Civic Center at the corner of Calle Tampico and Washington Street. Parking is free in nearby lots, with a shuttle to the fairgrounds.

Crossroads Renaissance Festival
Frances Stevens Park
Palm Canyon Drive and Alejo Road
(909) 735-0101, (800) 320-4736
This late-March event is a three-day annual trip back to the 1400s through 1600s—your chance to engage in make-

---

If you can't afford an original piece of art from one of the many art fairs and festivals, consider picking up a signature poster. The La Quinta Arts Festival and the Palm Springs International Film Festival are noted for outstanding poster designs that change each year.

---

believe and play as though computers, television, and traffic jams haven't even been dreamed of yet. All the vendors and entertainers dress in costumes of the period, speak their own (sometimes quite peculiar) versions of Elizabethan English, and encourage everyone to join in the spirit of fun and revelry. The nonstop entertainment includes magic shows, juggling, storytelling, plays, street theater, music, artisans, food, and drink. Though it's all in good fun, some of the performers really get into character, and their behavior and speech can get downright bawdy—be warned if you are visiting with small children or others who might be easily offended. Admission is $12.00 for adults and $7.00 for children 13 and younger. Parking is free on the street.

Indian Wells Arts Festival
Indian Wells Tennis Garden
78-200 Miles Avenue, Indian Wells
(760) 346-0042
www.iwaf.net
This three-day event at the end of March is a judged and juried show with arts and crafts from more than 200 artists across the country. It is trying mightily to reach the prestige and popularity of the La Quinta Arts Festival, though it isn't there yet. Still, there are some excellent artists, and it's a fun way to spend an afternoon. Refreshments, wine tasting, a beer garden, and live entertainment are offered from 10:00 A.M. to 5:30 P.M., with the last admission at 4:30 P.M. Admission is $7.00 for adults. Children 12 and under are admitted free. Valet parking, with shuttle service to the location, is available.

 The week of the Kraft Nabisco Championship is now a premier vacation and party time for thousands of lesbians, who come to the desert to play, dance, and enjoy the golf.

Kraft Nabisco Championship
Mission Hills Country Club
34-600 Mission Hills Drive
Rancho Mirage
(760) 324-4546
www.kncgolf.com
Starting in 2006, the Nabisco moved its tournament dates to the end of March and the first weekend in April in order to minimize conflicts with the NCAA basketball tournament, the PGA Tour Players Tournament, and several junior golf events. Originally known as the Dinah Shore Championship, this event is the first LPGA major tournament of the year and has been drawing huge crowds to the desert since 1972. It's one of four major LPGA tournaments and has been played for 33 years on the Dinah Shore Tournament Course at Mission Hills Country Club in Rancho Mirage. Only the men's Masters at Augusta has had a longer continuous run on either the men's or women's professional golf tours.

The usual schedule starts with a practice day and celebrity pro-am tournament, followed by four days of competition among the circuit's best women players. Throughout the week there are special events, such as Kids Day and the $1-million Hole-in-One Contest. Practice day tee times are at 7:00 A.M., and competition days have an 8:00 A.M. tee time.

Daily tickets are $15 to $20. Clubhouse badges are $60 to $70 for the week. Parking is free in a guarded lot with a shuttle to the course.

APRIL

Easter Egg Hunt
Ruth Hardy Park
700 Tamarisk Road
(760) 323-8186
The men and women of the Palm Springs Fire Department have been hosting this event for years, and they do a magnificent job of keeping the Easter Bunny magic alive for kids up to age 10. Fire trucks for

the kids to climb on, colored eggs to find, and simple contests make this a delightful morning. Admission and on-street parking are free. The hunt usually begins at 9:00 A.M. on Easter Sunday.

White Party
Various venues throughout Palm Springs
(760) 322-6000
www.jeffreysanker.com

This is the premier happening on the country's gay dance/party circuit. Promoter Jeffrey Sanker's brainchild, the White Party virtually takes over the city for Easter Week, with events in hotels and nightspots all over Palm Springs. The Palm Springs Convention Center is one of the venues and home of the two-room/two-dance-floor main party. Gay men from all over the country make this extravaganza a part of their vacation plans each spring, and it seems to get larger every year. For packages, prices, and detailed information on individual events, check the Web site.

Easter Bowl Tennis
Rancho Las Palmas Resort and Spa
41-000 Bob Hope Drive, Rancho Mirage
(760) 836-6040, (866) 423-1195
www.rancholaspalmasresortandspa.com
http://seenahamiltoninc.com/Easter_Bowl_Home.htm

This eight-day tournament has been held at the Palm Springs Riviera Resort in previous years, but it will be held at Rancho Las Palmas Resort and Spa for the first time in 2007. Dozens of the most famous American tennis players have been competitors in this junior tournament. Agassi, Connors, McEnroe, Austin, Capriati, and others have all slammed balls in the Easter Bowl, getting valuable experience on their way to the major tournaments. You'll see several hundred of America's best junior players, and you may be able to say you saw the world's next champion "way back in the beginning."

At press time, there was no charge for admission to preliminary matches, but the organizers may charge for the finals. Parking is by valet at the hotel only.

Matches start at 8:00 A.M., and finals begin at 9:00 P.M.

Joshua Tree National Park Art Festival
Joshua Tree National Park Visitors Center
74485 National Park Drive
Twentynine Palms
(760) 367-5522

This is a nice little arts event in early April with a folksy feeling and an eclectic collection of art and crafts. There are usually around 20 artists, each presenting a different and very personal view of the park in different media. All the works are for sale at prices far below what you might expect to pay in a glitzy art gallery in Palm Desert or Palm Springs. Admission and parking are free.

Indio International Salsa Festival
Various locations in Old Town, Indio
(760) 837-7230
www.salsafest.org

This community affair in mid-April draws locals and visitors from all over the valley to taste an amazing variety of salsas and other authentic Mexican foods. There's a full-scale farmers', market, artisan and merchant booths, a classic car show, midway carnival, and salsa dancing competitions. It's a perfect family outing and a chance to sample truly innovative uses of the fiery concoction. Admission and parking are free.

Opera in the Park
Sunrise Park
401 South Pavilion Way
(760) 325-6107
www.palmspringsoperaguild.org

This family-oriented event in mid-April was started by the Palm Springs Opera Guild in 1998 as a vehicle to introduce opera to the public. Various local and regional opera stars sing selections from the world's best-loved operas, playing to an appreciative audience of all ages. Seating is on the grass, cold drinks are usually available, and the only requirement is that you listen quietly and applaud loudly. Admission and parking are free.

Coachella Valley Music and Arts Festival
Empire Polo Field
81-800 Avenue 51, Indio
(800) 537-6986
www.coachella.com
Just a few years old, this multiday, multi-media event in late April has become one of the hottest international music fests around, showcasing young bands and groups on the cutting edge of alternative and rock music. Past groups have included Coldplay, Nine Inch Nails, Bauhaus, Weezer, Cocteau Twins, and many more.

One-day passes are $80 in advance and $85 at the box office. A limited number of two-day passes are available in advance for $150. They are not sold at the box office. Children under five are admitted free. On-site camping tickets are sold separately through Ticketmaster or at the campsite on show days if tickets are available, and prices for these are determined close to the event date. There is an extensive list of rules about what can and cannot be brought into the event, so it's a smart idea to study the Web site before going. That is also the best place to get updated information on groups and play times.

Palm Springs Tennis Club
Annual Tournament
Various venues in Palm Springs
(760) 323-7676
www.strokerecoverycenter.com
This tournament benefits the Stroke Recovery Center and has been a fixture in the desert for more than 20 years. Play is at the Palm Springs Tennis Club, Plaza Racquet Club, Riviera Resort & Racquet Club, and Smoke Tree Ranch, all in Palm Springs. It's a fun community affair that welcomes all players. The $50 entry fee includes lunch at one of the old-time elegant Palm Springs restaurants. Parking is free on the street.

MAY

Palm Springs Smooth Jazz Festival
O'Donnell Golf Club
301 North Belardo Road
(760) 323-6325
www.palmspringsjazz.com
This is a much-anticipated annual event, when major jazz artists entertain under the stars at historic O'Donnell, the valley's first golf course. The setting is magnificent, right up against the foothills of the San Jacinto Mountains just a block west of Palm Canyon Drive. This is a private club, and the Jazz Festival is one of the few times it is opened to the public. The event benefits Hanson House, a facility for families of critically ill patients at Desert Regional Medical Center. Friday Community Appreciation Night is $50 for general admission and $80 with dinner catered by one of the city's most elegant restaurants. The gala fund-raiser is held on Saturday night and runs $450 per couple.

JUNE

Film Noir Festival
Camelot Theatres
2300 East Baristo Road
(760) 325-6565
www.palmspringsfilmnoir.com
This campy, fun festival in early June celebrates the dark, sinister "B" films of the 1940s and 1950s—films that are appreciated today for their innovative use of lighting and camera work and their dramatic character studies. Festival producer Art Lyons, a lifelong Palm Springs resident and author of several popular crime-detective novels, is a huge fan of the film noir genre. In researching his book *Death on the Cheap: The Lost B Movies of Film Noir,* he formed the concept for a film festival and spent years scouring the country for original movie footage. Each year fans can expect to see films that were thought to have vanished, view a few familiar classics, and visit with some of the actors and actresses who starred in the original films.

Tickets range from around $11 to $13 and an all-access pass is $110. The all-access pass includes admission to parties and other special star events.

AUGUST

Idyllwild Jazz in the Pines
(No street address)
Idyllwild Arts Academy, Idyllwild
(909) 235-2093
www.idyllwildjazz.com
Taking a 45-minute drive up the winding mountain road from Palm Desert to the little town of Idyllwild is a favorite escape when summer temperatures start hitting the 100-degree mark. Hiking in the pine forest, shopping in charming boutiques, and dining at really good restaurants are reasons enough. When Idyllwild Jazz is on, there's just no excuse to stay in the desert. A two-day weekend festival in late August, this party on the Idyllwild Arts Academy campus attracts some of the world's top modern jazz masters to benefit the school's scholarship fund. Arts and crafts, great food, beer, wine, and dancing are a big part of the fun. Rooms in Idyllwild are scarce all through the summer, so book yours early if you don't want to drive down the mountain in the dark.

Tickets purchased before July 29 are $45 per day and $85 for both days. After July 29, prices are $50 per day and $95 for both days. Patron packages of two tickets for both days, dinner, dancing, and preferred parking and seating are $175 per person. The gates open at 9:30 A.M. on Saturday and 10:30 A.M. on Sunday, and music plays continuously until 5:00 P.M. both days. There is no reserved seating in the amphitheater. Seats are on the ground, so take a low chair or a pile of blankets.

Check the Web site for driving directions. Parking is $5.00 on the campus, and a shuttle runs from several locations in town. Limited reserved parking on-site accommodates vehicles with valid handicap plates. You are allowed to bring in food, but not alcohol.

Get CDs of past Jazz in the Pines festivals at Idyllwild online at www.parkhill music.com. Recorded and mixed by Park Hill Music in Hemet, these capture the energy and verve of the live performances. Part of the proceeds goes to the Idyllwild Arts Scholarship Fund.

Palm Springs International Festival of Short Films & Film Market
Camelot Theatres
2300 East Baristo Road
(760) 322-2930
www.psfilmfest.org
The largest competitive short-film festival in North America, this weeklong event held in late August or early September showcases film, video, and animation shorts by cutting-edge filmmakers from all over the world. The event is also a marketplace for short films looking for distribution, and more than 45 films in the lineup have gone on to win Oscar nominations. Entrants stand to win more than $30,000 in cash, film stock, and production services.

The works are arranged into programs by subject matter and scheduled so that it's actually possible to see them all. You won't even have to skip a few meals to do so, because the Camelot has an excellent snack bar with fresh sandwiches, salads, and hot coffee.

Opening- and closing-night programs and receptions are $25 per person. Advance purchase tickets are $45 for six programs. Individual tickets are $9.00 before 5:00 P.M. and $10.00 after 5:00 P.M. All-event access passes are $200 ($150 if purchased in advance).

SEPTEMBER

Fall Concerts in Sunrise Park
Sunrise Park
401 South Pavilion Way
(760) 323-8272
On Tuesday nights from mid-September

through mid-October, the City of Palm Springs hosts a weekly series of free fall concerts, featuring all types of music— from big band to rock, country and western, and bluegrass. Concerts start at 7:30 P.M. Food and drink vendors sell hot dogs and snack-type foods, but many concert-goers opt to bring their own picnic baskets and lawn chairs. Call for information.

Gram Fest
Hi Desert Playhouse
61231 Twentynine Palms Highway
Joshua Tree
(760) 366-3777
www.gramfest.com

A yearly musical tribute to '60s country rock legend Gram Parsons, this three-day event celebrates "cosmic American music" in the heart of the area where Parsons died of a drug overdose at 26. In a story that seems to become more elaborate and strange each year, Parsons's body disappeared from the Los Angeles International Airport, where it was waiting to be flown to Louisiana for burial. Phil Kaufman, Parsons's former road manager, believing that Gram would have preferred to be cremated in Joshua Tree, enlisted a cohort to steal the body and do just that. The two were arrested a few days later and fined for burning the coffin. Parsons's remains were later buried near New Orleans.

The event runs from 6:00 P.M. to midnight and features food, drink, and continual live music on two stages. A real throwback to the '60s.

All-event passes are $75 to $90, and day passes are $60. Early-bird ticket buyers get a chance to win a stay in the Joshua Tree Inn room where Parsons died. Parking is free on-site.

OCTOBER

Agua Caliente Cultural Museum Dinner in the Canyons
(No street address)
(760) 778-1079
www.accmuseum.org

The primary fund-raiser for the museum, this annual party in October has the best setting of any event all year—a natural rock plateau in Andreas Canyon, with a canopy of stars overhead and a grove of stately palms as a backdrop. This is the only time when the Canyons are open at night for an event, and it's truly special. Native American music, a silent auction, a brief awards program, and a gourmet dinner catered by the Spa Resort Casino are part of the evening.

Tickets are $300 per person. The event takes place in Andreas Canyon in the Palm Canyons, at the end of South Palm Canyon Drive, in Palm Springs.

American Heat Palm Springs Motorcycle and Hot Rod Weekend
Various locations on Palm Canyon Drive in downtown
(800) 200-4557
www.road-shows.com

This event in early October began a few years ago as a motorcycle fest, then added hot rods and vintage cars. Thousands of motorcyclists fill the streets during the three-day weekend, and virtually all of them are affluent, professional people riding bikes that cost more than most automobiles. There's a competition ride-in show, bike games, stunt shows, live music, and lots of vendors. Despite the noise, this is usually a very well-behaved crowd that adds a great deal of color and spice to the usually serene downtown. There is no admission charge for any of the events. Parking is free on the street.

Samsung World Championship
The Canyons Course at
Bighorn Golf Club
255 Palowet Drive, Palm Desert
(760) 341-9440, (888) 345-5742
http://product.samsung.com/golf

Since it began in 1980, the World Championship has become one of the most prestigious tournaments on the LPGA. The original format featured the world's top 12 women players and then expanded to 16 in 1996 and 20 in 1999. Each year the purse gets larger—$850,000 in 2005.

Day passes to this four-day event in mid-October are $15 to $20, and spectators are admitted to the Pro-Am Tournament for free during the annual Fan Appreciation Day. Parking is free, and a shuttle takes spectators to the course.

Tram Road Challenge
(No street address)
(760) 320–1341
www.tramroadchallenge.com

Billed as the world's toughest 6K, this race is uphill every step of the way. A desert tradition, it's gotten the better of many hardy runners, particularly if the weather is still in summer mode, as it can be in mid-October. Registration before October 2 is $20 for youth 14 and younger and adults 55 and older; and $25 for ages 15 to 54. Add $5.00 for registration after October 2. Parking is free, with shuttle service from the parking lot at the top of Tramway Road to the race start and from the race finish to the parking lot.

Walk-A-Thon "Footsteps for the Stroke Recovery Center"
Palm Springs High School Stadium
2401 East Baristo Road
(760) 323–7676
www.strokerecoverycenter.org

The walking here takes place in the Palm Springs High School Stadium, where spectators and tired walkers can also enjoy food booths, music, and a game area for younger children. All entry fees benefit the Stroke Recovery Center. Entry fees are $10.00 for adults and $5.00 for children 12 and younger. Parking is free on nearby streets.

Desert AIDS Walk
Begins at Sunrise Park
Sunrise Way between Ramon and Baristo Roads
(760) 323–2118
www.desertaidsproject.org

Heading into its second decade and now held in late October, this annual walk to benefit the desert organizations caring for

Golf carts are a big deal in the desert, and they're street-legal in Palm Desert. For the true aficionado, local dealers sell carts built to resemble Rolls Royces, Jaguars, Hummers, and other prestige autos.

AIDS patients is a festive affair for all ages and genders. It's pretty casual, meaning anyone can join in, though most walkers are there with their pledge cards in hand. Sign-up is at 7:00 A.M., followed by an easy walk downtown starting at 9:30 A.M. There is no admission charge, but pledges are accepted. Parking is free on the street.

Howl-O-Ween at the Living Desert
Living Desert Zoo and Gardens
47-900 Portola Avenue, Palm Desert
(760) 346–5694
www.livingdesert.org

Sponsored by the Berger Foundation, this is a gift to the desert's children, a fun way to celebrate Halloween safely with family and friends. All kids 12 and younger are invited to trick-or-treat at two dozen booths. Hot chocolate and other goodies are also available. The kids get bags to stuff with some of the 11 tons of candy that will be given out over the five-day event. Admission is $5.00 per person. Parking is free. Trick-or-treating is provided for children up to age 12. Check the Web site for exact days.

NOVEMBER

Rancho Mirage Art Affaire
Whitewater Park
71560 San Jacinto Drive, Rancho Mirage
(760) 324–4511
www.ci.rancho-mirage.ca.us

Around 100 fine art and crafts exhibits, jazz entertainment, food, and wine are the highlights of this two-day juried arts fair in early November. This is the city's biggest community event, and it attracts upward of 10,000 visitors each year. With its creation, the valley is well on the way to becoming a year-round venue for arts festivals and events. Admission and parking are free.

Greater Palm Springs Pride Festival
Parade on Palm Canyon Drive
downtown
Other events in Palm Springs Stadium
401 South Pavilion Way
(760) 416-8711
www.pspride.org
A local nonprofit group has been putting on Palm Springs Pride in early November for several years, arranging entertainment, booking vendors, and organizing the parade. The weekend festival celebrating gays and lesbians kicks off with this parade, a festive, lighthearted event that always packs the sidewalks with spectators and supporters. The fair in the Palm Springs Stadium is equally packed with vendors, food, and entertainment. No pets, coolers, or backpacks are allowed in the festival.

Admission is $10 per day at the festival gates. The event runs from 10:00 A.M. to 9:00 P.M. on Saturday and Sunday. The parade is scheduled for Saturday morning. Parking is free on nearby streets.

Palm Springs Veterans Day Parade
Palm Canyon Drive, downtown
(760) 323-8276
www.palm-springs.org
This rousing late-afternoon parade is sponsored by the City of Palm Springs to honor veterans of all wars. The Marine marching band is one of the big stars, and they provide a free public concert after the parade.

Dance Under the Stars
Choreography Festival
McCallum Theatre for the
Performing Arts
73000 Fred Waring Drive, Palm Desert
(760) 340-2787, (866) 889-2787
www.mccallumtheatre.com
Hosted by the McCallum Theatre Institute, the City of Palm Desert, and College of

the Desert, this is a two-day affair in mid-November that features professional and amateur dance companies and choreographers competing for cash prizes. Tickets range from $10 to $25 for the professional competition day and are free for the amateur day. Parking is free.

Phil Harris–Alice Faye Golf Classic
Desert Falls Country Club
1111 Desert Falls Parkway, Palm Desert
(760) 773-3076
This one-day tournament in November benefits the Arthritis Foundation. Prices and schedules are available in September.

Keith McCormick's Palm Springs Exotic
Car Show & Auction
Downtown Parking Garage
300 South Indian Canyon Drive
(760) 320-3290
www.classic-carauction.com
Held at the end of February and in mid-November every year, these classic car show-auctions often include as many as 400 cars for auction and an additional 200 cars for show. The 42nd car show-auction is scheduled for the end of February, 2007. If you can't make it to the venue, check out the excellent Web site, where you can preview and bid on the vehicles. Admission for the event is $10 per day or $15 for both days. On-street parking is free nearby.

AFI Comes to Palm Springs
Camelot Theatres
2300 East Baristo Road
(760) 325-6565
www.camelottheatres.com
This is a three-day event in mid-November that screens the audience and critical favorites from the American Film Institute's AFI Fest, a 10-day film extravaganza of screenings and special events held in Los Angeles each November. It's become a very hot ticket in town because it gives everyone a chance to see the top films without making the trek to Hollywood, thus avoiding both the hype and

extremely high prices of tickets and lodging. Ticket prices are not set until October, when the stars confirm their attendance.

Merrill Lynch Skins Game
Trilogy Golf Club
60-151 Trilogy Parkway, La Quinta
(760) 771-0707, (866) 754-6849
www.trilogygolfclub.com/skins
This three-day event pits the year's top PGA pro against three competitors vying for the title and a share of the $1-million purse. The first six holes are worth $25,000 each, the second six are worth $50,000 each, the next five pay out $70,000 apiece, and the final hole is worth $200,000.

Daily passes start at $20, and full weekend badges are $75. Tickets go on sale in September, and even though there are more than 14,000 spectators, tickets go very fast. The event is held over Thanksgiving weekend and is broadcast on ABC. Parking is free, and a shuttle takes spectators to the course.

Cabazon Indio Powwow
Fantasy Springs Resort Casino
84-245 Indio Springs Parkway, Indio
(760) 342-5000, (800) 827-2946
www.fantasyspringsresort.com
This three-day festival in late November is much the same as the one held here in late March. Visitors are encouraged to attend and are invited to join in intertribal dancing. The festival celebrates Native American dance, music, culture, and food. Artisans display and sell beadwork, paintings, pottery, leather crafts, jewelry, and more.

DECEMBER

Indio International Tamale Festival
Various locations in Old Town, Indio
(760) 342-6532
Held the first weekend in December, the festival takes place on Saturday and Sunday from 10:00 A.M. to 6:00 P.M. and kicks off with a parade on Saturday at 10:00

A.M. Live entertainment, mariachis, a carnival, fireworks, and more varieties of tamales than you thought existed make this one of the country's top 10 "All-American Food Festivals," according to the Food Network. It also holds the Guinness World Record for largest tamale—a foot in diameter and 40 feet long. Be prepared for crowds. It has attracted more than 100,000 people over the weekend in years past. Admission and parking are free.

Palm Springs Festival of Lights Parade
Palm Canyon Drive, from Ramon to Tamarisk Roads
(760) 325-5749
www.palm-springs.org
Held on the first weekend in December, this parade features lighted floats and displays of all kinds, marching bands, horseback riders, and lots of holiday spirit. It begins at 5:45 P.M. and can last as long as two hours.

Tree Lighting at the Top of the Tram
Mountain Station, Palm Springs
Aerial Tramway
One Tramway Road
(760) 325-1449
www.pstramway.com
A different celebrity has pulled the switch to light the mountaintop Christmas tree ever since the tradition began in the 1960s. Carolers, hot chocolate, and a jolly holiday atmosphere make this worth the trip. Tram tickets are $21 for adults, $14 for children 3 to 12, and $19 for adults 60 and older. Parking is free.

Dennis James Celebrity Golf Classic
The Golf Resort at Indian Wells
44-500 Indian Wells Lane, Indian Wells
(760) 321-8484
Ticket prices and schedules are announced a few months prior to this early-December one-day event, which benefits the Dennis James United Cerebral Palsy Center. The awards dinner is held at the Renaissance Esmeralda Resort and Spa in Indian Wells.

Wildlights at the Living Desert
Living Desert Zoo and Gardens
47-900 Portola Avenue, Palm Desert
(760) 346-5694
www.livingdesert.org
This is a wonderful holiday event for families with children. Huge light sculptures of different animals line the paths, and there's hot chocolate, cider, and cookies, as well as a jolly Santa to delight the small ones. Wildlights usually runs on various days throughout December and is a must-do for all ages. When you're there, be sure to stop by the nocturnal exhibit to get in the mood for exploring the desert at night. Admission is $6.75 for adults and $5.00 for children ages 3 to 12. Parking is free. Check the Web site for exact days.

ARTS AND ENTERTAINMENT

A rt is almost as big in the everyday life of the valley as is golf and shopping—a distant third, perhaps, but important in a big way for such a small area. Most cities now have an Art in Public Places (AIPP) program, following the lead of Palm Desert, which created the first AIPP back in 1986. That program requires developers to either install art in a public place or pay a fee for the arts program. The fee structure applies to every building project in the community and has become a national model for other cities.

From that program almost 100 works of art decorate the public places around Palm Desert and add to the already considerable beauty of the city. One of the largest collections of these pieces is installed every year on the grassy median that divides the two sides of El Paseo Drive. Sculptures of every genre decorate this strip, and a new exhibit is set up each January and is lighted at night—a nice accompaniment to dinner and drinks.

The city also has put together a sculpture walk as part of the visual landscape in the 72-acre Civic Center Park adjacent to City Hall and near College of the Desert. Palm Springs' AIPP program has its own particular flavor, which nicely ties the major pieces into the city's history and personality. The bronze statue of Lucille Ball on a park bench downtown at the corner of Tahquitz Canyon Way and Palm Canyon Drive is a must-stop for tourist photos, as is the larger-than-life statue of Sonny Bono next to the fountain a few blocks south on Palm Canyon Drive. Palm Springs tends to go with large, statement pieces, such as the enormous *Cahuilla Woman* that stands on the median across from the Spa Resort Casino. Elegant classi-cal bronze works and edgy modern pieces dot the downtown area and well-trafficked public places. Outside City Hall, Frank Bogert, the city's "cowboy mayor," is immortalized on his horse—a pose taken from a photo of the young wrangler when Palm Springs was just beginning to become known to the outside world. A fabulous construction by internationally famous glass artist Dale Chihuly hangs inside the Palm Springs Airport. Another Chihuly piece is the star attraction in the clubhouse for Palm Desert's public golf course, Desert Willow.

The Palm Springs area hosts a number of art events and festivals throughout the year. For listings, check the Annual Festivals and Events chapter.

GALLERIES

Adagio Galleries
**193 South Palm Canyon Drive
(760) 320-2230**

This spacious, airy gallery in downtown Palm Springs is known as the center for one of the country's finest collections of Southwest contemporary art. Modern masters with extensive representation include R. C. Gorman and Miguel Martinez. Paintings, sculpture, and watercolors are the predominant media.

If you fall in love with an art piece but are intimidated by shelling out the full price all at once, ask the gallery owners if they do payment plans. Many offer layaway arrangements that let you make regular payments over time until the piece is fully paid for.

A Gallery Fine Art
73956 El Paseo Drive, Palm Desert
(760) 346-8885

This contemporary-arts gallery has been around for more than 10 years. The collection of paintings, glass, sculpture, and jewelry features colorful, accessible pieces that highlight a few favorite returning artists as well as a changing roster of emerging, "trendy" ones.

Buschlen Mowatt Galleries
45188 Portola Avenue, Palm Desert
(760) 837-9668

One of the newest and most prestigious galleries in the desert, this is an 8,500-square-foot showcase for leading contemporary artists in fine painting and sculpture. This is truly a collector's gallery, and many of the works would be at home in the Palm Springs Art Museum. A select number of emerging artists are featured. The opening events for new exhibitions draw the wealthy and wannabes from all over the desert and are an entertainment worth attending.

Coda Gallery
73151 El Paseo Drive, Palm Desert
(760) 346-4661

Coda is a riot of color, featuring whimsical furniture, sculpture, paintings, glassworks, and jewelry. This is the place to go for the statement piece with a sense of fun and for a warm and casual atmosphere that never intimidates. Regular artists include Bye Bitney, E. David Dornan, Kent Wallis, and John Kennedy.

Denise Roberge Art Gallery
73995 El Paseo Drive, Palm Desert
(760 340-5045

A part of the Denise Roberge "empire" that includes Augusta restaurant and the Roberge jewelry salon, this large space always has a fine selection of well-known artists represented in painting and sculpture. Styles run from traditional to contemporary and postmodern.

Desert Art Center
550 North Palm Canyon Drive
(760) 323-7973

Located in what was the valley's first elementary school, this homey little place offers workshops, art classes, twice-yearly art fairs, and a small gallery featuring works by local artists. The selections are strictly beginning and a bit above, but there are still some charming pieces and the occasional stunner.

Dezart One Gallery
2688 Cherokee Way
(760) 328-1440

This little jewel box is the heart of the desert's emerging interest in innovative modern and contemporary art. The three artist-owners—Marian Moiseyev, Kim Chasen, and Downs—show their own pieces and have cultivated an outstanding roster of emerging and midcareer contemporary artists. They are the staff here and, as such, offer an unusual depth of warmth and knowledge for the novice or experienced collector. Their regular open studio exhibitions in their next-door workspace have a hip, bohemian feel and always draw lively crowds to meet the artists and see how the works come together.

Edenhurst Gallery
63655 El Paseo Drive, Palm Desert
(760) 346-7900

This lovely space features traditional work, including early California paintings by Guy Rose, William Wendt, Edgar Payne, Maynard Dixon, and Paul Grimm. Included on the walls are fine historical European works and a broad-genre selection of living artists working in traditional styles.

Though more galleries are staying open year-round, some still close for the summer months, particularly those run by longtime desert residents who make a practice of spending those dog days at the beach or in the mountains.

Elonore Austerer Gallery
73660 El Paseo Drive, Palm Desert
(760) 346-3695

Modern masters and international contemporary art are the focus here. The gallery specializes in original works on paper and rare graphic work by well-known 20th-century artists.

Gallery 1000
73400 El Paseo Drive, Suite 1
Palm Desert
(760) 346-2230

Noted European artists are represented here, with an emphasis on quality across a variety of media, including Impressionistic oil paintings, dry-point engravings, sculptures, and bas-relief. Major artists include Marcel Demagny, Duaiv, Anatoly Dverin, and Karl Jensen.

The Hart Gallery
73111 El Paseo Drive, Palm Desert
(760) 346-4243

This gallery specializes in fine prints, with a mixture of contemporary artists and acknowledged masters. This is the place to find rare and beautiful works by Pablo Picasso, Henri Matisse, Marc Chagall, and Joan Miró, as well as pieces by their peers.

Imago Galleries
45450 Highway 74, Palm Desert
(760) 776-9890

This avant-garde, hard-edged modern building caused a stir locally when it popped up behind the much more traditional El Paseo Drive. Outside, the sculpture garden and terrace exhibit outsize works that tend to unhinge jaws. Inside the 18,000-square-foot gallery, there are major exhibits of internationally recognized artists in painting, sculpture, glass, and photography, as well as artists' quarters where visiting artists can relax and make themselves at home. Like Buschlen Mowatt and Dezart, this place is known for its very upscale and energetic openings.

The artists who have studios on Corporate Way in Palm Desert—just a few miles from the middle of El Paseo— usually have an informal meet-and-greet event one night a month. Check the online guide, www.desertguide.com, for schedules.

Jones & Terwilliger Galleries
73375 El Paseo Drive, Suite A
Palm Desert
(760) 674-8989

The focus is on original, traditional art with a strong talent pool drawn from well-respected American, Italian, Chinese, and Spanish artists. A vast variety of styles is showcased in the paintings and sculpture, and a very knowledgeable staff will help you find the perfect piece.

Modern Masters Fine Art
73200 El Paseo Drive, Suite 3A
Palm Desert
(760) 568-9505

This is the type of gallery you might expect to find in La Jolla or Newport Beach—an elegant, intimate space with a charming courtyard and a delicious selection of major 20th-century artists. Works by Helen Frankenthaler, Pablo Picasso, Andy Warhol, Alexander Calder, Keith Haring, and other well-known artists establish this as a source for classic contemporary work.

Mountain Trails Gallery
73425 El Paseo Drive, Palm Desert
(760) 568-9505

Every good gallery town must have at least one place devoted to western art, and this is Palm Desert's. Works by Michael Albrechtsen, Simon Winegar, Scott Richardson, Stanley Proctor, Mark Pettit, and Ray McCarty offer a wide selection of fine landscapes and other art and establish this as a well-respected source for this popular American art form.

R. E. Welch Gallery
73680 El Paseo Drive, Palm Desert
(760) 341-8141
This gallery is more for beginning collectors or art lovers who just "know what they like" without regard for the fame of the artist or price of the piece. Contemporary European artists offer fresh and sophisticated works in an unpretentious space.

Ron Chespak Gallery/DKC Art and Design
139 East Tamarisk Road
(760) 416-7406
Ron Chespak's unusual white-on-white paper sculptures are the focal point in a space that also provides art consultation and interior design service. Fine art by others, including Andy Lakey, Herman Sillas, Carson Grier, and Anthony Villas, is primarily contemporary.

Tres Contemporary
73199 El Paseo Drive, Suite H, Palm Desert
(760) 568-2010
As the name says, the art here is quite contemporary, though not out on the edge. A number of emerging and midcareer artists are represented in changing exhibits throughout the year. The gallery is relaxed and upscale in an unobtrusive way, with a very savvy staff who can make even the novice feel at home.

ART MUSEUM

Palm Springs Art Museum
101 Museum Drive
(760) 325-7186
www.psmuseum.org
From a one-room facility in 1938 to today's 125,000-square-foot facility, the museum has greatly expanded its collections and programs. It now houses a collection of over 7,000 objects, including a significant collection of pre-Columbian artifacts and Native American baskets and tools, western American paintings and sculptures,

and major pieces from respected international artists in every media.

Each year the museum mounts several major exhibitions and has become known for its focus on bringing a multifaceted overview of the art world to the desert's residents.

PERFORMING ARTS

Annenberg Theater
In the Palm Springs Art Museum
101 Museum Drive
(760) 325-4490
Located in the art museum, the Annenberg Theater is an intimate 433-seat space with near-perfect acoustics and an excellent line of sight from every seat. The programmers try to mix it up with scheduling, combining comedy, jazz, classical, dance, and lectures each season.

One of the city's biggest events is the night when the theater opens for the season, usually in early November. It's black tie and glitzy, with a rising young performing star to draw the crowds. A number of different series run through the year, with package prices that can make admission very reasonable. The Musical Chairs series features celebrity guests, who join a revolving company of top local and national professionals to salute composers and musical themes. The small stage is an excellent showcase for winners of national and international competitions in voice, piano, violin, and other instruments, as well as small jazz and classical groups and standup comedians.

The valley's best value for performing arts is often the theater's Sunday Afternoon Concerts series, which presents outstanding chamber music by soloists and groups. Dress at the Annenberg runs the gamut from shorts to very presentable evening attire.

Cirque Dreams
Palm Springs Pavilion Theatre
123 North Palm Canyon Drive
(760) 778-1438, (866) 877-6779
www.palmsprings.com/cirquedreams/
The city of Palm Springs is still holding its

breath to see if this new venture will bring a key section of downtown back to life again. The Desert Fashion Plaza, once the hub of upscale retail, has been a "black hole" in the middle of downtown in recent years. Several attempts by developers to revitalize this prime parcel have fizzled, primarily because the city has been reluctant to commit public funds to the projects. Now, entrepreneur/producer Neil Goldberg of Cirque Productions has teamed up with Dick Taylor Productions to launch the Palm Springs Pavilion Theatre, an upscale, 1,000-seat tent at the rear of the Desert Fashion Plaza.

The venue is the home of Cirque Dreams, a Cirque du Soleil-type extravaganza that opened for a five-month run in the spring of 2006 and is set to ramp up again in the winter 2006/2007 season. Taylor hasn't shown a profit from these types of shows, which feature artists who often performed with the Montreal-based Cirque du Soleil, but he's received such a positive response from people who have seen them that he's enthusiastic about the future of Cirque Dreams. He also received a $300,000 interest-free loan from the city of Palm Springs to develop the show in a tent facility, and a three-year, $1.00-a-year lease from Desert Fashion Plaza. That feat alone should qualify as the show's most impressive performance.

Cirque Dreams is an 80-minute, fast-paced and elaborately costumed spectacle with no intermission. Tickets are $45 to $59 with validated parking, making the show and dinner at a nearby restaurant similar in cost to the $110 cirque and theater-style dinner shows at the Teatro ZinZanni tent theaters in San Francisco and Seattle.

The Fabulous Palm Springs Follies
The Plaza Theater
128 South Palm Canyon Drive
(505) 327-0225
www.palmspringsfollies.com

Riff Markowitz, a theatrical impresario of the old school, came up with the idea for this vaudeville-style revue, and he's been

The Palm Springs Art Museum usually offers at least one free day each month and may have special discount promotions, depending on the time of year. Check their Web site (www.psmuseum .org) to get the latest information.

packing them in since 1991. The Follies features perhaps the country's most unusual live entertainment premise. The elaborate shows are a modern-day, very slick version of old-time vaudeville, complete with what Riff calls the "signature line of long-legged lovelies" decked out in fabulous costumes and headdresses that rival the best in Vegas. Musical numbers call for these hoofers to dance, sing, and strut for as many as nine shows a week, Tuesday through Saturday, November through May. The show also highlights vocal groups, acts like ventriloquists, and performing animals.

All of the performers have had professional careers on Broadway and in musicals, movies, and live entertainment shows—and are now reviving those careers on the stage of the historic Plaza Theater, the valley's first movie house. The catch (and the draw) is that all of the performers are also what many producers would term "over the hill"—they're between the ages of 55 and 80. The show is an inspiration for anyone who has doubts about what their golden years might hold—and it's a remarkably well-done and entertaining creation. Tickets sell out fast, so if you're planning to attend when you visit, buy them online before you go.

Both Palm Desert and Palm Springs publish maps to the public art installations in their cities. Check the Web sites of both to get the latest version: www.palmdesertart.com and www.palm-springs.org.

CLOSE-UP

Riff Markowitz

Some say that Riff Markowitz is the very incarnation of Broadway showman and impresario Flo Ziegfeld. That may be, but Flo had the Great White Way as his territory and the most beautiful and talented young performers in the country vying for a spot in his shows. Riff has the distinction of breathing new life into a moribund downtown and doing it with performers whose stage days are far in the past. The Fabulous Palm Springs Follies, a vaudeville-style show with dancers and performers over the age of 55, was a concept that had a lot of doubters when Riff proposed it to Palm Springs in 1991. Riff wanted to put his show into the old Plaza Theater, a historical building with a lot of charm and a fabulous location downtown. But the Plaza was old, and refitting it to show modern movies just didn't make economic sense to any of the developers being wooed by the city's redevelopment people. It turned out to be the perfect venue for a variety show that, years later, has been written up in every major newspaper and magazine in this country and abroad and featured in dozens of broadcast programs.

Riff's background as a risk taker and entertainment genius stood him in good stead with the Follies. When he was just 15, he ran away from home and joined the circus as a tramp clown, moving on to become a radio deejay in northern Canada. He soon moved on to television and spent 30 years writing, producing, and directing variety TV shows, working with such big stars as Crystal Gayle, George Burns, Wolfman Jack, Abba, Tom Jones, Lauren Bacall, and Raquel Welch. In addition, he produced a number of specials starring cherished comedian Red Skelton, culminating in a Royal Command Performance at London's Royal Albert Hall. He also produced and cocreated HBO's award-winning dramatic hit series, *The Hitchhiker*.

He took early retirement in Palm Springs and sold his entertainment interests, including a Canadian pay television network and state-of-the-art postproduction studio. Quickly becoming restless without the excitement of producing, he came up with the Follies—an old-style stage show with Las Vegas–quality costumes and production values, and a cast of "a certain age."

Today his original pledge guides the

**McCallum Theatre for the Performing Arts
73000 Fred Waring Drive, Palm Desert
(866) 889-2787**
Barry Manilow is a regular performer here, and that says a lot about the age group of the audience. Each year there will be a few performers who rate a bit higher on the younger-and-hip scale, such as Seal, Lyle Lovett, and Trisha Yearwood, but this is not a cutting-edge venue. A look at the schedule for 2005–2006 shows Bill Maher, Daryl Hall and John Oates, Olivia Newton-John, Tango Nacional Argentina, the Gatlin Brothers, Little Shop of Horrors, Dame Edna, Paul Anka, and a good variety of musical and performing groups. Barry Manilow was the headliner for the holiday fund-raiser.

The Fabulous Palm Springs Follies prides itself on professional, highly elaborate staging, production, and costumes. PHOTO BY NED REDWAY

seasonal shows: "To remain true to the spirits of the '20s, '30s, and '40s, keeping alive and well the music, comedy, and dance of those eras. As well, you have our pledge of providing a world-class entertainment experience at every performance."

Many in the city of Palm Springs give Riff and the Follies credit for bringing new life into downtown, attracting new shops, restaurants, and nightclubs, and revitalizing the whole feel of the city. The show has earned international fame and is still packing the house for every performance. And Riff himself has become as well known in live entertainment circles as Ziegfeld was in his day. The onetime tramp clown and deejay produces, directs, and emcees one of the most enduring and popular live shows in the nation, astounding audiences with the agility, beauty, and talent of performers whose ages start at 55 and go up to 80.

A desert institution, the McCallum had its beginning in 1973 with a group that called itself Friends of the Cultural Center, Inc. They had a vision of creating a year-round permanent home for performing arts of all types for all residents. Named for a longtime desert family and supported with funding from all the desert cities, the McCallum opened in 1988 and has been expanding and improving its space and offerings ever since. The McCallum Theatre Institute introduces thousands of young people and adults to the joys of the performing arts, filling a void created by the elimination of arts programs in public schools. Each year the McCallum offers free performances and arts education programs to 43 local schools, involving almost

Bring a little extra cash for champagne and treats during intermission at the McCallum Theatre for the Performing Arts. This is a see-and-be-seen time, and it's great fun to people-watch with a glass of bubbly in hand.

35,000 kids and teachers.

With a growing reputation as one of the country's most beautiful and prestigious small theaters, the McCallum attracts more than 150,000 theatergoers annually, with an average occupancy rate of 86 percent, versus a national average of 60 percent.

The theater is a beautiful midsize venue with continental-style seating on three levels, a carpeted floor to improve acoustics, and a top seating capacity of 1,127. This is the desert, and it's a stretch to find anyplace where the crowd is consistently well dressed for evening events, so it's a treat to arrive at the McCallum and realize that almost everyone else took the same care in choosing their clothing and buffing up their appearance as you did. The McCallum's performances can be fairly pricey, so be sure to check for matinee tickets, which are often substantially cheaper than those at night.

Palm Canyon Theatre
538 North Palm Canyon Drive
(760) 323-5123
www.palmcanyontheatre.com
A nonprofit professional Actor's Equity theater, this little troupe is the essence of community theater. And because it's in the desert where a lot of professional actors live in retirement or semiretirement, the cast tends to have some serious acting chops. The plays are classics—*The Sunshine Boys, Sweeney Todd, Kiss Me Kate, Noises Off,* and similar well-loved productions. The setting is small and intimate, and the price is right—less than $30 for evening or matinee performances. The season runs from September through June, with a two-week run of a different play each month.

Senior Class—A Revue of the Golden Years
Palme d'Or Theatre
Westfield Shoppingtown, Palm Desert
(760) 838-3003
www.seniorclassrevue.com
Those who are nostalgic for days past will want to make their way to Palm Desert's Palme d'Or Theatre on Friday and Saturday from November through May, when *Senior Class—A Revue of the Golden Years* hits the stage. *Senior Class* is a series of witty and touching vignettes about seniors in their golden years in a musical format. Written by Saul Ilson, former Vice President of Comedy Development for NBC Television, the play looks at six senior citizens as they reflect on their past, present, and future, and the performers are as seasoned as the characters they portray. They include singer/actress Anna Maria Alberghetti; singer Julius LaRosa; television, film, and stage performer Ruta Lee; Broadway luminary and film and television regular Marcia Rodd; comedian and former *Gomer Pyle* regular Ronnie Schell; and singer/comedian Steve Rossi. The show is directed by Emmy-winning producer Geno Marcione and produced by television veteran Allan Blye.

KIDSTUFF

N ot so long ago, families visiting the Palm Springs area with small children would be hard-pressed to find entertainment beyond the pool and the movies. The destination was not only adult-oriented but also a place where people came to "just do nothing," and even the grown-ups found themselves pretty much limited to golf, sunning, and the odd game of tennis.

Today the desert's year-round residents as well as its visitors are younger than they were just 10 years ago. The perceived dangers of traveling out of the country and a general "nesting" trend in all aspects of life have meant that more and more families are taking their vacations together. All of this has not escaped the attention of the area's tourism businesses, which are increasingly careful to tailor at least some of their offerings to families traveling with children.

When you're in the desert with children, make sure to spend at least some of your time outdoors. In addition to its international reputation as a Hollywood "retreat" and golf capital, Palm Springs is finally becoming known for its wealth of natural resources. The mountains all around the valley are protected wilderness areas, with miles of hiking trails that go from the dusty desert into the cool pines and lush palm oases. The beauty of it all is that the wilds are just a few minutes from wherever you are in the desert. Very few tourist destinations offer such varied opportunities to really experience nature, from watching the lizards scamper over the rocks in the Indian Canyons to touching a majestic fir tree that smells like vanilla at the top of the Tram.

PRICE CODE

Price ranges apply to a regular season admission for one. Unless noted otherwise, assume that major credit cards are accepted at all locations.

$	Up to $10
$$	$11 to $20
$$$	$21 to $30

All the attractions listed are in Palm Springs, unless noted otherwise.

ATTRACTIONS

Big League Dreams Sports Park   **$$**
33-700 Date Palm Drive, Cathedral City
(760) 324-5600
www.bigleaguedreams.com
The big attraction here is baseball and softball—three of the fields are small replicas of Fenway Park, Wrigley Field, and Yankee Stadium—and pickup games are available if you call ahead. Among the activities and facilities are batting cages, four sand volleyball courts, a mini-soccer field, and a tot lot for the little ones, as well as a covered in-line hockey facility and a pretty good restaurant. Outside food and drinks are not allowed. It's a clean, safe, and well-run facility.

The park typically opens at 8:00 A.M. and closes after the last game is played. Call for exact hours. Admission is free for spectators 12 and younger; however, all activities require tokens, and these do add up quickly.

Boomers! Family Fun Center   **$$-$$$**
67-700 East Palm Canyon Drive,
Cathedral City
(760) 770-7522
www.boomersparks.com

Tour companies, particularly those that tour in jeeps, have age requirements, and many do not allow young children. Check for specifics before you book.

The Palm Springs Art Museum offers classes and special events for kids all summer. You can sign your kids up for a one-time class or movie and tour the museum while they're occupied.

More the typical amusement park/arcade setup than anything else, Boomers has miniature golf, go-Karts, bumper boats, batting cages, a rock wall for climbing, and a noisy, cheesy video arcade plus snack bar. This is not the best-kept place, but it's safe and may be a good option for the kids to let off steam on a slow summer night. Unless you have teenagers and they just have to get away for a bit, this is a parent-with-child facility, so plan on scrunching into those bumper boats and acting like a kid yourself.

Hours are Monday through Thursday 11:00 A.M. to 9:00 P.M., Friday through Saturday 10:00 A.M. to 11:00 P.M., and Sunday 10:00 A.M. to 9:00 P.M. You can choose an all-day admission pass or enter and pay for activities on an a la carte basis.

**Children's Discovery Museum
of the Desert** $
71-701 Gerald Ford Drive, Rancho Mirage
(760) 321-0602
www.cdmod.org
You and your young children can easily spend most of the day here, playing and learning. There are more than 50 hands-on exhibits, including the down-and-dirty Dig It, a kid-scale archaeological dig where children dig for actual Cahuilla Indian artifacts. There's a child-size grocery store where the kids can shop, act as cashiers, move the stuff around, and play grown-up. Vintage clothes and props are another fun make-believe activity. Everything here is geared to a child's imagination, and nothing is hands-off.

This is not a place where you can drop off the kids for a few hours, but rather a spot where the entire family is encouraged to play together. The gift shop is full of fun and educational gifts and toys that are perfect for entertaining small ones back at the hotel. Outside, there's an outdoor amphitheater where special events and activities are held, community gardens, and a covered picnic area.

Golf for Kids

Many of the local golf courses have junior golf leagues and provide lessons, play, and junior golf equipment for rent at very affordable prices. Some to try:

Desert Willow Golf Resort
38-995 Desert Willow Drive
Palm Desert
(760) 340-4057
www.desertwillow.com

Cimarrón Golf Resort
67-603 30th Avenue, Cathedral City
(760) 770-6060
www.cimarrongolf.com

Tahquitz Creek Golf Academy
1885 Golf Club Drive
(760) 328-1005
www.tahquitzcreek.com
This facility offers free adult and junior clinics daily, from January through May.

Check the Web site for such events as free family fun nights, toddler parties, and holiday activities. Classes and special programs for ages one through four are planned throughout the week. For more details, see the listing in the Attractions chapter.

The museum is open Monday through Saturday 10:00 A.M. to 5:00 P.M. and on Sunday noon to 5:00 P.M. It is closed on Monday from May through December.

Desert IMAX Theatre $
Highway 111 at Cathedral Canyon Drive
Cathedral City
(760) 324-7333

This is a typical IMAX, which means lots of amazing nature and adventure documentaries, plus great animation on staggeringly large and lifelike screens. Be sure to check *The Desert Sun*'s movie listings, as this facility regularly runs specials and offers discount coupons that can save a lot for a large family.

The Indian Canyons $
38-500 South Palm Canyon Drive
(760) 325-3400, (800) 790-3398
www.indian-canyons.com

Tahquitz Canyon $$
500 West Mesquite Avenue
(760) 416-7044

The Indian Canyons are the ancestral home of the Agua Caliente Band of Cahuilla Indians, the original Palm Springs residents. Thousands of years ago they developed complex communities here, relying on the abundant water, plants, and animals that flourished in these natural palm oases. Today many remains of that ancient society—rock art, house pits, foundations, irrigation ditches, trails, and food preparation areas—still exist in the canyons.

The three canyons at the south end of Palm Springs—Andreas, Murray, and Palm—are listed on the National Register of Historic Places. They are the only places in North America where the California fan palm grows naturally, and they are quiet

Sacred to the local tribe, Tahquitz Canyon is said to be home to an evil spirit who will snatch up wandering children. The "Witch of Tahquitz" appears as a shadow in the shape of a witch on a broomstick in the early morning or late afternoon. Look west from the intersection of Farrell Drive and Vista Chino.

spots from which you can escape the diversions of resort life.

Located on Agua Caliente tribal land, just a few minutes' drive from downtown, Andreas, Murray, and Palm Canyons are true, natural palm oases, with waterfalls, streams, and cool canopies of towering palm trees. Palm Canyon and Andreas Canyon also have the world's largest stand of naturally occurring palm trees. This is one of the desert's three "must-see" attractions, along with the Living Desert and the Palm Springs Aerial Tramway.

Pack a picnic and wear your walking shoes because you'll want to spend the day here, exploring, hiking, or just dreaming.

To reach the canyons, follow South Palm Canyon Drive in Palm Springs until it dead-ends, just a few minutes from downtown. Andreas Canyon is the easiest spot to access, just steps from a paved parking lot. About a half mile away is Murray Canyon, with unusual rock formations, and Andreas Creek, which runs year-round.

At the end of the canyons road is majestic Palm Canyon, one of the most beautiful wild areas in the country. At the top of the canyon, the trading post sells maps, refreshments, Native American arts and crafts, and books. A lovely little waterfall is a short walk away. A paved, moderately graded footpath winds down into the canyon and its 15 miles of hiking trails, waterfalls, and picnic areas.

Ranger-led interpretive hikes provide a wealth of information about the canyons and the Agua Caliente Band of Cahuilla Indians. The hikes are usually about a mile in total and will accommodate most ages

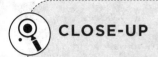

Children's Discovery Museum
of the Desert

The desert was not always a family place. In the early days of Palm Springs, those who could afford it sent their children off to boarding schools. Those who could not had to work to make sure their kids grew up with a sense of discovery and curiosity about the world. For working parents without the time to spend exploring the mountains and deserts, there were few places to go for a solid learning experience that was also fun.

Twenty years ago a group of concerned valley residents took up the challenge of creating a place where kids could learn and express themselves through play and without commercialism. These visionary founders could see the time when arts and music programs would drop off the public schools' list of necessities, and they set to work. The City of Palm Desert, long the valley's leader in quality-of-life issues, put up money for a needs assessment in 1987, and by 1990 the museum opened its office and first exhibits and started an exciting school outreach program.

The museum always has been a collaboration with kids and their families, schools, and communities. In 1991 Rancho Mirage and Indian Wells joined Palm Desert to create a $1.6-million building trust fund, and in 1992 the organization won the California Teachers Association State Gold Award.

Innovative programs with *Scholastic*, Microsoft, Crayola, and the *Los Angeles Times,* a family theater series, and a constantly changing smorgasbord of hands-on exhibits and activities have kept the museum fresh and kept the kids coming back. Before the permanent building opened in 1998, more than 20,000 children and their families took advantage of the fun. A look at the most recent statistics shows that this has grown to almost 100,000 a year.

Private and public donations paid for the current building, an elegantly designed 18,000 square feet of fun and learning. It sits on four acres donated by the Honorable Walter Annenberg and another two and a half acres that were also donated. In addition to the exhibit gallery, the campus includes a multipurpose facility named the Dinah Shore Center, an outdoor covered performance area/amphitheater, horticultural gardens, and a "logo grove." In its first six years of operation, the museum has served over 350,000 visitors, including 60,000 children on school field trips. Held regularly are summer and holiday camps; toddler, art, and dance programs; classes; performances; family fun days; birthday par-

Painting an old VW bug—over and over again—is one of the fun activities at the Children's Discovery Museum of the Desert. PHOTO BY TOM BREWSTER, COURTESY OF THE CDMOD

ties; museum store events; and more.

In 2001 the Children's Discovery Museum of the Desert was ranked number 20 in the nation and number 2 in California, important recognition on a wide scale that its mission of generating a "spark of lifelong learning" is being fulfilled.

Rangers at Joshua Tree National Park conduct free guided hikes and presentations on desert animals and plant life. This is also the best spot to view the stars in the night sky, and the locals often come out for free, family-oriented "star-watching parties." Check the Web site, www.joshua.tree.national-park .com, for dates and times.

and abilities. Call for the daily hike schedule and register at the trading post.

Tahquitz Canyon is just a few blocks from downtown Palm Springs and is famous for its spectacular 60-foot waterfall, rock art, wild setting, and amazing view of the city. The only access to Tahquitz is on a ranger-led hiking tour over rocky trails. The hike takes about two and a half hours total and is not appropriate for young children, who may have a hard time keeping up. For families with active kids older than eight or nine, though, it is a wonderful adventure. For more details, see the listing in the Attractions chapter.

The Indian Canyons and Tahquitz Canyon are open daily from 7:30 A.M. to 5:00 P.M. August through June; in July they're open from 8:00 A.M. to 5:00 P.M. Friday through Sunday. Tahquitz Canyon may close in the summer; beginning in June, be sure to phone to get up-to-date information. Reservations are required for the guided tours to Tahquitz Canyon. The last tour of the day begins at 3:00 P.M. Call for hours and a tour schedule.

Joshua Tree National Park   **$–$$**
Joshua Tree National Park
Visitors Center
74485 National Park Drive
Twentynine Palms
(760) 367–5522
www.joshua.tree.national-park.com
Located just south of the town of Twentynine Palms in what's referred to as the "high desert," Joshua Tree National Park is a pristine desert wilderness area covering

794,000 square miles. The park's enormous boulder formations draw rock climbers, photographers, and visitors from all over the world; locals who have spotted UFOs here say that the park is attracting visitors from other galaxies as well. This is an ideal spot to watch the summer meteor showers, as it's miles from the light pollution of the lower desert and the skies are clear virtually all year.

In the spring the park can be carpeted overnight with dozens of species of wildflowers, and if the rains have been particularly propitious in the winter, the many cacti and Joshua trees will be showing off blooms that range from white through brilliant fuchsia. Hikers will find 35 miles of trails, and campers can spend the night at nine primitive campsites with fire grates and picnic tables.

Home to the Pinto Native Americans hundreds of years ago, the area saw an influx of explorers, cattlemen, and miners in the late 1800s. Though gold was discovered and mined here, there was never a big "strike," and the lack of water made life too rough for most settlers.

Bill and Francis Keys were hardy types, though, homesteading 160 acres in the early part of the last century and building the Desert Queen Ranch on the site of the defunct Desert Queen Mine. Park rangers lead tours of the ranch grounds, which include the ranch house, schoolhouse, store, workshop, orchard, and piles of mining equipment that help tell the story of life almost a hundred years ago. Whether you're coming to climb, shoot photos, hike, or picnic, Joshua Tree is well worth a full day. Permits are required for backcountry camping. Pets must be on a leash and attended at all times and are not allowed on nature trails.

The park is open year-round. The visitor centers are open daily from 8:00 A.M. to 5:00 P.M. The Oasis Visitor Center is located at the Twentynine Palms entrance. The Cottonwood Visitor Center is at the south entrance. The Black Rock Canyon Visitor Center is at the campground southeast of Yucca Valley.

If you're planning on multiple visits, you might consider the $125 individual annual pass. The seven-day pass, at $10 per vehicle, is a good value, particularly for families.

Knott's Soak City U.S.A. & Rocky Point $$$
1500 Gene Autry Trail
(760) 327-0499
www.soakcityusa.com

Admission to the Knott's Soak City water park includes unlimited use of all water rides and attractions. There's an additional charge for parking and locker rentals. If you're going for the day and want to splurge, cabana rentals give you a large private cabana and your own private, relatively uncrowded sunning area to use as home base in between rides and swimming.

There are 18 major water "attractions," including big and little water slides and an 800,000-gallon wave pool that mimics the ocean surf well enough to call for boogie boards. For future surfers there's Gremmie Lagoon, a kids' water playground, and Kahuna's Beach House, a family-interactive water playhouse.

You are not allowed to bring in food or beverages, so budget for some burgers and soft drinks. Men's and women's changing rooms offer lockers for a small fee. Life vests and tubes are provided free. This isn't the beach; so don't bring chairs, barbecues, or much of anything extra besides standard swimwear and towels. Other rules ban long pants, denim, and swimwear with metal or plastic ornamentation in the pool and activity areas. Soak City is a well-kept, orderly family attraction. If you've got kids longing to cut loose from the quiet of the hotel pool, this is the place where they can scream and giggle to their heart's content.

Adjacent to Knott's is Rocky Point, an outdoor, shaded, and micro-cooled facility with 7,500 square feet of man-made rock walls to climb—a total of 125 different routes up to 55 feet long. Classes and programs are geared to all skill levels and are suitable for children as young as four years old. The two facilities share a parking lot.

Knott's Soak City offers nicely discounted admissions after 3:00 P.M. With summer days that don't get dark until almost 9:00 P.M., you can save money and enjoy the water when the sun's rays are less likely to create instant sunburn.

Admission is separate for the two operations. For more details, see the Attractions chapter.

Knott's is open from March through October.

Living Desert Zoo and Gardens $$
47-900 Portola Avenue, Palm Desert
(760) 346-5694
www.livingdesert.org

Established in 1970, the Living Desert today is one of the most successful zoological parks in the country, attracting more than 275,000 visitors each year. At the Living Desert you'll discover nearly 400 fascinating desert animals representing more than 150 species, including coyotes, bighorn sheep, Arabian oryx (also known as the "unicorn of the desert"), zebras, cheetahs, and meerkats.

One of the facility's many strong points is its organization. Depending on your available time and attention span, you can tour the entire park or focus on one or two special areas, such as Eagle Canyon, with its streams, mountain lions, bobcats, Mexican wolves, and golden eagles. The African exhibit, Village WaTuTu, is an authentic replica of a 19th-century Nigerian village, with mud huts, an Elders Circle, and a storyteller's area. Little children will be thrilled with the Petting Kraal, where they can feed and pet sheep, goats, and Ankole cat-

The Living Desert has a full schedule of activities and events planned especially for children. The golden eagle exhibit is amazing and allows kids to get up close to these magnificent birds.

> The best time to see the animals at the Living Desert is when the park opens in the cool morning hours. Most of the animals are at their most active before noon; in the afternoon the intense sun drives them to seek shade and rest.

tle. Other animals here include leopards, camels, hyenas, giraffes, and ostriches. There's a very good casual restaurant, a snack bar, and a gift shop as well.

Because there are so many different activities and events going on, it's a good idea to call before you visit or check the daily schedule on the excellent Web site for updated events, programs, special tours, demonstrations, or lectures. Regular tram shuttles, guided tours, gift shops, first aid stations, restaurants, baby-changing stations, and ATMs make this a full-service attraction for the family. For additional information, check the Attractions chapter.

The Living Desert is open daily from 9:00 A.M. to 5:00 P.M. September 1 through June 15, with the last admission at 4:00 P.M.; it is closed on December 25. It's open daily from 8:00 A.M. to 1:30 P.M. June 16 through August 31, with the last admission at 1:00 P.M. Regular, non-narrated shuttle service is available throughout the park for an extra charge. Parking is free.

Palm Springs Aerial Tramway $$
One Tramway Road
(760) 325-1391, (888) 515-8726
www.pstramway.com
A trip to the top of the Tram in Palm Springs is like a ride on the Staten Island Ferry in Manhattan—you've just got to do it. This is one of the world's longest tram

> Guided hikes at the Palm Springs Aerial Tramway are easy enough for all skill levels and an excellent way to introduce your children to this mountain wilderness.

rides, almost straight up from sea level to the Mountain Station at 8,516 feet. The ride up is in a very stable, 80-person car that rotates 360 degrees over the course of the 15-minute ride, giving everyone a stellar view of the desert below.

At the top, the views are even more breathtaking from the balcony and dining areas, both inside and outside. There's a good cafeteria-style restaurant, a gift shop, and a short educational film, plus viewing platforms with telescopes. A short walk down a steep incline leads you right into the Mount San Jacinto State Park and Wilderness, a cool pine forest with lovely meadows that are dotted with flowers in the spring and covered with snow in the winter.

In the colder months (the Tram top is always 30 to 40 degrees colder than the desert), the Winter Adventure Center rents snowshoes and cross-country skis. Free guided hikes are held daily, and the trails are gentle and clearly marked. It's a great place for a cool picnic in the summertime and a bracing snowball fight in the winter. Overnight camping and backpacking are by permit only. For additional information, check the Attractions chapter.

Tram cars depart at least every half hour, starting at 10:00 A.M., Monday through Friday, and starting at 8:00 A.M. on weekends and during holiday periods. The last car up is at 8:00 P.M., with the last car down being at 9:45 P.M. Ride 'n' Dine specials that give a discount for a ride and a meal are available after 3:00 P.M.

Whitewater Trout Farm $–$$$
9160 Whitewater Canyon Road
Whitewater
(760) 325-5570
www.campingfriend.com/whitewater troutfarm/
For families wanting a bit of an outdoor camping experience, and a little guaranteed fishing thrown in, Whitewater is a good option. The facility grew up around a commercial trout-farming operation and still supplies trout to the desert's restaurants, so you can be sure that the fish

you're catching are in very good company. Whitewater is a far cry from the wilds, but the location is secluded and quiet, the staff is quite accommodating, and it's a wonderful experience for young children or those who've never caught a fish.

You can come for the day, drop a line in the pond, and—voilà!—bragging rights. It's a "catch and keep" facility, and all the fish are sold by the pound. You can have the staff clean and pack your fish in ice, or you can lay claim to one of the barbecue pits and cook them on the spot. For those who want to fly fish, there's a pretty lake for sportsmen. Fishing there is catch and release, so you can only fish with your own tackle and barbless hooks. There is a per-hour fee for fly fishing.

Even if you don't fish, admission is just $1.00, and there's a nice little picnic park to spread out on and relax. Camping sites are available for RVs and tents, and there are a few cabins to rent as well, all with access to clean restrooms and hot showers. Other facilities include a seasonal swimming pool, a convenience store with fishing supplies, and a small cafe.

In many ways, Whitewater exists in a little bubble world unto itself—it's not remotely related to the high-toned glamour of the desert, and it's a much more "citified" spot than the wilderness areas in the mountains around Palm Springs. In a survey of American culture, it would wind up squarely in the 1950s on the outskirts of a small town in Colorado. To reach Whitewater, take I-10 to the Whitewater exit, then go 5 miles north on Whitewater Canyon Road. Definitely worth the drive.

RESTAURANTS

Big Willie's Down Home Cookin'   **$$**
83-214 Requa Avenue, Indio
(760) 347-9446
Big Willie's started out in Palm Springs, then moved out to Indio, where it seems all the real "down-home" places put down roots. It's definitely a family place, and the staff is used to small children and big appetites.

Afternoons are bargain matinee times at most area movie theaters. With kids in tow, you can save a lot by seeing a matinee, then eating during the ubiquitous "early-bird dinner" time, usually before 6:30 P.M. in area restaurants.

Southern soul food is the specialty, and there's not really a menu, just a huge buffet with a few options on price and number of entrees, side dishes, and desserts. You'll find succulent ribs, fried chicken, cornmeal-fried catfish, sweet potato pie and cobblers, and such southern staples as biscuits, greens, black-eyed peas, and whatever vegetables are in season locally. Get a big glass of iced tea or cold milk and settle in for a laid-back feast. Open for lunch and dinner. No reservations.

California Pizza Kitchen   **$-$$**
73-080 El Paseo Drive, Palm Desert
(760) 776-5036

123 North Palm Canyon Drive
(760) 322-6075
A long step above the fast-food regulars, CPK has consistently good food, good prices, and a fun, friendly atmosphere that's a lot more civilized than the usual noisy pizza place. The CPKids Menu features kid-size pizza, pastas, and desserts, so everyone gets their own choice of the many different toppings. Both CPKs in the desert are sparkling clean, offer quick service, and have enough of a variety that they're good for much more than one or two stops. Open for lunch and dinner. No reservations.

Cheesecake Factory   **$$**
The River at Rancho Mirage
71-800 Highway 111, Rancho Mirage
(760) 404-1400
Like CPK, the Cheesecake Factory is a chain, and one that knows how to do a moderate-priced menu well. In this case, there are more than 200 menu items, with some excellent burgers, sandwiches, sal-

ads, and children's items. The big draw is the dessert menu. Cheesecakes and other sweets aren't inexpensive, but the portions are huge. You may decide that this is the place to go for a special treat, particularly if you've been eating at the more hum-drum spots or cooking in your condo. The cheesecake with seasonal fruit topping is just too good to pass up. There's also an extensive bakery section, so keep that in mind when you're planning picnics. Open for lunch and dinner. No reservations.

Don & Sweet Sue's Café   **$$**
68955 Ramon Road, Cathedral City
(760) 770-2760
Breakfast at Don & Sweet Sue's is a desert tradition, and lines are very long on the weekends. It's a big place, though, and the service is spot-on, so you won't be waiting long. When you have the yen for great platters of fluffy pancakes, crispy waffles, fresh eggs and slabs of ham, homemade biscuits and gravy, a side of spicy salsa, fresh grapefruit picked locally, steaming coffee—well, it's all here, from early in the morning until late at night. The lunches and dinners are also beautifully cooked and reasonably priced, but the breakfast is legendary. It's a friendly, noisy place with a lot of bustle and a high tolerance for restless kids. No reservations.

Las Casuelas Nuevas   **$$**
70-050 Highway 111, Rancho Mirage
(760) 328-8844
www.lascasuelasnuevas.com

Las Casuelas Terraza
222 South Palm Canyon Drive
(760) 325-2794

Las Casuelas Quinta
78-480 Highway 111, La Quinta
(760) 777-7715
www.casuelasquinta.com

Las Casuelas Café
73-703 Highway 111, Palm Desert
(760) 568-0011
"Las Cas," as the locals know the Las Casuelas spots, started as a small lunch and dinner spot in downtown Palm Springs. The Delgado family, under the inspired cooking tutelage of matriarch Mary, went on to open Terraza a few blocks from the original, then Nuevas in Rancho Mirage, Quinta in La Quinta, and Café in Palm Desert. The Café is the only one to offer breakfast, and it's the most reasonably priced, although they are all firmly in the moderate range.

This is the place to go for good, solid, border Mexican food—fajitas, fattening platters of nachos with guacamole and cheese, traditional enchiladas and burritos, and so on. A family can eat very well here, and even the pickiest eater will find some-thing yummy, as there's a nice selection of chicken, burgers, and salads, and the kitchen is happy to tone down or spice up anything on the menu. All the restaurants except for the Café also have mariachi music during happy hour and outside din-ing areas that let you enjoy the fabulous weather. Open for breakfast (the Café only), lunch, and dinner. No reservations.

Ruby's Diner   **$$**
155 South Palm Canyon Drive
(760) 416-0138

The River, Highway 111, Rancho Mirage
(760) 836-0788
Another chain, Ruby's takes the diner theme and goes all the way—jukeboxes; bright red, white, and black decor; wait staff in carhop uniforms; and an all-American burgers-shakes-fries-salads menu. It's a fun place for the kids, with trains that circle the ceiling and a light, open atmosphere. In truth, the food is not so special, but it's consistently appetizing,

and the prices are moderate. There's also a good children's menu, and the kids get coloring books and crayons to keep them occupied while waiting. Open for lunch and dinner. No reservations.

Sherman's Deli & Bakery   **$$**
401 East Tahquitz Canyon Way
(760) 325-1199

Plaza de Monterey Shopping Center on Country Club Drive, Palm Desert
(760) 568-1350
A kosher-style family restaurant, Sherman's in Palm Springs has been packing in the locals for more than 20 years. The Palm Desert Sherman's is also building a reputation, but if you want to get a real feel for the "old-time" desert, find a table at Sherman's in Palm Springs and watch the kibitzing among the locals and out-of-towners. The waitresses don't take any guff, and they really know the menu.

Bring the swimsuits, no matter the time of year. If there's a desert motel or hotel without a swimming pool, it's keeping itself a secret. Be aware, though, that few pools offer lifeguards, so you should plan on being with your children or arranging for adult supervision.

Fresh-baked breads, pies, and cakes, full dinners, and a truly massive sandwich menu mean that everyone gets what they want. You can easily spend $20 on a simple meal here, or you can take advantage of the early-bird and daily specials. Don't bother ordering the chicken soups, because they are usually the one mediocre item in the house. Open for breakfast, lunch, and dinner. No reservations.

DAY TRIPS AND WEEKEND GETAWAYS

After decades of being a day trip and weekend getaway destination itself, the desert is also becoming the home base for vacationers who want a reliably warm and sunny spot and a relaxed lifestyle to be the center of their "hub and spoke" ventures in Southern California. Those who live in the desert year-round usually have their favorite day trips and getaways, and the choices are plentiful, encompassing city life, the beaches, mountains, and major tourist attractions.

Palm Springs is really the ideal location to use as a hub for exploring Southern California, with everything from Los Angeles in the north to San Diego in the south within two or three hours' drive, depending on the traffic. This means that every destination can be a day trip as well as a weekend getaway—the choice is up to you.

The chapter is organized into broad geographic areas, such as Los Angeles, Santa Monica, and Long Beach; Orange County, Laguna Beach, and Newport Beach; San Diego; and nearby mountains and deserts. Within each area, we'll take a look at major attractions, activities, and any special annual events of note.

Without exception, you'll find smaller crowds and lighter traffic on weekdays. Sometimes it feels as if the entire population of Southern California is on the road heading to the beaches in the summer and the mountains in the winter. All the spots

you may want to visit are open seven days a week (except museums, which are often closed on either Monday or Tuesday), so plan to stay off the freeway from Friday morning through Sunday night and enjoy the desert. You might also want to plan your driving time around the morning and evening commuting hours, which are most hectic from 7:00 to 9:00 A.M. and 3:00 to 7:00 P.M.

Freeways were born in Southern California, and the highway system is impressive in terms of safety and quality. Driving is the major mode of travel throughout the state, and the public transportation system—buses, trains, and rapid transit—is sketchy at best. A car here means freedom. If you do not want to drive or cannot do so, there are still ways to get where you want to go, primarily with tour companies and a combination of commuter airline and taxi. If this is your choice, you will have to do a lot of homework on your own, plan ahead, and be patient.

LOS ANGELES, SANTA MONICA, AND LONG BEACH AREA

You could spend the entire year doing day trips and weekend getaways in this broad area and never repeat yourself. There are literally hundreds of events, some of the country's most famous tourist attractions, world-class shopping and museums, movie and TV studios, sports, gardens, and zoos. It's not possible to list them all here, so we're picking out highlights that will appeal to a wide variety of ages and tastes.

Los Angeles is a sprawling community—more a concept than a sharply defined geographic area. There's downtown LA,

---

Always take a cell phone and map with you, even when you're driving to the most urban of areas. Pay phones are practically nonexistent in Southern California, and asking for directions from strangers can be dangerous.

---

the "Westside" and Santa Monica, Burbank and Long Beach, all distinct areas but referred to as "the LA area."

Downtown is the oldest section, and over the years it's become a bit gritty around the edges, as new communities grew up on all sides. Many of California's most important architectural treasures are here, home to everything from banks to run-down bodegas and trendy restaurants. A move toward containing Southern California's urban sprawl is behind what many residents hope will be a renaissance of the downtown, and a few intrepid developers are finding an eager market for lofts and condos in renovated buildings.

The famed **Jewelry District** is downtown, as is the heart of California's retail apparel industry. The Jewelry District is renowned for wholesale prices on precious gems, watches, and all types of fine jewelry. If you have the stamina and persistence to visit dozens of shops to compare and bargain before you buy, you can take advantage of savings ranging from 50 to 70 percent by purchasing from the source and cutting out the middleman.

The LA **Fashion District** covers 90 blocks in the downtown area. Access to the high-end fashion offices is reserved for wholesale buyers, but there's plenty on the street to keep you amazed and shopping. From bridal accessories to flip-flops, flowers to thousands of bolts of silk, this area has it all. The action is fast-paced and bargaining is expected, even though the prices are already quite good.

Both the Jewelry District and the Fashion District close up early—usually around 5:00 P.M.—and are not open on Sundays or major holidays.

Also downtown is world-famous **Olvera Street,** a Mexican marketplace for more than 75 years. It's lined with historic buildings, authentic Mexican restaurants, and vendor stalls selling everything from leather goods to artwork, clothing, imported crafts, candles, traditional Mexican wares, and colorful souvenirs.

Downtown attractions include Watts Towers, the life work of artist Simon Rodia

Most TV shows offer free tickets to their tapings. A painless way of getting tickets to be in the live audience at your favorite show is to go to the Web site www.tvtix.com. All tickets are free.

and a landmark in the community; the Geffen Contemporary at MOCA, a museum of cutting-edge contemporary art; the Japanese American National Museum, with its extensive history center and exhibitions; and the Natural History Museum of Los Angeles County, the largest natural and historical museum in the western United States.

The **Westside** includes Hollywood and Beverly Hills and has a wonderfully eclectic assortment of museums, shopping areas, and celebrity hangouts. One not to be missed is the **Farmers' Market,** open every day and selling fresh meats, poultry, seafood, produce, flowers, bakery goods, and specialty foods. The market is a weekend tradition for many locals, from just regular folks to movie stars, all enjoying the scene, picking up something good for dinner, and enjoying a coffee and brioche at one of the many outdoor cafes.

Hollywood is home to the famous Hollywood sign, the Walk of Fame, Grauman's Chinese Theater, the Guinness World of Records museum, the Hollywood Wax Museum (with its famous Chamber of Horrors), and the huge Los Angeles Zoo and Botanical Gardens.

The **La Brea Tar Pits** are on the Westside, and it's well worth the trip to visit this slice of the prehistoric past, right in the middle of the urban jungle. The bubbling tar pits have been seeping out of the ground for at least 40,000 years, and the adjacent museum displays some of the more than three million fossils found here, including mammoths, saber-toothed tigers, and giant ground sloths.

The stunning hilltop Getty Center has an extensive collection of art, but the building and the views are the real draw. The Los Angeles County Museum of art has more than 120,000 works in its permanent collection and is recognized as the premier visual arts museum in the western United States. A must-see is the Museum of Tolerance, with high-tech, interactive exhibits that explore the dynamics of discrimination, the legacy of the Holocaust, and current human rights issues. Another unique museum is the Petersen Automotive Museum, which uses exotic and ordinary cars from Hollywood and Detroit to illustrate important milestones in history.

As you might expect, the shopping on the Westside is extraordinary. Two Rodeo, and its neighbor, Rodeo Drive, is a pedestrian area that includes such shops as Gucci, Gianfranco Ferre, Versace, Tiffany, and more. Melrose Street, with its jumble of small retailers selling apparel, jewelry, gifts, and souvenirs, is in this area, as is the glitzy **Hollywood & Highland Center.** A destination unto itself, Hollywood & Highland includes the Kodak Theatre, Renaissance Hollywood Hotel, a six-screen cinema, 12 bowling lanes, some excellent restaurants, over 60 specialty shops, a television production studio, and two radio stations.

Burbank and the **San Fernando Valley** are home to the motion picture studios, including Universal and Warner Brothers. **Universal** has become an attraction in itself, with theme rides and what they call "full sensory" experiences built around blockbuster movies. At **Warner Brothers,** tours include behind-the-scenes looks at working studios.

Also in the San Fernando Valley is the Los Angeles Equestrian Center, a huge facility with horse shows and events, a riding academy and rental stables, retail

---

Major attractions do not allow outside food or drinks. Given the steep prices for everything inside a park's gates, you may want to plan to eat a hearty breakfast and dinner outside and just have a snack or two while you're playing.

---

shops, and a restaurant/bar.

On the shopping end, Universal has also developed the Universal Citywalk shopping/entertainment complex, with dozens of restaurants and specialty shops, an 18-screen multiplex, an IMAX 3-D theater, and several nightclubs. Shopping in the LA area doesn't get any more varied than at the upscale Glendale Galleria, with five major department stores and 250 specialty stores.

In the **San Gabriel Valley,** star attractions include Santa Anita Park, with top thoroughbred racing from October through April; the Norton Simon Museum of Art and its far-ranging European art collection; and the Los Angeles County Arboretum & Botanic Gardens. The Huntington Beach Library, Art Collections, and Botanical Gardens are 200-plus acres featuring art galleries and a library, gorgeous gardens, a bookstore, and daily English tea. Pasadena, of course, is home to the annual Tournament of Roses New Year's Day parade. The Rose Bowl is also the site of one of the largest continuing outdoor swap meets in the country.

Farther west—right on the ocean—is **Santa Monica,** a beautiful, friendly little city that's just made for walking. It's home to zillon-dollar movie star beach retreats, excellent shopping, and a lovely little beach that's more urban than any other beach along the Southern California coast.

If you're going for the day, look for a pay lot near the beach and head to the walk-in Visitor Information Center at 1620 Main Street, where you can pick up a special events schedule and a trip schedule for the Big Blue Bus, a locally run bus system that is all you'll need to get around for the day. There's also a visitor information kiosk in the stretch of beachfront that runs right between the Pacific Ocean and Ocean Avenue.

A pedestrian shopping/dining area a few blocks from the beach, **Third Street Promenade** is the heart of the town. Major retailers such as Abercrombie & Fitch, Banana Republic, Borders Books & Music, Anthropologie, Levi's, and Old Navy share space with independent boutiques selling everything from motorcycle gear to jewelry and designer clothing. Fred Segal, the upscale men's, women's, and home boutique that is the star of the city, also has its main store and several mini-boutiques on and around Third Street. Street entertainers of all types lend a festive air, and most shops stay open late—until 9:00 P.M. on weekdays, 10:00 P.M. on Friday and Saturday, and 6:00 P.M. on Sunday. There's also an excellent farmers' market adjacent to Third Street on Wednesday and Saturday mornings. The Third Street promenade is anchored by Santa Monica Place, a traditional indoor shopping mall with Macy's and Robinsons-May department stores and the usual assortment of mall specialty stores and kiosks.

Another good shopping/dining district is the more laid-back **Main Street,** a few blocks from the beach and a haven of beautiful old buildings that have been converted into boutiques, restaurants, and sidewalk coffee shops. This is the place where locals go to read the paper and lounge around on a weekend morning.

Mid-City is a growing art hub, with the renowned 18th Street Arts Complex and Bergamot Station Arts Center, the latter of which houses the Santa Monica Museum of Art as well as the largest collection of art galleries on the West Coast. You'll need the bus to get here, but it's a short ride and well worth it if you love browsing in galleries.

At the northern edge of town but still an easy walk from downtown is **Montana Avenue,** perhaps the quintessential Southern California shopping/dining experience. On 10 blocks in the middle of an upscale family neighborhood, luxury boutiques, high-priced home furnishing stores, bakeries, restaurants, wine bars, and cafes are populated by a distinctly upscale crowd of locals and celebrities. Shops here close around 6:00 P.M., and the restaurants and bars become the hub of the action.

Santa Monica is a big dining-out town, and you'll find just about every type of food and price point here, from inexpen-

Expect to encounter "June gloom" at the beaches through late June. This is a thick layer of fog that settles overnight and usually lingers until early afternoon. Dress in layers you can peel off when the sun comes out.

sive Mexican to very high-end concept cuisine. This is the city where "California cuisine" was born, and the competition for the newest, most popular, best, most exotic fare is fierce.

The **Santa Monica Pier** and adjacent **Pacific Park** are worth a day's trip in themselves. The Santa Monica Aquarium offers hands-on fun for children, and the Carousel at the Pier is a beautifully restored 1922 ride for everyone. Pacific Park is the LA area's only free-admission amusement park, although you'll pay for individual rides inside, including the famous roller coaster and a nine-story, solar-powered Ferris wheel. The park also has a lot of smaller rides and games, as well as typical amusement park food and souvenir shops.

Nearby **Venice Beach,** long famous for its artist hangouts and Muscle Beach, is definitely worth a side trip. The various street entertainers and artists on the beach promenade are friendly, funky, and frenetic—this is California people-watching at its best.

Just off the coast is lovely little **Catalina Island,** just 18.5 miles long and 7 miles wide. It's edged with beautiful sandy beaches, and the town is a gem of small shops and cafes. Take a ferry ride over and rent a golf cart to tour around—no cars are allowed.

Back on land but still by the ocean, **Long Beach** is home to the famous *Queen Mary* ocean liner, as well as the Long Beach Aquarium, a fabulous place with more than 12,500 creatures in 50 different exhibits. A highlight is the Shark Lagoon, with more than 150 sharks that you can actually touch. Also check out the Museum of Latin American Art, the only one in the

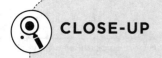

CLOSE-UP

The High Desert

Pick a crisp, sunny day, pack a lunch, and leave the Saks card and golf clubs at home. You're on an expedition in your own backyard, venturing into the High Desert, where bikers, space aliens, orchid growers, rock climbers, U.S. Marines, and Old West gunfighters spin out their days under wandering clouds. In this vast, dusty landscape, a lawn- and Starbucks-free zone, personal eccentricities and dreams flourish to an astonishing degree.

Start from the west end of the valley, going 14 miles north on Indian Avenue from the heart of Palm Springs. Indian Avenue curves to the west and intersects with Highway 62 (29 Palms Highway). As you drive up the hill, you'll spot antiques shops, small diners, and a "dig your own cactus" nursery. A good way to weave together the threads of this indefinable area is to go all the way through the towns of Morongo Valley, Yucca Valley, Joshua Tree, and 29 Palms, and then start exploring on the return trip.

At first sight 29 Palms is just another modest little highway town, nothing special. But its heart beats with a rare patriotism fueled by its neighbor, the Marine Air Ground Combat Center, the world's largest Marine combat training center and a complete town unto itself. With today's heightened security, individual and group visits are tightly scrutinized.

In 29 Palms itself, the Mural Project has been busy creating huge outdoor murals on business building walls since 1994. The murals depict the city's history since 1910 and showcase the work of world-famous artists. Most are on buildings located on 29 Palms Highway, and all are well worth a look.

The North Entrance Station for Joshua Tree National Park is also in 29 Palms, just off the highway on Utah Trail, which becomes Park Boulevard directly past the Oasis Visitor Center. This is the best path to take for a "quick" look at a serenely beautiful expanse of 800,000 acres where the ecosystems of the Colorado Desert and the Mojave Desert come together. There's often snow in the winter, and spring can bring spectacular displays of wildflowers.

Five different palm oases, "forests" of Joshua trees and cholla cactus, granite monoliths, and immense mosaics of boulders dot the landscape. A few miles in from the North Entrance you'll pass through Jumbo Rocks and Hidden Valley, both spectacular spots for exploring, having a picnic, and watching the climbers who come here from all over the world.

Head back out of the park on the continuation of Park Boulevard past the West Entrance Station and into the town of Joshua Tree. Continue to the middle of Yucca Valley and turn north on Old Woman Springs Road (Highway 247). Keep on this road for 10 miles, turn right on Reche Road, drive another 2.5 miles, and then turn left on Belfield Boulevard, an easy-to-miss road that leads to the Mysterious Integratron. Three miles north of that building is Giant Rock.

These two spots have made the High Desert legendary among those who believe in extraterrestrials, UFOs, and all things unseen. For a closer look at the Integratron, see the chapter on Attractions.

Right across the road is Gubler Orchids. A world-famous orchid grower, Gubler also grows and ships bromeliads, ferns, and carnivorous plants. Tours are always free, and there are some great spots outside to loll around on picnic benches in the sun.

The real goodies, of course, are the

High-desert foliage offers rugged beauty. PHOTO BY TOM BREWSTER, COURTESY OF THE PALM SPRINGS DESERT RESORTS CONVENTION AND VISITORS AUTHORITY

orchids. Dozens of varieties are for sale, each perfect and perfectly tempting, from the vanilla-scented "dancing ladies" to the lusty magenta "prom corsage" flowers. The prices are outstanding, and the quality is superb. Gubler ships all over the world and guarantees the plant will arrive fresh and healthy.

Even if you've already consumed a picnic lunch, you can still make room for real barbecue on the way back. Take Pioneertown Road north from the middle of Yucca Valley, travel 4 miles, and slow way down—the speed limit on Pioneertown's wide dirt streets is 5 miles per hour.

When it was built as an all-inclusive movie location in the late 1940s, the adobe and wooden storefronts along Mane Street housed cast and crew. A sound stage for interiors, the Golden Stallion Restaurant, The Red Dog Saloon, and a bowling alley made it a very practical movie town.

Because most of the buildings there were built to last, the town looks much as it must have in 1950. The storefronts now house a film production studio and sound stage, Web services company, post office, church, photo studio, and homes for many permanent residents.

The undisputed star of Pioneertown and the one "must stop" on a visit here is Pappy and Harriet's, a little adobe bar and grill that serves as local watering hole. It's been the center of town for almost 30 years and remains the place of choice on Saturday and Sunday afternoons.

Motorcycles, pickups, and sleek sports cars surround the building on weekends, their drivers drawn here for the cold beer, backyard barbecue, and live music. Eric Burdon, Donovan, and Eddie Veddor of Pearl Jam are a few of the singers who have dropped in to jam and entertain.

Even if you're staying at an independent boutique hotel, it pays to ask if they have connections or reciprocal relationships with hotels in your weekend destination. The California tourism industry is close-knit, and you just may find an excellent value.

western United States to exclusively feature contemporary Latin American art.

ORANGE COUNTY, LAGUNA BEACH, AND NEWPORT BEACH

Anaheim in Orange County is home to Disney's **California Adventure Park** and the Disneyland Resort, the granddaddy of all American man-made tourist attractions. The park concentrates on California, re-creating elements of the gold rush days and the early years of moviemaking magic in Hollywood. Rides, parades, and shows go on all the time.

At the **Disneyland Resort,** site of the original Disneyland, you can explore the eight different "lands" in the Magic Kingdom, from Mickey's Toontown to Main Street. The nightly Parade of Dreams is spectacular. Admission is separate for each park.

Also in Anaheim is **Six Flags Magic Mountain,** famous for its 16 roller coasters and known as a heaven for thrill seekers. There are more than 100 different rides and games, plus dozens of places to eat and shop.

According to the experts at South Coast Plaza, the best days to shop, whether you go to an outlet mall or a big department store, are Tuesday and Thursday. If you get your shopping done by early afternoon, you'll really avoid the crowds.

Just a little south of all this excitement is some of the country's best shopping in two very different "malls." The first, **South Coast Plaza,** is like a small city. Department stores include Macy's, Robinsons-May, Nordstrom, Saks Fifth Avenue, and Sears. There's a concierge, valet and taxi services, tons of ATM machines, a carousel, and a staggering array of shops. You'll find European couture, American athletic gear, fine jewelry, exquisite home furnishings, art, and much more. If you're shopping here, you may want to spend two days—one to reconnoiter and one to actually buy.

Fashion Island, in Newport Beach, is home to Southern California's only Bloomingdales, as well as Neiman-Marcus, Macy's, Robinsons-May, and more than 100 other shops. It's an open-air "village," laid out in nine different sections that encourage wandering, browsing, and often getting lost. This is the place to go for people-watching and it's a lovely excursion on a sunny day.

In nearby **Newport Beach** and **Laguna Beach,** the atmosphere is just made for vacationers. Like Santa Monica, these are mostly walking towns, with the main shopping and dining districts stretched out along Pacific Coast Highway, which is just a few steps away from the sandy beaches. Both towns are noted for their fine art galleries and laid-back, casual atmosphere. In the summer the Laguna Arts Festival, Sawdust Arts Festival, and Pageant of the Masters pack in visitors from all over. It's a crush, but never hectic or stress-inducing. If you're in the area around Christmastime, the Newport boat parade is a magical collection of lighted and decorated yachts and small boats that goes on for several evenings.

Heading south, you'll find **La Jolla** and **Del Mar,** two more lovely and very upscale beach communities. The Birch Aquarium at Scripps features a tide-pool center, revolving exhibits, a live coral reef, dive shows, a simulator ride, and, best of all, seasonal full-moon walks on the La Jolla Pier, which is closed to the public except for these evenings. Art galleries abound in La Jolla, as do excellent bars and restaurants.

Del Mar is most famous for the summertime Del Mar races. Opening day in July at the Thoroughbred Club is an elegant, dress-up affair, especially if you have tickets to the much-coveted box seats.

SAN DIEGO

Down in **San Diego,** a visit to the historic **Gaslamp Quarter,** or old downtown, is a must. This is a lively entertainment and dining district full of wonderful old buildings that have been restored to their original beauty. Downtown San Diego, once a seedy and forgotten neighborhood surrounded by the high-tech companies in the suburbs, is coming into its own as a vibrant, fun place to eat and play all week long.

Seaworld San Diego has seen more than 100 million visitors since it opened in 1964. It's a full day of rides, shows, and attractions such as the world-famous Shamu.

In the heart of the city, **Balboa Park** is home to 15 museums, various arts and international cultural associations, and the San Diego Zoo, making it one of the nation's largest cultural and entertainment complexes. The **San Diego Zoo** is one of the country's biggest and best, with more than 100 acres and the famous Wild Animal Park. Some of the world's rarest animals live here, including giant pandas, koalas, and the country's only panda cub.

Beaches around San Diego are usually clean and crowded—it seems like everyone in the city is an ocean lover. One of the nicest spots for a stroll on a Sunday morning is the strand by the historic **Hotel Del Coronado.** The "Del," as locals call it, was built as a luxury resort in 1888 and has since been designated a National Historic Landmark. If you go to San Diego, this is a must, whether you stop in for tea or dinner or just amble through the lobby and look into the gift shop.

December through May is the season for whale-watching, and there are several tour companies that arrange regular boat trips to view these extraordinary creatures. Check the local paper or do an Internet search for "whale watching."

NEARBY MOUNTAINS AND DESERTS

With their pine forests and winter sports, Idyllwild to the south and Big Bear and Lake Arrowhead to the west offer a complete change from the desert and make fun little excursions just about any time of year.

Idyllwild is a rustic mountain village where many "flatlanders" have purchased summer homes or cabins. The downtown is small, with pretty little art galleries, shops selling crafts, and excellent restaurants. The big draw here is a summer escape from the desert heat, and the August Jazz Festival is always packed with well-behaved music lovers.

In the San Bernardino Mountains between Palm Springs and Los Angeles, **Lake Arrowhead** and **Big Bear** are also very popular summer "escape" destinations. Because the lake in Lake Arrowhead is privately owned, visitors have very limited use. If you have a friend who belongs to a beach club or owns a house there, you can water-ski and loaf around on the lake as much as you like. If not, you'll be limited to taking a boat out and gazing at the lakeside mansions from a distance.

It's a different story in Big Bear, which is more of a "real world" place and also happens to have an excellent downhill skiing facility at Big Bear Mountain. Big Bear Lake is public and open to power boating and jet skiing. The little town itself has some cute shops and a handful of good restaurants. Outdoor recreation is the attraction here, with more than 50 group camps in the area. Stream and lake fishing,

Most museums have frequent free days, and some will offer reduced admission if you go late in the day. This can be a considerable savings if you're going in a family group and want to see several museums. Check each museum's Web site for details.

hiking, and golfing are all available in the summer months.

Desert natives say that **Borrego Springs** is "Palm Springs 50 years ago."

Located in the middle of the Anza-Borrego desert around 60 miles from Palm Springs, this little town is the ultimate "relax and do practically nothing" hideout. You'll find golf, some tennis and four-wheel exploring, hikes in the desert, and a few good restaurants, but not much else. This is a place where you can hear the coyotes howl every night and soak up the silence and beauty of the desert away from lights and traffic. If you go in the spring, odds are good that the wildflower show will be spectacular.

RETIREMENT AND RELOCATION

Making the decision to relocate, whether for retirement or a different lifestyle, involves considering a lot of factors, from the availability of health care to the cost of living and quality of life. Many a desert visitor has fallen in love with the Palm Springs area and become a permanent resident. If you're thinking about moving here, take your time. Visit at all times of the year, not just in the lovely winter months. Talk to people who have lived here for a few years and can give you the good and not-so-good—the real "insider" information. Some of the happiest retirees and relocatees are those who, over the course of several years, spent months at a time in the desert, getting used to the rhythm of life in the different seasons and learning the quirks of each city.

This chapter gives you the basic information you'll need to start your research. Here, we give you a brief overview of each city, moving from Palm Springs in the west to Indio in the east; touch on the general "personality" of each; and give some pros and cons to consider if you are thinking of relocating. This is followed by sections that round up information on the desert's health care, libraries, police and fire service, senior centers, utilities, child care, schools, media, and worship. You'll find a lot of variation in all of these amenities from city to city, and some may be the "deal breakers" or "deal makers" you're looking for.

THE COMMUNITIES

Palm Springs

Incorporated in 1938, Palm Springs is the flagship of the desert, carrying the famous name that is now used to refer to the entire valley. It's got a lot of depth going for it, including the Palm Springs International Airport, Palm Springs Art Museum, Palm Springs Aerial Tramway, Moorten Botanical Garden, Mizell Senior Center, Desert Regional Medical Center, Spa Resort Casino, Indian Canyons, and the valley's only real downtown. The city has very little buildable land left, and housing prices have shot into the stratosphere lately, as real estate investors have discovered the area. Following Palm Desert's lead, the city established an excellent Art in Public Places program, installing a large selection of important sculptures in public areas. Developer fees pay for this program, and as the new condos go up, the fees go up as well.

At the last census the population was around 45,000, with about the same number of seasonal residents. In terms of household income, Palm Springs ranks above Indio and Cathedral City and below Palm Desert, Rancho Mirage, and La Quinta.

Palm Springs has a decidedly more liberal and varied population and attitude than most of the other valley cities, as evidenced by the large gay population and the increasingly diverse ethnic makeup. It's still rather homogeneous, as the desert always has been, but compared to Palm Desert, Palm Springs is a virtual United Nations.

Despite budget woes that have plagued the city since the retail migration to the east began more than 20 years ago, the city still fights to keep the parks, library, and public services at the top of the quality scale, and it succeeds very well. It's a very easy city to navigate, compact and logically laid out, with a lot of neigh-

When you're buying a house, make sure you know whether it's "lease land," which means it is Indian-owned. Homes on lease land may appear to be less expensive, because you are paying a monthly lease payment rather than a mortgage payment. However, you have no control over lease renewal, and that could be extremely costly down the road. "Fee land" is land that you actually own.

borhood centers that offer such necessities as groceries, cleaners, movies, and more within a walkable distance.

Cathedral City

Cathedral City is more similar to Indio than it is to its next-door neighbors, Palm Springs and Rancho Mirage. Originally developed as a planned subdivision in 1925, the city grew up in the shadow of Palm Springs and incorporated in 1981. For years it was known as a blue-collar place, with few amenities for its residents. The lack of either a major hotel or a golf course meant it missed out on lucrative tourist dollars, and the absence of a central downtown area meant it had the feeling of a bedroom community.

With an estimated population of 53,000 in 2005, Cathedral City is the desert's third-largest city, behind Indio and Palm Springs. In recent years Cathedral City has become the center of the valley's automotive businesses and has worked hard to leverage those tax dollars and redevelopment funds to clean up and modernize many neighborhoods. The biggest improvement is in the area around City Hall, just off Highway 111. A planned shopping, dining, and entertainment complex is slowly taking shape, with an IMAX theater, an upscale multiscreen movie house, and a few restaurants.

Housing in Cathedral City is among of the most affordable in the valley, and more

than half of the housing units are rentals. With its convenient location close to the middle of the valley and the large hotels, this is a popular spot for the many service workers who keep the hotels and restaurants running. Median household income in 2005 was estimated at $45,000, with a median age of 32, making it one of the youngest cities in the desert. There are a lot of family neighborhoods full of well-kept homes and streets where children can play safely. The city is still struggling with its blue-collar image, though, and the city's amenities for residents—parks, public arts, and recreation programs—are pretty skimpy when compared to other cities in the desert.

Rancho Mirage

More a retail and dining center than a city with a center and defined neighborhoods, Rancho Mirage calls itself the "playground of millionaires," and that says a lot about the makeup of the community. There is very little accommodation for families, with the few parks offering minimal amenities and no community center, though it helps fund the Joslyn Cove Center. Its relatively new library is one of the best small libraries in the state. The city incorporated in 1973, the same year as Palm Desert. Though it boasts the new River entertainment and dining complex, the Children's Discovery Museum of the Desert, and Eisenhower Medical Center, the city is hampered by the lack of a coherent downtown and walkable neighborhoods.

Palm Desert

This city incorporated in 1973 as a general law city and changed its basic form of government to that of a charter city, a designation that helps cement the city's ability to self-govern. Like many other valley cities, it has a council-manager government, with five citizens elected to staggered four-year terms. Unlike other cities, voters don't choose a mayor; rather that post falls to each council member on a rotating basis each year. According to the last census, the city has around 42,500 permanent residents and another 32,000 who live there in season.

Palm Desert prides itself on its balance—in business, real estate, and quality of life. It's the only city in the valley to boast a complete spectrum of education, including kindergarten, middle school, private and public high school, community college, and the new four-year college campus.

Apartments, condos, single-family homes, and luxurious golf country clubs are in the real estate mix. Like many other cities, Palm Desert struggles with the state's requirements for a certain amount of affordable housing, trying to strike a balance between ghettoized low-income housing and vast tracts of expensive homes. It was the first city in the desert to create an Art in Public Places program, which requires developers to either pay a fee for public art or install significant pieces.

The city has an active affordable-housing program that helps low- to moderate-income individuals and families prequalify for resales of single-family homes in its pilot project, Desert Rose. This subdivision has 161 homes with three to four bedrooms, in a mix of townhome-style and detached units. Amenities include common areas, an adult pool and spa, a children's pool, a volleyball and basketball court, and a YMCA-run child care center on-site. The city also owns and operates over 900 affordable rental units. To see if you qualify for Palm Desert's affordable-housing program, call the Redevelopment Agency (760-346-0611), or visit www.cityofpalmdesert.org and click on Housing.

The Palm Desert Community Garden opened its gates in the spring of 1999 and was the first in the Coachella Valley. Open to novice as well as experienced gardeners, the gardens are aimed at strengthening community ties as well as providing fresh, inexpensive produce for those who share their time and work. The city is an active partner in the whole garden program, bringing in speakers to teach about design, nutrition, cooking, and soil and sponsoring field trips to local farms.

Palm Desert also has an excellent public parks and recreation program. For details on that, check the Parks, Recreation, and Sports chapter.

Indian Wells

Incorporated in 1967, Indian Wells has a full-time population of just 4,433 spread over 15.04 square miles. An additional 5,000 to 6,000 part-time residents call the city home during the winter months. The average age of residents is 63, and the median family income is $134,237, the highest for any city in Riverside County. Home to the Indian Wells Tennis Garden and a great supporter of cultural events and institutions throughout the valley, Indian Wells has established itself as the conservative culture hub of the desert. There is virtually no buildable land in the city, and certainly no affordable housing. In many ways the city is much like a very large, very exclusive country club.

La Quinta

The fastest-growing city in the desert and one of the most rapidly expanding in California, La Quinta is becoming known as an attractive family community. PGA West and the La Quinta Resort are the undis-

---

Earthquake insurance is getting increasingly hard to obtain in California. Some areas of the desert, however, are considered out of the earthquake zones—a good thing to know when you're buying a home. Same thing for flood insurance.

ℹ️

---

puted economic engines of the city, attracting thousands of visitors each year. A lot of those visitors return to relocate or retire, or just to invest in the relatively affordable land and beautiful setting.

When it incorporated in 1982, La Quinta had a population of just over 5,200. Today the population has grown to approximately 30,450. New homes are now available in La Quinta at prices ranging from the high $90,000s to more than $1 million. A wide range of older, established housing, condominiums, and town houses is also available for rent or purchase.

Indio

Indio was the Coachella Valley's first incorporated city, taking this step in 1930, with a population of 1,875. At the last census, Indio counted a little more than 59,000 permanent residents, with another 8,800 who spend the winter months there. It's one of the valley's youngest cities, with a median age of a little more than 27. Around 75 percent of the residents are Hispanic, reflecting the area's agricultural heritage and close ties to Mexico. Median family income is a little more than $33,000.

As the valley's growth continues to move to the east, Indio is seeing strong growth in single-family homes, with more than 25,000 new homes and apartments approved for construction in 2004. Prices here are probably lower than anywhere else on the desert floor, making Indio a very attractive location for young families and others on a budget.

HEALTH CARE

For such a small population, the desert's medical facilities are outstanding, owing in large part to the many famous and wealthy men and women who have retired here and donated time and money to make sure they are cutting edge.

Hospitals

Desert Regional Medical Center
1150 North Indian Canyon Drive
(760) 323-6511
www.desertmedctr.com
This 367-bed acute care facility houses the only designated trauma center in the Coachella Valley. It has the distinction of being located at the site of the old El Mirador Hotel, once the most famous "hot spot" in the Palm Springs social scene.

The Comprehensive Cancer Center here provides patients with outpatient surgery facilities, a radiation oncology treatment area, a medical oncology infusion center, a "stat" laboratory for quick processing of treatment related labwork, physician offices and exam rooms, a pharmacy, a comprehensive breast center, a research department, a patient resource center, psychosocial and nutritional support services, and financial counseling services. Satellite facilities are located in nearby Yucca Valley and Indio.

Other special services and facilities include treatment for low- and high-risk obstetrical patients at the Women and Infants' Center, including central fetal monitoring; the Orthopedic Institute; weight-loss surgery; and a community fitness program at the Wellness Center. A free club for desert residents age 50 or older provides health and education programs, a referral service, claims application assistance, discounted preventive health screenings, and hospital pre-registration.

Eisenhower Medical Center
39000 Bob Hope Drive, Rancho Mirage
(760) 340-3911
www.emc.org
Dolores and Bob Hope donated the original 80 acres of land for this hospital and Dolores spearheaded the formation of the Eisenhower Medical Center Auxiliary when ground was broken in 1969. The hospital opened in 1971. Over the years Dolores has been president, chairman of the board, and chairman emeritus of the board of trustees.

In the last 30 years the medical center campus has grown tremendously. In 2005 the center was named one of the country's top hospitals by Solucient, a company recognized as the premier source of health-care intelligence in the United States.

Eisenhower Medical Center is now home to a number of world-class facilities, including:

Annenberg Center for Health Sciences (760-773-4500; www.annenberg.net). This accredited center provides continuing education for health-care professionals and includes a 500-seat auditorium. Professional video production as well as graphic design, videoconferencing, and satellite uplink/downlink services are available.

Barbara Sinatra Children's Center (www.sinatracenter.org). This nonprofit facility has received international recognition for being an advocate for abused children and provides help regardless of a family's ability to pay for services. The Sinatra Center address issues of child abuse detection and prevention, as well as counseling, through its Web site, outreach programs, and a speakers bureau.

Betty Ford Center (www.bettyford center.org). Founded in 1982, the Center is a licensed 100-bed recovery hospital that has treated thousands of patients and family members from all over the United States and throughout the world. All aspects of drug and alcohol dependency are addressed in residential, outpatient, family and children's programs so that patients' physical, spiritual and psychological needs can be met.

The Hearing Institute (www.hearing-institute.com). The staff of this facility, located on the Eisenhower Medical Center campus, evaluate and treat hearing loss, tinnitus, and dizziness. This was the first Coachella Valley clinic to provide cochlear implants.

Additional special centers at Eisenhower include the **Eisenhower Lucy Curci Cancer Center,** providing full cancer care and support services; the **Eisenhower Smilow Heart Center** for advanced cardiac

The desert has excellent traditional medical facilities. However, the choices are pretty slim when you are looking for alternative medicine providers such as acupuncturists, naturopaths, and the like.

care services; and the **Eisenhower Ortho-pedic Center** for care and surgery in sports medicine, total joint replacement, and spine, as well as hand and foot, disorders.

Educational services are offered through the **Diabetes Program,** the first program in the Coachella Valley to achieve recognition by the American Diabetes Association and the **Phillip & Carol Traub Center,** for help with Parkinson's disease. The **Center for Healthy Living** is a free club for permanent and seasonal desert residents aimed at promoting healthy lifestyles. The center offers education, information, screening, and wellness programs. Members can receive discounts on services at local businesses and Eisenhower Medical Center, counseling on how to file Medicare and supplemental health insurance claims, and help in filling out advance health care directives.

John F. Kennedy Memorial Hospital
47-111 Monroe Street, Indio
(760) 347-6191
www.jfkmemorialhosp.com
This 145-bed acute care hospital has a 24-hour emergency room and a daily express care center. There is a 16-bed intensive care unit and a 24-bed medical surgical unit. Specialties include maternity and obstetrical services, with prenatal classes and private labor and post-partum rooms; the multidisciplinary Arthritis Institute; neurosurgery and spine care; orthopedic, general, and vascular surgery; urology services; and an array of standard radiology and laboratory services.

The hospital also has a pediatric asthma management program, which educates individuals about asthma in both

English and Spanish. The program serves both inpatient and outpatient children.

Urgent Care Center

These are stand-alone clinics for urgent but not life-threatening health situations and are used frequently when individuals don't have a regular doctor or can't get in to see one. All are open 24 hours. They are not emergency rooms. Each clinic does routine physical exams, vaccinations, and other routine medical office procedures.

Desert Urgent Care
74990 Country Club Drive, Suite 310
Palm Desert
(760) 341-8800

EMC Immediate Care Center
78-822 Highway 111, La Quinta
(760) 564-7000

67-780 East Palm Canyon Drive
Cathedral City
(760) 328-1000

Palm Desert Urgent Care
73-345 Highway 111, Palm Desert
(760) 340-5800
www.palmdeserturgentcare.com

Specialty Facilities

Braille Institute
70-251 Ramon Road, Rancho Mirage
(760) 321-1111
www.brailleinstitute.org
A local chapter of the national organization, this offers free educational, social and recreational programs, Low Vision Rehabilitation consultations, a Vistas shop, a youth program and library services.

Veterans Administration Medical Center
Palm Desert CBOC
41-865 Boardwalk, Suite 103, Palm Desert
(760) 341-5570
This is a community-based outpatient clinic under the auspices of the VA's Loma Linda Healthcare System in Loma Linda, California. Outpatient services available here must first be approved through the Loma Linda facility or another full-service VA hospital. Contact the Veterans Administration Medical Center at 11201 Benton Street, Loma Linda, (800-741-8387 or 909-825-7084; www.va.gov) for more information.

LIBRARIES

Palm Springs Public Library is one of the best in Southern California and definitely the best in the desert. Its extensive collections, special events, and unstintingly professional service make it a pleasure to visit.

Cathedral City's library, a new (opened in 2005) $12.8-million library in Rancho Mirage, and the long-standing facility in Indio round out the valley selection.

POLICE AND FIRE

In 1984 Cathedral City's own municipal Police Department was created. Cathedral City boasts the lowest crime rate in Coachella Valley. The city has three Community Police Services Offices in busy shopping center complexes, each offering accessibility and high visibility to the community. The city's award-winning GRASP unit uses traditional enforcement methods, state laws, and local ordinances to focus on curfew and truancy enforcement and gang suppression.

The Cathedral City Fire Department currently operates three fire stations and also provides paramedic and ambulance service within the city limits.

The Palm Springs Police Department consists of one police station and one substation and more than 125 full-time personnel.

In addition, 53 part-time employees act as school crossing guards, volunteer auxiliary officers, and reserve police officers. In addition to their on-the-job duties, department personnel are also actively involved in teaching self-defense and personal safety skills, conducting drug and crime awareness programs, and serving on specialized rescue teams.

The Palm Springs Fire Department staffs five fire stations throughout the city and provides paramedic and ambulance service within the city limits.

Indio also has its own police department, with 60-plus sworn officers, 44 civilian employees, and more than 50 volunteers. The emphasis is on community policing, with special neighborhood watch and education programs.

The Indio Fire Department staffs four fire stations in the city, with paramedic and ambulance service provided within the city limits.

The rest of the valley cities contract for their police services through the Riverside County Sheriff's Office and also contract for fire and rescue services through a variety of providers. Over the years this has yielded considerable savings, though there is an ongoing debate about the quality of service and response time for city-housed services as opposed to those provided by the county.

SENIOR CENTERS

Indio Senior Center
45-222 Towne Street, Indio
(760) 347-5111
www.indio.org
The center's programs are available to anyone age 50 and older, and the building is open on weekdays from 7:30 A.M. to 4:30 P.M. Resources include the Meals on Wheels program, information and referral services, health screening, exercise and

> *All of the local libraries have borrowing privileges with larger systems in places like Riverside, so you can order and enjoy materials that aren't readily available on the shelves.*

arts and crafts classes, bridge, a variety of counseling and educational programs and workshops, bingo, a library, and a program of catered lunches and breakfasts.

Joslyn Senior Center of the Cove Communities
73750 Catalina Way, Palm Desert
(760) 340-3220
www.joslyncenter.org
A wellness center and health screenings, fitness and dance classes, all types of games from mah-jongg to bridge and lawn bowling, language lessons, art classes, bingo, legal counseling, and a vast array of excursions and special events keep the members busy all year. Membership is just $20 a year and open to everyone 50 years and older.

Mizell Senior Center
480 South Sunrise Way
(760) 323-5689
www.mizell.org
A top-notch facility supported heavily by local donors, Mizell offers a wide range of activities and programs, including daily lunch, support and counseling groups, exercise and dance, excursions, music, special-interest groups, computer instruction, table games and bridge, bingo, and special events.

UTILITIES

WATER: Desert Water Agency serves Palm Springs and approximately one-third of Cathedral City. The Coachella Valley Water District serves approximately two-thirds of Cathedral City and all of Rancho Mirage. Imperial Irrigation District, a community-owned utility, supplies water to

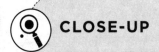

CLOSE-UP

Palm Springs Art Museum

The history of the Palm Springs Art Museum, the oldest cultural establishment in the desert, says a lot about the quality of life for those who choose to retire or relocate here from more urban areas.

The Palm Springs Art Museum was founded in 1938 as the Palm Springs Desert Museum, a one-room showcase for Native American artifacts and the natural sciences, specializing in the environment of the surrounding Coachella Valley. Soon the growing museum found temporary new quarters in a section of the town's library; it then expanded again in 1947 into a section of a converted wartime hospital.

With the war over, the desert started experiencing its first population boom. New residents were looking for a sunny, beautiful place to spend at least half of the year, and many of them hungered for the art and culture that were a part of their lives in Chicago, New York, or Los Angeles.

A modern 10,000-square-foot structure was built in downtown Palm Springs in 1958, and in 1962 it expanded to include an auditorium and galleries for contemporary art exhibitions.

A significant fund-raising effort marked by large donations from all manner of celebrities, business tycoons, and everyday people built the museum's first modern home on Museum Drive, in the middle of downtown and right up against the foothills of the San Jacinto Mountains.

E. Stewart Williams, a Palm Springs resident and internationally famous architect, was the mastermind behind the new facility. Williams, one of the country's most renowned midcentury architects, captured the magic of the desert with references to sand dunes and liberal use of the rocks from the surrounding moun-

tains. The soaring space is filled with light at all hours and somehow manages to create a feeling of intimacy and openness at the same time.

In 1960 Williams designed a new theater for the site, and in 1976 he added a wing for art, one for natural science, and the expanded Annenberg Theater. He was back again in 1982 to design the administration building so that staff could free up museum space for the western American art wing.

As his latest achievement for the museum, Williams came out of retirement to design a major expansion to incorporate the Steve Chase Art Wing and Education Center, which opened in 1996. Every addition came together seamlessly—visitors can't tell where the original building ended and the new parts began.

Williams is just one of the extraordinary people who have made the desert their home and have given huge amounts of time and skill to make it a better place to live. When the expansion to the museum opened in 1996, he said it would not be complete until the building, the art, and the people came together. To him, the vitality of the museum and its role in enriching the lives of everyone in the desert were the crowning achievements.

From a one-room facility in 1938 to today's 125,000-square-foot facility, the museum has greatly expanded its collections and programs. It now houses a collection of over 7,000 objects; the Marks Administration Building is home to the administrative staff and library; Frey House II was a bequest to the museum in 1999; and the Buddy Rogers Box Office opened in 2000. Buddy Rogers, Albert Frey, and Walter Marks all had homes in the desert, loved it, and contributed sig-

The Palm Springs Art Museum has an excellent and extensive collection of Native American pottery, baskets, and other crafts. PHOTO BY TOM BREWSTER, COURTESY OF THE PALM SPRINGS DESERT RESORTS CONVENTION AND VISITORS AUTHORITY

nificantly to the museum, in both time and money.

Nine active councils—devoted to Architecture and Design, Artists, Contemporary Art, Docents, Museum Associates, Museum Service, Performing Arts, Sunday Afternoon Concerts, and Western Art—attract an amazing talent pool from current community leaders and those who have retired and now spend their days improving the valley's quality of life. A major fund-raising arm of the Board of Trustees, the Museum Associates Council boasts exceptional success in planning and carrying out innovative fund-raising events.

In April 2004 the museum made a major shift in its focus, from a multidisciplinary museum to a world-class art museum with a vibrant theater program. It became clear that the art collections were growing and that the art audience was expanding—primarily in the areas of architecture, photography, and contem-

porary glass. In April 2005 the museum officially changed its name from the Palm Springs Desert Museum to the Palm Springs Art Museum, to reflect its emphasis on the visual and performing arts.

Accredited by the American Association of Museums, Palm Springs Art Museum has 28 galleries, two sculpture gardens, four classrooms/resource centers, an artists' center, five storage vaults, a 90-seat lecture hall, a 433-seat theater, a 1,000-square-foot store, and a locally popular cafe.

The museum has more than 4,000 members, and the institution has come to be one of the most egalitarian cultural organizations in the valley. Exhibitions, education programs, and performing arts productions at the museum are constantly changing and improving, made possible by admission fees, private funds, donations, memberships, grants, and volunteer efforts from all over the desert and the nation.

Palm Desert and communities to the east.

GAS: Southern California Gas Co. serves the entire valley.

ELECTRIC: Electricity rates are a huge sore point for desert residents, most of whom are served by Southern California Edison, which charges one of the highest rates in the nation. It's not uncommon for summer electric bills to run into the hundreds of dollars, even with the thermostats set on high. Edison serves Palm Springs, Cathedral City, Rancho Mirage, and part of Palm Desert. Imperial Irrigation District, with rates that are actually affordable for the normal working person, services part of Palm Desert and all areas east through Indio.

Coachella Valley Water District
(800) 262-2651
www.cvwd.org

Imperial Irrigation District
81600 Avenue 58, La Quinta
(760) 398-5811

Southern California Edison
73540 Highway 111, Palm Desert
(800) 655-4555

Southern California Gas Co.
(800) 427-2200
http://www.socalgas.com

CHILD CARE

For the past several years, the population of all of the desert cities has increased and has included more families. In turn, the new younger families have created a demand for dependable, professional child care services. Where once this was limited to a neighbor's home, there are now several full-service facilities offering care for infants to preteens. Often, desert churches also offer child care during the school-holiday times.

Desert Day Care Resources
www.desertdaycares.com
The Web site lists all the desert day care facilities that are licensed by California's Community Care Licensing Division. It's an excellent first stop in researching up-to-date availability of child care.

Desert Sonshine
1800 Via Negocio
(760) 320-9533
www.desertsonshine.org
Established in 1980, Desert Sonshine is a private, nonprofit, nondenominational preschool and kindergarten.

First Schools of the Desert
2300 East Racquet Club Road
(760) 327-5005

69440 McCallum Way, Cathedral City
(760) 321-0090

44996 Adams Street, La Quinta
(760) 772-2996
www.firstschool.com
Child care is available for kids from 18 months through age 12. Classes are small, with a ratio of six to one for toddlers. Maximum size is 15 children for the kindergarten ages. A fourth school in Indio will open soon.

Kiddie Kollege
490 Compadre Road
(760) 327-3767
One of the oldest and most respected facilities in the desert, Kiddie Kollege specializes in preschool.

If you're retiring and want to make sure your grandkids are welcome in your new home, be diligent about researching the rules for condo or planned community developments you're considering. Many are downright uptight about allowing kids.

EDUCATION

Public Schools

Desert Sands Unified School District
47950 Dune Palms Road, La Quinta
(760) 771-8502
www.dsusd.k12.ca.us
This school district serves part of Palm Desert, plus La Quinta and Indio. It contains 14 elementary schools, six middle schools, three high schools, and one alternative school.

Palm Springs Unified School District
980 East Tahquitz Canyon Way
(760) 416-6000
www.psusd.us
This school district serves the communities of Palm Springs, Cathedral City, Rancho Mirage, Thousand Palms, and parts of Palm Desert. There are 15 elementary schools, four middle schools, three high schools, and six alternative schools.

Private Schools

Christian School of the Desert
Desert Christian High School (Pre-K-12)
40-700 Yucca Lane, Bermuda Dunes
(760) 345-2848
With around 450 students in preschool through high school, this nondenominational Christian school bases all of its goals on scriptural "directions" and includes Bible study as a significant part of the curriculum. The 10-acre campus offers small classroom size (17–24 students), a computer lab, a library, a gymnasium, athletic fields, and a swimming pool.

Desert Chapel Christian (K-12)
630 South Sunrise Way
(760) 327-2772
There are around 350 students in small classes that emphasize daily Bible study along with academics. A strong sports program focuses on football and volleyball. The campus is a few blocks from downtown Palm Springs and across the street from the public Palm Springs High School.

Desert Torah Academy (1-8)
73-550 Santa Rosa Way, Palm Desert
(760) 341-6501
Desert Torah Academy offers secular and Jewish studies program to children from Reform, Conservative, Orthodox, and unaffiliated families. Extended care and hot lunches are available.

The Learning Tree (Pre-K-5)
42-675 Washington Street, Palm Desert
(760) 345-8100
There are about 190 students in this school, which has a 1-to-12 teacher-student ratio. It is a nonsectarian, nondenominational early-learning program aimed at preparing students for top placement in public schools.

Marywood-Palm Valley (Pre-K-12)
72-850 Clancy Lane, Rancho Mirage
(760) 346-1197

35-525 Davall Road, Rancho Mirage
(760) 328-0861
These two independent schools merged in 2005. Classes for prekindergarten through grade 5 are held on the Clancy Lane campus; classes for prekindergarten and grades 6 through 12 take place on the Davall Road campus. The 40-acre Davall Road campus includes classrooms, athletic fields and courts, and a gym and stage complex. The 19-acre Clancy Lane campus includes permanent and modular classrooms, athletic fields and courts, playgrounds, and an eating area. Classes are aimed at college prep and are nondenominational.

Montessori School of Palm Springs
(Pre-K-3)
3692 East Chia Road
(760) 323-2502
Just three teachers comprise the faculty at this small Montessori school, which generally has a student body of 30. Tradi-

tional Montessori techniques focus on developing each child's individual talents.

**Montessori School of the Valley
(Pre-K–5)
43250 Warner Trail, Palm Desert
(760) 345–1889**
Another traditional Montessori school, this has around 65 students and five teachers.

**Sacred Heart School (K–8)
43-775 Deep Canyon Road, Palm Desert
(760) 346–3513**
This is a traditional Catholic school, with around 300 students from kindergarten through grade 8. Academic instruction is aimed at preparing students to go into a standard college prep program in high school.

**St. Margaret's Episcopal School
(Pre-K–8)
47535 Highway 74, Palm Desert
(760) 346–6268
www.stmargarets.org**
Academics are emphasized here, with advanced math, science, and language arts classes. Weekly faith-based classes on religion and ethics are also part of the curriculum. The 10-acre campus includes athletic facilities, classrooms for 120 or so, a gym, and a theater. Classes are small—usually around 10.

**St. Theresa School (K–8)
455 South Compadre Road
(760) 327–4919
www.stsps.org**
The curriculum is based on traditional Catholic faith, and the staff believes in educating the whole child academically, socially, physically, emotionally, and spiritually. The school has been educating students for more than 50 years. Enrollment is approximately 321 students, from kindergarten through grade 8.

**Xavier College Preparatory High School
34-200 Chase School Road
Thousand Palms
(760) 370–9274**
This will be the first Catholic high school in the Coachella Valley. Classes began in the fall of 2006 at the Palm Desert Campus of Cal State University, San Bernardino, while workers put finishing touches on the first classroom building and gym. Those buildings were expected to be completed by the end of 2006. The full campus is set for completion by 2011.

Colleges and Universities

**California State University, San Bernardino, Palm Desert Campus
Cook Street near Frank Sinatra
Palm Desert
(760) 341–2883
www.pdc.csusb.edu**
A new addition to the education environment of the desert, CSU offers less than a dozen undergraduate degrees, all aligned closely with the curriculum at College of the Desert in a master plan that will add degree options over the years. Students at this campus are assumed to have taken their basic requirements at COD or another two-year college so they are ready to embark on a two- or three-year course of study ending in an undergraduate degree. The sprawling campus is brand-new, and the buildings are gorgeous—it's an important part of the City of Palm Desert's master plan and sits on several acres donated by the city.

**Chapman University
41-555 Cook Street, Suite 100
Palm Desert
(760) 341–8051
www.chapman.edu**
Chapman classes are aimed at the adult student who wants to get a certificate or degree while still working full time. Associate, bachelor's, and master's degrees as well as several professional certifications are available, and terms start every 10 weeks. A number of classes are offered online, and the entire library system is a

virtual one, with online access to a large research database.

College of the Desert
43-500 Monterey Avenue, Palm Desert
(760) 346-8041
www.desert.cc.ca.us
Full-time enrollment in this community college is almost 4,000, and there are several thousand more part-time students working for associate degrees or certificates. Campus facilities include a gym/pool complex, athletic facilities, a library, a golf driving range, a student center, and use of the McCallum Theatre for the Performing Arts. The College of the Desert Alumni Association puts on the highly successful weekend street fair and farmers' market, with booth rentals benefiting the college. Nursing and education are top certificate programs, and the curriculum is designed to allow students to get the standard classes required by four-year colleges at a very affordable tuition rate.

MEDIA

There's a selection of local daily newspapers as well as home delivery and newsstand availability of the *Los Angeles Times, USA Today, Riverside Press Enterprise, Wall Street Journal,* and even the *New York Times.* The local business news publication, *Public Record,* is available to subscribers only. The free *Desert Post Weekly,* available every Thursday at paper boxes throughout the valley, provides the latest in movies, restaurants, club openings, theater, music, and everything fun. The local daily, *The Desert Sun,* is a Gannett publication and has excellent local sections as well as general national and international coverage.

If you really want to call yourself a "local," *Palm Springs Life Magazine* is a must-read. This glossy publication is packed with the latest in fashion, art, home, and the local social scene. The September issue, hardbound and placed in select hotel rooms, is a piece to savor and save. Its companion piece, the *Desert*

If you're hungering for a culture fix and don't want to negotiate the drive to Los Angeles or San Diego, check into the many day trips and overnight excursions offered by local travel agencies.

Guide, is bound into the full magazine and is also available free in restaurants, shop, attractions, and hotels. It is the official visitor guide of the Palm Springs Desert Resorts Convention & Visitors Authority and an excellent source for up-to-date event news.

The electronic media are also well represented in the valley, with some 15 radio stations broadcasting the gamut from news and talk to the top 40. All three of the major television networks also have affiliates in the desert. Public access television is available in each city to keep up with local government.

Publications

The Bottom Line
312 North Palm Canyon Drive
(760) 323-0552
www.thebottomline.com
This glossy monthly, targeting the gay and lesbian market, is in its 23rd year, with a circulation of more than 100,000. This is the bible for everything to do with the gay scene in the desert, from parties to politics.

Desert Golf
P.O. Box 1158, Rancho Mirage 92270
(760) 324-2476
This publication is devoted to the more than 110 golf courses in the valley.

Desert Post Weekly
68625 Perez Road, Suite 6
Cathedral City
(760) 202-3200
This is a weekly publication of *The Desert Sun* and is aimed at the 20- to 30-something group, with in-depth pieces

Earthquakes are a fact of life in the desert, so get up to speed on how to prepare and survive the dreaded "big one." The Governor's Office of Emergency Services has a good tip sheet on its Web site, www.oes.ca.gov.

on local music and independent entertainment, as well as some spicy opinion columns.

The Desert Sun
750 North Gene Autry Trail
(760) 322-8889
www.thedesertsun.com

111 Magazine
69730 Highway 111, Rancho Mirage
(760) 770-5033
A former editor of *Palm Springs Life Magazine* started this slick monthly several years ago. It is a shameless worshiper of the local society scene, with articles on high rollers, charity bashes, and luxury homes and goods. It is only available to the select few who live in the most expensive neighborhoods.

Palm Springs Life Magazine
303 North Indian Canyon Drive
(760) 325-3333
www.palmspringslife.com

The Public Record
303 North Indian Canyon Drive
(760) 416-9709
www.publicrecord.com

Radio

KPSC 88.5 FM
P.O. Box 7913, Los Angeles 90007
(213) 225-7400
www.kusc.org
University of Southern California–sponsored station playing classical music.

KHCS 91.7 FM
P.O. Box 2507, Palm Springs 92263
(760) 864-9620
www.joy92.org
Christian broadcasting, noncommercial.

KKUU 92.7 FM
1321 Gene Autry Trail
(760) 345-92FM
Top 40, today's hottest music.

KWXY 98.5 FM, 1340 AM
68700 Dinah Shore Drive
Cathedral City
(760) 328-1104
www.kwxy.com
Easy listening, "beautiful music," same format for 37 years.

KPSI 100.5 FM, 1010 AM
2100 East Tahquitz Canyon Drive
(760) 327-0977 (FM)
(760) 325-2582 (AM)
www.mix1005.fm
www.newstalk920.com
The FM station plays the top 40, and the AM station is news and talk, including national and local talk hosts.

KJJZ 102.3 FM
441 South Calle Encilia
(760) 320-4550
www.kjjz.com
Smooth jazz, Palm Springs style: lots of Sinatra.

KEZN 103.1 FM
72915 Parkview Drive, Palm Desert
(760) 340-9383
www.ez103.com
The format is "adult contemporary," which translates to soft rock.

KDES 104.7 FM
2100 East Tahquitz Canyon Way
(760) 325-2582
www.kdes.com
This station has been playing the "oldies" format for many years.

KPLM 106.1 FM
441 South Calle Encilia
(760) 320-4550
An established country station.

KNWZ 970 AM
1321 Gene Autry Trail
(760) 864-6397
www.knewstalk.com
This is another venerable desert station, with the same successful news and talk format for several years.

Television

CBS TV (2), CBS
31276 Durham Way, Thousand Palms
(760) 343-5700
www.cbs2tv.com

KESQ TV (3), ABC
42650 Melanie Place, Palm Desert
(760) 773-3333
www.kesq.com

KMIR TV (6), NBC
72920 Park View, Palm Desert
(760) 568-3636
www.kmir6.com

WORSHIP

With nearly 100 places of worship throughout the valley, you certainly can find what you're looking for. Some of the more famous ones are St. Theresa's in Palm Springs, the site of Sonny Bono's funeral, and St. Louis Catholic Church in Cathedral City, home to the Sinatra clan. Whatever you choose, from nondenominational Christian-based teaching to Jewish temples or Episcopalian churches, you will be at home.

The best way to locate the service of your choice is either by reading the Saturday edition of *The Desert Sun*'s Religion Section or, of course, by looking in the Yellow Pages.

INDEX